CANADA'S DEL. ___ ___ ...

Beyond Elizabeth II, The Crown's Continuing Canadian Complexion

The Crown in Canada has had a profound influence in shaping a country and a constitution that embraces the promotion of political moderation, societal accommodation, adaptable constitutional structures, and pluralistic governing practices. While none of these features themselves originated through legislative or constitutional action, David E. Smith, Christopher McCreery, and Jonathan Shanks propose that all reflect the presence and actions of the Crown.

Examining how a constitutional monarchy functions, *Canada's Deep Crown* discusses how the legal and institutional abstractions of the Crown vary depending on the circumstances and the context in which it is found. The Crown presents differently depending on who is observing it, who is representing it, and what role it is performing. With a focus on the changes that have taken place over the last fifty years, this book addresses the role of the Crown in dispersing power throughout Canada's system of government, the function the sovereign, governor general, and lieutenant governors play, and how the demise of the Crown and transition to a new sovereign is likely to unfold.

DAVID E. SMITH is adjunct faculty in the Department of Politics and Public Administration and a member of the Yeates School of Graduate Studies at Ryerson University.

CHRISTOPHER MCCREERY is the private secretary to the lieutenant governor of Nova Scotia and executive director of Government House Halifax.

JONATHAN SHANKS is senior counsel at the Privy Council Office Legal Services Sector of the Department of Justice Canada.

CANADA'S DEEP CROWN

Beyond Elizabeth II, The Crown's Continuing Canadian Complexion

David E. Smith, Christopher McCreery, and Jonathan Shanks

UNIVERSITY OF TORONTO PRESS

Toronto   Buffalo   London

© University of Toronto Press 2022
Toronto Buffalo London
utorontopress.com
Printed in the U.S.A.

ISBN 978-1-4875-4075-3 (cloth)   ISBN 978-1-4875-4078-4 (EPUB)
ISBN 978-1-4875-4076-0 (paper)   ISBN 978-1-4875-4077-7 (PDF)

Library and Archives Canada Cataloguing in Publication

Title: Canada's deep Crown : beyond Elizabeth II, the Crown's continuing
    Canadian complexion / David E. Smith, Christopher McCreery, and
    Jonathan Shanks.
Names: Smith, David E., 1936– author. | McCreery, Christopher, author. |
    Shanks, Jonathan, author.
Description: Includes bibliographical references and index.
Identifiers: Canadiana (print) 20210329378 | Canadiana (ebook)
    20210329440 | ISBN 9781487540753 (cloth) | ISBN 9781487540760
    (paper) | ISBN 9781487540784 (EPUB) | ISBN 9781487540777 (PDF)
Subjects: LCSH: Monarchy – Canada. | LCSH: Monarchy – Great Britain. |
    LCSH: Federal government – Canada.
Classification: LCC JL88 .S54 2022 | DDC 320.471 – dc23

This book has been published with the help of a grant from the
Federation for the Humanities and Social Sciences, through the Awards
to Scholarly Publications Program, using funds provided by the Social
Sciences and Humanities Research Council of Canada.

University of Toronto Press acknowledges the financial assistance to its
publishing program of the Canada Council for the Arts and the Ontario
Arts Council, an agency of the Government of Ontario.

 Canada Council **Conseil des Arts**
for the Arts **du Canada**

 ONTARIO ARTS COUNCIL
CONSEIL DES ARTS DE L'ONTARIO
an Ontario government agency
un organisme du gouvernement de l'Ontario

Funded by the   Financé par le
Government   gouvernement
of Canada   du Canada

 Canadä

To the governors general and lieutenant governors who have served to represent the Crown

The Crown is an idea more than a person and I want the Crown in Canada to represent everything that is best and most admired in the Canadian ideal.

Queen Elizabeth II
26 June 1973
TORONTO

Contents

Foreword

We are delighted to welcome an insightful new book, one of several in recent years on the Canadian Crown.

At a time of global threat and disruption, and for all the challenges we face as a nation, Canada's constitutional monarchy is one of the world's most successful democracies.

But the Crown is inherently elusive to many Canadians. It is not primarily based on codified rules but extensively on tacit understandings. It is constitutionally entrenched and a deeply woven symbolic presence; at the same time, it is also pragmatic, incremental and responsive to local realities. Multi-faceted and dispersed, the Canadian Crown can indeed be hard to grasp.

We are therefore particularly indebted to David Smith, Christopher McCreery and Jonathan Shanks. They have brought together political science, history and law in a wide-ranging, accessible and well-researched effort that shows how the Crown works, and how it has been a unifying voice and a moderating influence in our evolution as a country.

Her Majesty Queen Elizabeth II, Queen of Canada, has been one of the most remarkable sovereigns in modern history. From Her first public speech more than 80 years ago at the onset of the Second World War, to Her recent addresses on the pandemic and VE Day, Her constancy and dignity calls on our strengths and inspires us to a higher purpose. She has personified, for longer than most Canadians have been alive, the strengths of constitutional monarchy.

This book is especially welcome because it reveals a deeper understanding of the ideals that the Crown represents: a sense of justice rooted in one thousand years of law; the striving for excellence; the importance of history and symbols as a core part of identity; the exercise of executive authority as a trust; and the summoning together of Canadians in a non-partisan commitment to nation building.

As a young country, we look to the future but do not turn away from our past. Canada is at its best in human purpose and compassion when it embraces its past and mirrors its geography: broad, expansive and diverse.

We know that trust grows when diversity becomes inclusion. Increasingly, this has been a defining quality of vice-regal appointments and we were pleased to see the profile given to the work of the vice-regal family in this book. We have always been impressed by their sense of service, their ability to combine tradition with modern day innovation, and of their deep love of country. It is no accident that eight of eleven vice-regals and all three territorial commissioners are currently women. These offices are most often characterized by a modest degree of formality and limited budgetary resources, juxtaposed with a high degree of civic engagement and public access. *Canada's Deep Crown* refers to this as *monarchy light*. How Canadian.

Our warmest congratulations go out to the authors of *Canada's Deep Crown*. Thank you for shining a light on a system of constitutional monarchy that has worked surprisingly well for Canada and that continues to adapt to a changing world.

The Right Honourable David Johnston,
PC, CC, CMM, COM, CD
Governor General of Canada, 2010–17

Stephen Wallace, CVO
Secretary to the Governor General, 2011–17

Preface

The Crown is everywhere. So why don't we understand it?
Patricia Treble, *Maclean's*, January 2016

Why does the Crown in Canada matter and why has it functioned effectively in Canada, the third-oldest continuous democracy in the world? These questions have often been examined by political scientists, historians, lawyers, and other interested practitioners and commentators when dissecting the role and operation of Canada's constitutional monarchy, yet there remains something lacking. Certainly, much focus has been placed on the reserve powers: how, when, and under what circumstances they are exercised – all highly important questions. However, the means by which the Crown has survived, evolved, and remained quietly present in civil society is too often reduced to discussion of its longevity as a vestigial relic of Canada's evolution from colony to nation. Surely the Crown is more than Canada's proverbial tailbone.

Modern practitioners and students of the Crown in Canada naturally rush to pull Peter Hogg's *Constitutional Law of Canada* and Andrew Heard's *Canadian Constitutional Conventions* off the shelf to find out how and why the Crown has behaved in the past – to discern what should be done now.[1] These works, along with David Smith's *The Invisible Crown*, are the familiar touchstones of our understanding of the mechanics of the Crown. John Fraser, in his popular examination of Canada's constitutional monarchy and its future, *The Secret of the Crown: Canada's Affair with Royalty*,[2] delved into the Crown's place in our imagination and also, to a degree, its function. While Fraser's work is not academic, it is relevant to anyone seeking a more holistic understanding of Canada's constitutional monarchy. This monograph does not seek to replicate any of the aforementioned publications; rather we seek to provide a multifaceted understanding of this subtle, yet ubiquitous element of the Canadian state and society.

Often nuances of the Crown's role and function have been written about as though the various components of the institution – legal, constitutional, symbolic, and ceremonial – all took place within distinctive watertight compartments, yet the actual operation of the Crown is fluid and dynamic. The accretion of the Crown as an institution and the activities carried out by the sovereign, governor general, and lieutenant governors are of particular relevance to any examination of its role and function. Despite the inevitable cycles of the demise of the Crown and accession of a new monarch, much focus and commentary has been directed to the person of the present Queen of Canada, Elizabeth II – who has been the lodestar of Canada's monarchy for more than *sixty* years. Given the length of her reign, pervasive changes experienced since 1952 to all of society, and the compelling nature of the person of the sovereign, who not only wears the physical crown, but is the outward embodiment of the institution, this is natural – it helps to personalize an institution, which, like all structures of authority and governance, can seem distant, abstract, and shrouded in mystery.

The Crown is part of the rhythm of Canadian life – like white noise in the background, it is always there and part of the hum of our national existence and identity, although it is not always appreciated for this quality or its subtle ubiquity. There is something practical about the Crown's role, function, and evolution in Canada, even if it does not fit neatly into a box. As the introduction explains, this modest work seeks to explain the profound and ingrained nature of Canada's constitutional monarchy, hence the title *Canada's Deep Crown*.

This collaborative project came about almost by accident, following the launch of *The Canadian Kingdom*, which was hosted at

Queen's Park in May 2018 by the lieutenant governor of Ontario, the Honourable Elizabeth Dowdswell.[3] All three authors were present and, following the niceties of a vice-regally sponsored book launch, discussion ensued about what had yet to be written about the Crown and its flexible characteristics. One can now make a joke about what happens when a political science professor, private secretary, and constitutional lawyer walk into a reception and are plied with ample quantities of Ontario's fine wines, all while in the presence of one of the Queen's representatives.

The challenges of writing a book by distance were made up by the friendship and cooperative spirit of the authors – and a sense of conviction that there remains much to be explored about the Crown in Canada. For the authors, this was their first trifurcated work of this type to be undertaken. Lack of ideas or clashes of personality were never an issue – in those areas this book has been a fluid and dynamic project. The distances between Halifax, Ottawa, and Niagara-on-the-Lake did prove a slight challenge, as did the inevitable intrusion of work or personal duties upon the writing and editing. This was a particular challenge for Jonathan and Christopher, who were often sending slightly cryptic notes to each other, and David noting that certain events in Ottawa or Halifax were going to trespass upon evenings and weekends that would have otherwise seen this work completed several months earlier.

To the authors there is a symbolic symmetry that our first formal meeting to develop the overall idea behind the work took place at Government House in Halifax, not far from the very room where responsible government was first practised in 1848, and the very room where the Prince of Wales, future King of Canada, was sworn into the Queen's Privy Council for Canada. One would like to think that Sir John Harvey and Joseph Howe were somehow smiling upon our deliberations and the evolution of Canada's deep Crown over the past two centuries.

Acknowledgments

The authors acknowledge the assistance of a number of individuals for their support of this project, notably Daniel Quinlan from University of Toronto Press. Thanks are also owed to the Honourable Serge Joyal, PC, OC, OQ, former member of the Senate of Canada, and formerly secretary of state for Canada; Warren Newman, senior general counsel in the Constitutional, Administrative, and International Law Section of the Department of Justice of Canada; and Charles Robert, clerk of the House of Commons (formerly clerk of the Senate and clerk of the Parliaments). Their critical reading and suggestions did much to improve the content, tone, and structure of this work. Joyal, in particular, ensured the authors took into account the present political landscape with a realpolitik lens on how this study will be received by legislators, practitioners, and other interested parties alike.

During the course of the research and writing of this manuscript, David Smith wishes to acknowledge the support he received from the head and faculty of the Department of Politics and Public Administration, and the office of the Dean of Arts at Ryerson University. As well, the scholarly contribution of friends and colleagues in Canada and abroad who share his interest in the Crown is sincerely appreciated.

Christopher McCreery is grateful to his partner Matthew Malone, who, while appreciating the architectural references contained herein, was somewhat put out at the idea of a cottage weekend transpiring in his absence. Thanks is also owed to two friends and mentors, John Fraser, CM, and Michael Bliss, OC, each whom in his own way coaxed him into thinking of the Crown, and alternatives to it, outside of his genetic inheritance as a Family Compact Upper Canadian. Former secretary to the governor general, Stephen Wallace, CVO, is thanked for his comments on the draft manuscript and support in the last phase of this project.

Jonathan Shanks owes a debt of gratitude to Sanam Goudarzi, who has endured more extracurricular focus on the Canadian Crown than she ever imagined possible, but has otherwise been a loving life companion and also a dedicated and successful Crown servant in her own right. Ann Chaplin and Warren Newman are simply the best mentors and role models that a young lawyer could have hoped for upon joining the federal public service. Like so many other colleagues, they have also become cherished friends. There is not space to single out all of the many others who have been supportive, collegial, and courteous throughout the years, or the peculiar few who have provided examples of what not to do. However, particular thanks are due to Stephen Zaluski, Joanne Klineberg, Jenna MacDonald, Laurie Wright, Edward (Ted) Livingstone, Julie Wellington, Ted Murphy, Rob Rishikof, Alissa Malkin, Alan Cliff, Jenna Wates, Jason Harrington, Ray MacCallum, Nicholas MacDonald, Daniel Roussy, and Jodie van Dieen. From 2010 to 2020, students taking the introductory course to public and constitutional law, first at the University of Ottawa and later at Queen's, provided academic stimulation and challenged orthodoxy about the Crown. Above all, gratitude is owed to Robert and Sharon Shanks for their love and support throughout this and every other project. The usual disclaimer applies: the views expressed in this book are personal to the authors and do not necessarily represent the views of the Department of Justice or the Government of Canada.

The authors acknowledge with gratitude the contribution of a foreword by the twenty-eighth governor general of Canada, the Right Honourable David Johnston, PC, CC, CMM, COM, CD, and Stephen Wallace, CVO who served as his secretary throughout his time in office. The lieutenant governor of Nova Scotia, the

Honourable Arthur J. LeBlanc, ONS, QC, who graciously allowed our initial deliberations to take place in the historic and meaningful setting of Government House, is thanked for his generosity and interest in the development of this book. We are also indebted for the work of Paul McCreery in ensuring that we were supplied with running water during our November 2019 deliberations on the snowy shores of Lower Beverly Lake in Ontario.

David E. Smith
NIAGARA-ON-THE-LAKE

Christopher McCreery
HALIFAX

Jonathan Shanks
OTTAWA

CANADA'S DEEP CROWN

Introduction

Although the Crown today remains an integral part of Canada's Parliament, in company with the Senate and the House of Commons, and although the Crown has performed a constitutive function in the development of the British North American colonies that later comprised Canada, as well as playing a central role in the evolution of the federal and provincial constitutions following the achievement of Confederation in 1867, its place and significance in the governing of the country remain mysteriously ignored or misunderstood. Several reasons may be offered for the apparent disinterest or confusion. First, although the sovereign of the United Kingdom is the sovereign of Canada, the Crown is viewed by many observers as a vestigial relic of a bygone era. Or, when it is not so viewed, then the "royal stewardship of the Commonwealth" helps perpetuate "an image of the British that was drawn by the end of the nineteenth century."[1] Second, the Crown in Canada is obscured by the monarchy in the United Kingdom – by its spectacle and longevity. In the matter of the Crown, Britain, in Canadian eyes, is still the place where things happen! As a result, Canadians do not see the institution in their own country, whose characteristics in truth are quintessentially Canadian – multifaceted and dispersed with one governor general and ten lieutenant governors; nor when it is presented to them – admittedly, as more circumstance than pomp – do they recognize it. In consequence, the Crown is not perceived to be Canadian. Paradoxically, and in contrast to Australia, another federation with a constitutional history parallel to Canada's, this condition has nothing to do with competing support for republicanism; except for Lower Canada in the period of the 1830s, there has never been an organized movement or even visible sympathy of any enduring strength for that cause.[2] There have been sporadic outbursts of opposition to the monarchy, such as when Peter Donolo (the long-serving director of communications to Prime Minister Jean Chrétien) commenced discussions within the Prime Minister's Office of what a non-monarchical system of government could look like for Canada.[3] The plan was to "introduce the idea to test public opinion, without actively promoting it,"[4] and this later expanded to active consideration of abandoning the monarchy as a key millennium project for the year 2000. After much internal discussion and engagement, along with a number of trial balloons in the media, the project was eventually shelved at Chrétien's direction, who decided not to "stir up a hornet's nest about the fate of the monarchy or the Americanization of Canadian institutions."[5] The absence of a robust and organized pro-republican/anti-constitutional monarchy movement[6] does accurately reflect the ability for such sentiment to be expressed or to eventually capture the public mind, especially when the present Elizabethan era draws to its natural conclusion.

This book focuses on Canadian experience with the Crown because this is a neglected area of study. While in recent years there has been increased scholarly attention paid to the Crown as a constitutional entity (as, for instance, in the exercise of prerogative powers), there has been no exploration of why the Crown matters – recognized or not – in how Canadians govern themselves. It is that silence that explains this book's title, *Canada's Deep Crown*. The authors advance the proposition that the Crown has been a fundamental contributing influence in creating a country and a constitution whose distinctive characteristics embrace, among other matters, the promotion of political moderation, societal accommodation, adaptable constitutional structures, as well as governing practices that favour cultural and linguistic pluralism. None of these features themselves, it should be emphasized, have originated through legislative or constitutional action but all, it is maintained, reflect in important respects the presence and actions of the Crown.

Canada faces major political and societal challenges. One obvious example is how to come to terms with past government practices and relations with the country's Indigenous peoples. Inordinately complex and the source of strong grievances, these matters and their remedy invariably lie close to the Crown because of the legacy of treaties concluded by the Crown with original inhabitants of what is now Canada.[7] According to David Arnot, a former treaty commissioner for Saskatchewan, "The legal framework for making treaties with First Nations in the last 250 years is the Royal Proclamation of King George III," which, he says, is "regarded by Canada's First Nations as their *magna carta*."[8] That primacy finds support from Lord Denning, who, as master of the rolls in 1982, said that the proclamation was "ranked by the Indian peoples as their Bill of Rights, equivalent to our own Bill of Rights in England 80 years before."[9] As dominant as relations with First Nations may be, they are not now, nor have they been, singular in their claims on the Crown. Consider, for instance, the succession of apologies for past actions recently made to Acadians, Japanese Canadians, and more.[10] The potential competence of what this book refers to as *Canada's Deep Crown* to meet these pressing challenges is beyond the scope of the investigation envisioned here, although the very reference to them underlines both their temporal and demographic continuity.

Another challenge, without being accused, one hopes, of committing an act of lese-majesty, is to recognize that in the next decade or so, Prince Charles will accede to the throne. At that point it is certain that there will be a discussion, if not some controversy, over whether Canada should retain its "British" sovereign. While republican sentiment has perennially been weak, periodic criticism of the imputed British connection may still be found: "Even if the Queen is only symbolic in Canada, the reality of a foreign monarch in our Constitution should raise some objections.... What relevance does a colonial figure still have in 2017?... Saying goodbye to our British monarchy ... is only a matter of common sense and political maturity."[11] The constitutional and historical accuracy of that indictment will be probed in chapter 1, "The Crown and Metaphor." A second question, usually prefaced by the statement that a majority of Canadians favour the outcome, is whether or not Canada should have a Canadian as its "head of state."[12] At this point, however, media coverage of the Crown, which overwhelmingly is of the monarch and, more precisely, her family, is on evidence in every convenience and drugstore magazine display across the country. That the princes and princesses of the House of Windsor have only the most tangential relationship to the governing of Canada and its provinces goes unacknowledged. Indeed, with the advent of online platforms, it is even easier today than in the past to disseminate the celebrity perspective of the personalities associated with the Crown.

Thus the person becomes the matter as opposed to the Crown, which is perceived not to matter. One explanation for the personality-driven coverage of the monarchy is the longevity of British kings and queens. As of 2021, nearly 260 years since ratification of the Treaty of Paris, 1763, three monarchs (George III, Victoria, and Elizabeth II) have occupied the throne for 182 years. Successions are infrequent, if not rare, in the life of the monarch's subjects, with the Crown in consequence appearing almost permanent: "It is being, rather than doing, as the Queen once observed."[13] Decades of distance separate the appointment, by Queen Victoria, of Lord Durham to investigate and report on the causes of the rebellions in Upper and Lower Canada in 1837–8 and the death of the Queen in 1901, by which time Sir Wilfrid Laurier, Canada's first prime minister of French-speaking lineage, had been in office for five years. Similarly, Queen Elizabeth II had been on the throne for five years before John Diefenbaker became prime minister, since whose time in office she has had ten additional prime ministers. Yet, notwithstanding that long history, it will be argued that the Crown lives in the present, and it is that reality, as it applies to Canada's dispersed Crown, that will be examined in the following chapters.

The brilliance of the British monarchy eclipses not only the Crown in Canada and elsewhere in the Commonwealth, but other constitutional monarchies as well, many of which are in countries whose political systems are not well known in Canada; Denmark, the Netherlands, Norway, and Sweden are prime examples. The demise of Continental monarchies in central Europe after the First

World War contributed to this parochial perspective. A contrary perspective nonetheless may be found, as illustrated in an article in the *New York Times*, "The World Could Use More Kings and Queens," citing Canada as an alternative (to the United States) that "demonstrates that democracy is perfectly compatible with constitutional monarchy."[14] The piece neglects to say what needs to be recalled, which is that "the Crown was crucial to Canadian self-identity because it provided ballast," not least in the country's relationship with the United States.[15] Large and powerful, the United States, which rejected through revolution the constitution Canada inherited, is Canada's only neighbour, for there are oceans in three other directions. A recurring theme of the *World Happiness Report*, since it was first published in 2012, has been the high performance of constitutional monarchies in many of the areas taken into the calculation of the overall happiness of populations by country. As of the 2020 report, nine out of fifteen of the happiest countries are constitutional monarchies.[16] One key factor is what the report's authors define as the "institutional quality" of government in each country. Institutional quality is divided into two components: "access to power … such as the ability to participate in selecting the government, freedom of expression, freedom of association and political stability … and exercise of power, including the rule of law, control of corruption, regulatory quality and government effectiveness."[17]

While the report includes a lengthy discussion of "Nordic exceptionalism" and why Nordic countries are consistently among the happiest countries in the world, there is no similar discussion of the perennial high-performance of Australia, Canada, New Zealand, and the United Kingdom as being in the same cohort; yet institutional quality is certainly a key factor in every instance.

As important as the longevity and pre-eminence of the sovereign may be, the Crown in Canada also presents a contradictory profile. At any moment in time there are eleven members of the Canadian vice-regal family, each of whose tenure in his or her position is on average five years. As a consequence, there have been approximately 140 representatives of the Crown in Ottawa and the provincial capitals in the nearly seven decades of the Queen's reign. Chapter 5 examines the vice-regal family from the perspective of how accurately it reflects the Canadian population – linguistically and ethnically, of course – but also from the perspective of the different roles members of "the family" play, for example as convenors of groups of Canadians with varied interests or as promoters of diversity, which, given the distribution of Canada's heterogeneous population, results in an inordinate range of contacts between the Crown and Canadians. And as a result, the Crown visibly contributes to providing unity in a diverse and decentred country.

Writing in 1922, Stephen Leacock commented that "[The English] have seen so much of the mere outside of his [George V's] kingship that they don't understand the heart of it as we do in Canada."[18] An astute observation nearly a century ago, it remains so today, in large part because the Crown in Canada is so diverse. There are in Canada many more opportunities than in the United Kingdom for myriad events to arise that engage the Crown, whether it be the results of an election where no party has a majority and the Crown must select its chief adviser nonetheless, as following the British Columbia election in 2017 or New Brunswick in 2018, or a first minister advises the representative of the Crown to use the prerogative power, for instance to prorogue Parliament or a provincial legislature. Invariably such advice is controversial, as witness the title of an edited book of essays following the 2008 prorogation (requested by then prime minister, Stephen Harper, and granted by the governor general, Michaëlle Jean) *Parliamentary Democracy in Crisis*; moreover, it is subject to comment, as witness the injunction offered by Robert Hazell, director of the Constitution Unit at University College London: "The golden rule is not to draw the Monarch into controversy or political negotiations; especially in light of recent difficulties in Canada."[19] In short, Canadians see more of the Crown than people in Great Britain do because there is more of it to see. Chapter 2, "A Realm of Opposites," and chapter 3, "The Dispersal of Power," make that abundantly clear, while at the same time chapter 6, "Yet Symbols Still Matter," reinforces the cardinal point that, despite differences in appearances and presentation, the Crown in question is the same Crown, even if the sum of its activities exceeds those of its British counterpart. Still the distinctions are important, and a reassessment of Walter Bagehot's *The English Constitution*[20] and its applicability to Canada historically, but more so today, is a predictable although necessary topic requiring examination, and is found in chapter 4: "Beyond All That Glitters: Reassessing Bagehot's Efficient and Dignified Crown."

The aesthetic preference in Canada has always been for monarchy. Indeed, who can picture Canada in the Crown's absence? It is the object of this book to explain why that is the case and in what respect it affects the governance of the country. Its authors are of diverse ages, possess wide experience, and bring to their task knowledge from different disciplines, the last covering history, law, and political science. One of their number has worked on the front lines, so to speak, and has acquired practical knowledge of the Crown as it functions in Canada. Given the range of experience and expertise, the reader will find subtle differences in the writing style used between chapters, a natural by-product of a collaborative work of this nature.

In his classic work, *The Government of Canada*, first published in 1947, R. MacGregor Dawson included the following passage:

> "Once upon a time," runs the fairy tale, "there was a King who was very important and who did very big and very important things. He owned a nice shiny crown, which he would wear on especially grand occasions; but most of the time he kept it on a red velvet cushion. Then somebody made a Magic. The crown was carefully stored in the Tower; the King moved over to the cushion and was transformed into a special kind of Crown with a capital letter; and this new Crown became in the process something else, no one knows exactly what, for it is one thing today, another thing tomorrow, and two or three things the day after that. The name given to the Magic is Constitutional Development."[21]

No subject has been more important to that development than the Crown. If the weight of monarchy has never been heavy in Canada, it is weightless today. For that reason it is difficult to imagine Canada in the absence of the Crown. Nonetheless, the authors of this work must dissent from the effusive and somewhat theatrical assessment, offered by Vincent Massey in an address to the Canada Club in London in 1953, that "the influence of the Crown on our national life is so great and pervasive as to elude all efforts to appraise it."[22] On the contrary, they believe that it is vital to explore and analyse the Canadian elements of the Crown and to posit reasons why they are foundational to the stability of Canadian society and government today. One consequence of adopting such a perspective is that in contrast to much that is written about the subject, which often uses the sum of its past as the traditional frame of reference, the present manuscript challenges that perspective: it is equally interested in the Crown and the future. In short, the Crown and time is a recurring theme in the chapters that follow.

1

The Crown and Metaphor

According to the *Concise Oxford English Dictionary* a metaphor is "a thing regarded as symbolic of something else." There can be few terms that have as many metaphors applied to them as the word "Crown." To be clear, and in the language of literary critic James Wood, "a metaphor is a fictional alternative, a likeness, another life."[1] For the Crown, "symbol," "stamp," "figurehead," and "idea" are examples of words customarily associated with the term, but also of vocabulary incomplete in offering a full sense of its range of meaning. The Crown may not be the sole instance in political language of metaphorical attraction, but it is an outstanding exemplar of the difficulty the veil of metaphor may present.

Relatedly, in its advisory opinion on the Harper government's proposal to introduce a scheme of indirect Senate elections, based on consultative votes in the provinces, the Supreme Court of Canada found the initiative prejudicial to the "Constitution's architecture."[2] In subsequent public discussion that metaphorical phrase proved to be contentious because it was deemed ambiguous and permissive. As well, some critics saw it as artificial – "a delicate construct the Supreme Court conjured … out of the air."[3] As a corrective to that perspective, it is instructive to read a review of "real" architecture that has nothing to do with the Senate or Canada but nonetheless speaks aptly to the controversy – and to the utility of metaphors in political literature: "The creation of architecture is a balancing act that contends not only with physical forces like stress, resilience, and gravity, but also with psychic forces like

confidence, inspiration, and, often enough, sheer persistence. Ultimately, in order to work at all, an architectural design must come
to terms with the world around it."[4] One might say the same of the
Crown in Canada. And it is the purpose of this book to probe that
reconciliation, emphasizing, on the one hand, the extent to which
the Crown has given shape to Canada and, on the other hand, the
degree to which Canada has altered established understanding of
the Crown. Stephen Leacock's observation from 1922, cited in this
book's introduction, that "the English have seen so much of the
mere *outside* of kingship that they don't understand the *heart* of it
as we do in Canada,"[5] may have changed in detail, as subsequent
chapters will illustrate, but his perspective still holds true: the
greater the distance – and the viewing point is traditionally from
the banks of the River Thames – the more general the perception.
For that reason, the Crown in Canada must be looked at up close
if its distinctive characteristics are to be appreciated. In short, it is
not a mirror of the British Crown, nor are the governor general or
lieutenant governors impersonators of the sovereign.

Most books about the Crown in Canada say little about how it
works or about its influence; rather they concentrate upon exceptional aspects of its activity, such as the exercise of the prerogative
when there is a request, for example, to dissolve or prorogue Parliament. As a result, and for the general public, the Crown leads
an almost underground existence. Here is what might be called a
subterranean metaphor, with the Crown as the tap root of the Constitution: what you know about it depends on how deep you go.
In other words, it is about more than an exploration of prerogative
powers. Much more, since the Crown is the *symbol* of cohesion in
Canada: there is no instrument of integration more public than the
Crown, although it must be emphasized that the Crown does not
intrude on, or conflict with, private initiatives that reinforce that
cohesion. Consider, for instance, church union in the 1920s, which
reflected not only denominational tolerance but also striking disre-
gard for the geographic variations of a country as huge as Canada.[6]
Appositely, author Cynthia Ozick has argued that "the prevailing
temper of a society and a time is situated in its minor voices, in
their variegated chorus, but above all in their collective presence."[7]

There is no evidence or reason to believe that the Crown played any part in the move to church union, except that in this instance, as in others to be cited in later chapters, the Crown may be seen as an impetus to or model for a collective or community response to policy questions – in other words, a community leadership role through example. In this context, it is of significance that "all three of the uniting churches had been independent self-governing bodies for some time, and the vast majority of their clergy were Canadian-born. They emphasized not the British roots of the Canadian churches but the extent to which imported institutions had adapted themselves to meet Canadian needs in the Canadian environment."[8]

Where the Crown has exercised restraint on public initiatives may be found in what might be termed Canada's "narrow seam of direct democracy." In the opinion of the Judicial Committee of the Privy Council (JCPC), speaking in 1919 about the validity of Manitoba's *Initiative and Referendum Act*, which would have compelled the lieutenant governor "to submit proposed laws to a body of voters instead of to the Legislature of which he is the constitutional head, and render him powerless to prevent such proposed laws, if approved by such voters, from coming into effect," Lord Haldane wrote, "The Lieutenant-Governor is as much the representative of His Majesty for all purposes of Provincial Government as is the Governor-General for all purposes of Dominion Government.... [D]irectly representing the Sovereign in the province, renders natural the exclusion of his office from the power conferred on the Provincial Legislature to amend the constitution of the Province."[9]

The Canadian Crown is not a subsidiary crown, nor even before the grant of Letters Patent in 1947 – when "the King made a complete delegation of all powers to his representative the governor general, so that the latter, acting on the advice of the Canadian Privy Council, may now legally exercise *all* the prerogative powers so far as they affect Canada if and when the Canadian cabinet so desires" – was it ever of minor importance to the development and expansion of Canada.[10] The legitimacy of Canada's political system predates the formation of the federal state. It resides in the actions of the Crown's representative, the governor, who in the

1840s agreed to take advice from the leader who commanded the support of the legislative assembly in each colony, even if, as Lord Metcalfe in Upper Canada subsequently informed the colonial secretary in London, "he was compelled to govern Canada by a party, and by a party with which he had no sympathy."[11] That event and the acceptance as a *principle* of government of a symbiosis between things or individuals once thought as opposites (the Crown and elected persons), and its subsequent dissemination through Canadian history texts, proved singular in influence. In the words of the distinguished political scientist J.R. Mallory, "It was one of the few concepts about Canadian politics that stuck in the minds of generations of Canadian schoolchildren. It became a central part of the mythology of Canadian history, an outstanding example of the use of the past to create a sense of national identity in a colonial people."[12]

In this discussion it is important to remember that Canadians, unlike their neighbours to the south, brought no sense of newness to their political situation in 1867, or afterwards. Federalism was intended to escape old problems, not to improve conduct, or to build virtue, or, in the words of American author, Bernard Bailyn, "to begin the world anew."[13] Thus, Canadians (unlike Americans) turned to – not away from – their history. This is why understanding the country's history is so important to governing today. It cannot be exaggerated that Canadian loyalty derived from politics. In the words of Alan Cairns and Cynthia Williams, "The Fathers of Confederation did not view the individual citizen as the source of political legitimacy."[14] On the contrary, it was "British political institutions which have served as the greatest single unifying force in our history."[15] Here was the basis for MacKinnon's claim that if French-speaking Canadians "had their institutions, their language and their religion intact today, it is precisely because of their adherence to the British Crown."[16] Furthermore, it is in light of this political attachment, and more particularly this continuing *British* political attachment, that legal scholar Peter C. Oliver could describe the Parliament at Westminster as Canada's "constituent assembly."[17] The virtual unanimity in Canadian public life before and after Confederation on maintaining a continuing connection with the British Parliament, of which the Crown was pre-eminent, cannot be stressed too greatly. It explains, for instance, the orderly calm of the Charlottetown conference, captured in Sir John A. Macdonald's remark that "here we are now, in a state of peace and prosperity – now we can sit down without any danger threatening us, and consider and frame a scheme advantageous to each of these colonies.... I will feel that I shall not have served in public life without a reward, if before I enter into private life, I am a subject of a great British American nation, under the government of Her Majesty, and in connection with the Empire of Great Britain and Ireland."[18] Sir Wilfrid Laurier, visiting Britain in 1897, used similar inclusive language when he pointedly described Canada as a "nation of a new type – a nation within the Empire."[19]

That phrase "nation within the Empire" is extraordinarily important, for it was within that physical and political context that Canada evolved. The country's history in the twentieth and twenty-first centuries is taught, indeed celebrated, by reference to "milestones of independence," such as, among others, membership in the League of Nations and later the United Nations, the *Canadian Citizenship Act* (1947), the *Statute of Westminster* (1931), and the adoption of the Maple Leaf flag, proclaimed by the Queen in 1965. In contradistinction to the unifying influence often claimed for the Crown, the Canadian Crown and its prerogatives were used to elevate Canada's distinctiveness as an autonomous country. Yet through these events the Crown continues without interruption. More than that, it was the Crown that helped unite the parts that together formed Canada. Indeed, the legitimacy of the Canadian political system originates in the Crown and predates the formation of the federal state (or the provinces). Joseph Howe and other Nova Scotians, who feared that Confederation would make their province a very junior partner in a new and unwelcome nationality, eventually realized, in Richard Gwyn's words, that "in order to remain British, they had to become Canadians."[20] (Nor, it should be noted, was this a uniquely Canadian response. David Malouf has written of Australian experience that "the tie with Britain was sometimes seen not as a threat to independence but as a guarantee of it against what we would now call 'Canberra' and the other states."[21]) Thus the Crown is as interwoven with geographic governance in Canada as it is with the temporal evolution in Great Britain. Indeed, as students of the scholarship of Harold Innis and Northrop Frye learned, if Canada evidenced a "longitudinal mentality" (in Frye's words), it owed a major debt to the Crown for keeping that linear perspective focused and its influence integrative.[22] It needs to be remembered as well that this perspective is not antique but extended into the last century. Witness, for example, an address by the Prince of Wales (later Edward VIII) at Massey Hall in 1919:

> Since I was last in Toronto I have been right across the continent to Vancouver Island and back again which enables me to look better at Canada as a whole, and I think I can best express myself in military terms. The western provinces are like the outposts of the nation, held by most gallant and enterprising outpost troops, who are continually pushing forward into the No Man's Land of the great Northwest. Ontario and the east is still the main body of the nation and the main line of resistance, and I congratulate you on the way in which your fine position is organized.[23]

The circumferential unity of Australia, whereby six states each with a capital city on the ocean united into a Commonwealth in 1901, stands in stark contrast to Canada's slower (1867 to 1949), continental-wide sequential unification. Confederation, said Harold Innis, was "an instrument of steam power."[24] This was why it took time to complete, and why it might be viewed as an industrial-age instance of what W.L. Morton described as "the basic rhythm of Canadian life," that is, penetrating the wilderness and then returning to civilization, whether the goal was fish, fur, timber, grain, or minerals, and whether the civilization, depending on the century, was found in Europe or Canada.[25] In striking contrast to Australia, Canada's "great stretches of wilderness" acted in a manner, wrote Northrop Frye, that made "its frontier... a circumference rather than a boundary; a country that has made a nation out of the stops on two of the world's largest railway lines."[26] Here the frontier was not a line of settlement, stretching north to south and moving west in Frederick Jackson Turner fashion, but rather composed of different parts, largely explained by the history of the Hudson Bay Company territories. Its charter, granted by Charles II in 1670, conferred a monopoly over the region and its territory included not only northern Canada but Vancouver Island and parts of coastal British Columbia: "In the 1857 parliamentary enquiry into the HBC, Rupert's Land was one of three 'descriptions' of territories held by the company: 'land held by charter.' Another was Vancouver Island, also chartered, but in a different and later arrangement. The other was the territory 'held by licence,' or 'the Indian Territory.'"[27] As a result, Canada's history includes a frontier moving not only westward but eastward (and with global warming, perhaps northward too). Remember, in Pierre Berton's words, "the Great Canadian Photograph" of Donald A. Smith hammering home in 1885 "the last spike" of the Canadian Pacific Railway, at Craigellachie in the Rocky Mountains, hundreds of miles *east* of its terminus at Vancouver on the Pacific Ocean.[28]

Over all of this vast terrain, much of it isolated from European settlement, the presence of the Crown was nonetheless tangible. It was not necessary to have the institutions and visible practices instantly associated with the Crown of today or even a century ago for its influence to prevail. There is a tendency, when speaking of the Crown, to see it as our parents and grandparents saw it: "Our elders have talked their memories into our memories until we come to possess some sense of a continuity exceeding and traversing our own individual being."[29] When it comes to the Crown in Canada, and perhaps elsewhere in the Commonwealth, this promotes an astigmatism in historical perspective that seeks to transpose a preconceived image, drawn from popular interpretation, usually British, on present and local practice. Doubtless, there is a legitimate pedigree to this disposition: legal scholar R.C.B. Risk, for instance, stated that in the matter of governance "the story began with the Constitution Act of 1791, which divided Upper and Lower Canada, and sought to reproduce in each the eighteenth century British constitution."[30] Yet the Crown is not, nor has it ever been, linear. The quintessential Canadian Crown is plural and, for that reason, it is more complicated and sophisticated than is customarily acknowledged.

W.L. Morton described the Confederation scheme of government as "a union monarchical in principle, parliamentary in form, and traditional in spirit."[31] "Principle," "form," and "spirit" are highly permissive and adaptable terms as regards meaning. One of the authors of this book, David E. Smith, has argued elsewhere that, notwithstanding the preamble of the *Constitution Act, 1867*, which speaks of the desire of provinces of Canada, Nova Scotia, and New Brunswick to secure "a Constitution similar in Principle to that of the United Kingdom," Canada today is in the position of evolving in a distinctive direction away from the United Kingdom in the matter of the Crown.[32] "Before the passage [in Great Britain] of the *Fixed-term Parliaments Act 2011*, Parliament was dissolved by the monarch, using prerogative powers. Under the 2011 Act a statutory mechanism was introduced to dissolve Parliament."[33] The debate in the British House turned on whether it was desirable that the prime minister should or should not have the discretion to seek dissolution of Parliament whenever he or she saw fit. In Canada, in 2007, an amendment to the *Canada Elections Act* established a fixed date for federal elections. When later, the government nonetheless sought and received from the governor general a dissolution in 2008, at a time when it still commanded the confidence of the House of Commons, this action was challenged in the courts as violating the terms of the "fixed date election law." Ultimately, both the Federal Court of Canada and the Federal Court of Appeal rejected the suit, on the grounds that the legislation established an expectation of fixed-date elections but preserved the prime minister's ability to advise the governor general to dissolve Parliament at any time.[34]

Does this contradictory approach to elections make the Canadian Constitution more British than the British? Or might the question about lack of symmetry be rephrased as follows: the matter at hand is not to what degree the Crown changes Canada but rather to what extent does Canada change the Crown? The answer to both questions is no. Instead, it is the procedure for amending the Constitution, set down in Part V of the *Constitution Act, 1982*, that requires the consent of all Canadian legislative assemblies to an amendment "in relation to ... the office of the

Queen, the Governor General and the Lieutenant Governor of a province." This provision is one of only five subjects (the others are provincial representation in the Commons, certain constitutional guarantees relating to the use of the English and French languages, the composition of the Supreme Court of Canada, and the amendment of this part [Part V of the 1982 Act] to be so treated). Yet, if change is reality, then the Crown today in Canada has changed: it is now deeply, almost permanently, protected. Over a comparatively short span of time, "English Canada shed its definition of itself as British and adopted a new stance as a civic nation, that is, without ethnic particularities, and erected this as the Canadian model."[35] Contemporaneously, it has been stated that "with the decline of the Empire, the paraphernalia of power that once went with it has been allowed to fade away, and the office of governor general has become more consciously low-key, deliberately unostentatious, and accessible to the general public."[36] It is the purpose of this study to evaluate the degree to which these changes have become manifest and to assess their implications for governing in Canada. To what extent, one wonders, does Canada echo Australian practice, where, it has been said, the governor general has evolved "from being an expression of Imperial bonds to 'interpreting' an independent Australian nation 'to itself.'"[37]

Even if the Crown may be said to be drifting apart – like continents – it is open to question if this movement in any respect is undermining the Crown. This chapter opened with a discussion about metaphors and alluded to the challenge for understanding that is presented by the abstraction associated with them, since analogies make one point at the expense of another. And yet, perhaps the Crown is more acceptable, or less objectionable, today because it presents itself as an abstraction. The regalia of imperialism has disappeared; the pattern now is heterogeneity. In *McAteer v Canada (Attorney General)*,[38] the subject in dispute was the oath (or affirmation) of allegiance found in the *Citizenship Act*, which the appellants in the case argued violated their rights under sections 2(a) freedom of conscience and religion, 2(b) freedom of expression, and 15(1) equality of the Charter of Rights and Freedoms.

They sought to make the oath optional. The Court of Appeal of Ontario rejected the appellants' argument, reasoning that

> the oath in the [Citizenship Act] is remarkably similar to the oath required of members of Parliament and the Senate under The Constitution Act, 1867. In that oath, the reference to the Queen is symbolic of our form of government and the unwritten principle of democracy. The harmonization principle of interpretation leads to the conclusion that the oath in the Act should be given the same meaning. (para. 6) Moreover, the Court found that the oath is secular and is not an oath to the Queen in her personal capacity but to our form of government of which the Queen is a symbol. (para. 7)

Furthermore, citing with approval, as had the lower court, the judgment quotes the late chief justice of Canada Bora Laskin: "Her Majesty has no personal physical presence in Canada.... [O]nly the legal connotation, the abstraction that Her Majesty or the Crown represents, need be considered for the purposes of Canadian federalism. Giving the term 'Her Majesty' or 'the Crown' a personal meaning is [an] anachronism" (para. 52).[39] The Supreme Court of Canada refused to hear an appeal of the case.

How has Canada come to this distinctive position with regard to the Crown and monarchy? Unlike the assessment offered by the British scholar Ben Pimlott that the republican movement in Australia would result in the Queen's "civic death," this is neither sought nor probable in Canada.[40] Canada's independent view on monarchy today has nothing to do with republican sentiment, but rather needs to be placed in the larger context of its independent disposition on imperial and Commonwealth matters in the past, when the country was far more closely aligned with South Africa (and sometimes the Irish Free State) than with Australia and New Zealand in the first six decades of the last century.

As the following chapters of this book will demonstrate, the subject of the Crown is multifaceted in Canada, with the result that it is not at all unusual to find, within weeks of each other, articles that speak, on the one hand, of "End of a Royal Era" and, on the other, of how the "Crown Proves Its Use."[41] With that breadth of interpretation on display, it was not exceptional to read, at the time Julie Payette was appointed governor general in 2017, an announcement by a "senior Liberal official" that she was "perfectly aligned with the image that we want to project."[42] Writing in the same paper, Campbell Clark described the "vice-regal role" as "a national symbol," with equal emphasis placed presumably on both terms.[43] As for actual duties, Clark maintained, in matters of governance, the governor general is "like a third-string goalie: You want them to be sharp in case it ever really matters, but it rarely does."[44] In literature on the Crown, a metaphor that equates a hockey goalie with the sovereign's representative is unique: it complicates rather than explicates the meaning of the word for which it is being employed. Moreover, it is a mystifying analogy for foreigners and an inaccurate and confusing one as well, because it depreciates what the authors of this book maintain is the pivot of the Constitution, for, among its other functions, "it is the Crown that gives legitimacy to what the politicians have worked out among themselves."[45]

The Crown completes (even concretizes) the legislative process, and for that reason, the metaphor of a neutral umpire or referee is inapplicable. On the contrary, the Crown *always* participates in the "game" – if the sporting image is employed – but not as a contestant. Its contribution is to the efficiency of the contest. In addition, as the following chapters of this book will substantiate, the Crown is involved in much more than the legislative process (federal or provincial) and its presence – in a phrase, its "demonstration effect" – has grown more visible in Canadian society in the half-century since the centennial of Confederation.

2

A Realm of Opposites

St. Edward's crown and the Imperial State crown, among other precious objects, are usually on display in the Tower of London in the United Kingdom. Contemporary visitors view them on a moving footpath, which carries sightseers from one end of the room to the other. As one is moved along, one sees the crowns in different ways and from different perspectives. What was initially distant becomes nearer, and what was once unfathomable becomes tangible – before fading back into the distance. This human reaction to perceiving the physical crowns as objects is congruent with the different perspectives on how "the Crown" is perceived as an institution. The legal and institutional abstraction of the Crown also varies, depending on the circumstances and the context in which it is found. The Crown presents differently, depending on who is observing it, who is representing it, and what role it is performing.

Some of the characteristics of the Crown are the result of constitutional history and development. It was the evolution from personal rule by kings and queens to a system of representative and responsible government that motivated Walter Bagehot to characterize the Queen as a dignified rather than efficient part of the British constitution.[1] These particular labels are reassessed in chapter 4. There are several other dichotomies that contrast aspects of the Crown, its function and operation. It is hereditary yet democratic, a symbol of colonialism and a symbol of independence, and it presents as both British and Canadian – and we should not forget that it is also an institution shared with fourteen other countries as well. The Crown enables incremental constitutional development, but prevents precipitous departures from past practices. Its powers and position are vulnerable to ordinary legislation in the United Kingdom, but its constitutional status and central powers are constitutionally entrenched in Canada.[2] Viewed from a Canadian perspective, the Crown can appear to be in a realm of opposites.

Individual and Institution

In Canada's modern constitutional monarchy, the sovereign is both an individual person, Elizabeth II, and the personification of both the state embodied by Canada as a country, and the Crown as an institution of government. The Queen is a physical person, capable of personally exercising the powers vested in her by the Constitution of Canada, by statute and pursuant to the royal prerogative or the common law. Through constitutional practice, interpretation, and development, the Queen also personifies the Crown, which has become in most senses a legal abstraction that can be distinguished from the person who is the sovereign at any given time through succession to the throne.

It is relatively straightforward to appreciate the Queen's role in Canada's system of government when she acts personally by visiting Canada, approving the creation of national honours, reading the speech from the throne (as she did in 1957 and 1977), appointing the governor general, or approving the appointment of additional senators (as she did in 1990). It is more challenging to appreciate the nature of the Crown as an institution of government, in part because the development of the Crown as something distinct from the Queen owes less to deliberate choices about how Canada should be governed than to the particular trajectory of the historical development of the United Kingdom and Canada.

The British constitution both embraced and eschewed abstraction: "The Crown became a corporation or body politic" but "retained the use and elaboration of familiar or common terms such as person, body or Crown."[3] There remains a distinction between the physical object of the crown and the abstraction that it symbolizes: historian and legal scholar F.W. Maitland wryly commented, "As a matter of fact we know that the crown does nothing but lie in the Tower of London to be gazed at by sight-seers."[4]

Over time, the Crown's personal and institutional survival was ensured as a result of the accommodation of parliamentary sovereignty, representative and responsible government, and the rule of law. While many of Europe's Continental monarchs were deposed, the British monarchy survived.[5] Familiar monarchical forms were retained, but power shifted from the sovereign to chief ministers, Parliament, and the courts. It was during the reign of Queen Victoria that the modern form of constitutional monarchy was cemented in the United Kingdom. Vernon Bogdanor summed up the sovereign's role as one of "constitutionally restricted influence rather than power."[6] By wielding this influence "not for partisan purposes, but in a neutral and detached way … [t]he sovereign came to be seen as head of the nation as well as head of state."[7]

The concept of the Crown as an institution is remarkably resistant to grand unifying theories. Exceptions, aberrations, anomalies, and expedients thwart most attempts to capture in any comprehensive abstract terms the nature of the Crown as an institution. Attributing to the Crown the characteristics of an institution distinct from the person of the sovereign is a legal fiction for which it is sometimes necessary to suspend disbelief. As Sir William Wade stated in relation to the United Kingdom, "Our law has failed to produce a coherent theory of the State," and the treatment of the Crown in British constitutional law has been characterized as "rules legitimated by history," but "unsatisfying to political theorists."[8] Similarly, Canada's pre-eminent constitutional scholar, the late Peter Hogg, observed that the "juristic nature of the state (or the government) has given rise to controversy among legal theorists."[9]

As an organizing principle of government, the Crown has been adaptable. The dispersal of the Crown, first throughout the empire and now throughout the Commonwealth, has permitted the Crown to adjust to different constitutional structures, governing practices, and local realities. The flexibility of the Crown has allowed it to function in federations as well as in unitary states, with varying degrees of regional devolution. The Crown has been exported to countries with a range of electoral systems and varying approaches to democratic and rights-based societies. It has also served as the interface with many different Indigenous peoples. In Australia, Canada's closest constitutional cousin, the Crown has been likened to a chameleon, changing its appearance to suit the political environment, with the consequence that its influence also became camouflaged and poorly understood.[10] A related charge could be made that undue fascination with and attention to the Canadian Crown as an abstraction obscures what transpires beneath the surface, by concealing the work and conduct of the Queen's representatives as well as the interactions between the political actors and the vice-regals. The celebrity status of the sovereign and the members of the Royal Family end up distracting from the nature and function of the Crown as the load-bearing structure of an entire system of government.

The potential ambiguity over the theoretical nature of the Crown as an institution seldom poses any meaningful practical difficulties. For example, in criminal cases where the liberty of the subject is at stake and where the burden of proof is the most onerous standard known to law (proof beyond a reasonable doubt), there is no metaphysical soul-searching about the nature of the Crown. Criminal prosecutions are conducted in the name of Her Majesty the Queen as represented by the appropriate attorney general. Similarly, in a handful of cases where individuals have attempted to challenge the oath of allegiance to the Queen, the courts were not concerned with medieval philosophy about the King's two bodies or the corporate attributes of the Crown. Instead, they reasoned that the oath of allegiance is "a symbolic commitment to be governed as a democratic constitutional monarchy unless and until democratically changed."[11] When an officer of the Canadian Armed Forces alleged that it was "a form of institutional harassment" to be required to "pay respect to the Queen as the Head of State of Canada" because such practices were "politically offensive and in conflict with his personal views," the Federal Court held that, given the constitutional role and status of the Crown, there is "legitimacy within our institutional structures for demanding, in appropriate circumstances, expressions of respect and loyalty to the Crown."[12]

Prompted by the litigation surrounding the *Succession to the Throne Act, 2013*, co-counsel for the attorney general of Canada, Warren Newman, cogently characterized the approach of the courts to cases about the nature of the Crown in an insightful and elegant manner:

> The practice of Canadian constitutional law before the courts is, at bottom, a pragmatic and prudential exercise. In the context of litigation, our courts have generally neither the time nor the inclination to become deeply immersed in broad philosophical and theoretical debates about the divisible and indivisible, corporeal and incorporeal nature of the Crown. It should not be surprising, then, that in the course of adjudicating disputes, the courts may often be content to rely upon a few well-canvassed constitutional principles and conventions, as well as the occasional legal fiction, in construing and applying the terms and provisions of the Constitution of Canada to the extent that it may be relevant or necessary to the case at hand, without striking off in bold new directions. Nor do constitutional anomalies born of historical facts and political compromises necessarily trouble our courts. It is not their role – certainly not in most contexts – to overcome lacunae by over-theorizing the grand scheme of things. Judges, especially those trained in the common-law traditions of public law, work incrementally, through a slow process of accretion over time and over a range of cases, in developing the law, notably as it relates to the Crown.[13]

The need to understand the Crown in a broader context and perspective was evident in the Supreme Court's 2017 decision in *Clyde River (Hamlet) v Petroleum Geo-Services Inc.*[14] The court was faced with having to decide whether the Crown's duty to consult with Aboriginal peoples arose in the context of hearings before the National Energy Board (NEB) to authorize offshore seismic testing for oil and gas in Nunavut. If it did, the question for the Court was whether or not the NEB, which is neither the Crown nor a Crown agent, could discharge the duty. During oral argument, then Chief Justice Beverley McLachlin questioned counsel for the attorney general of Canada: "As I understand your submission, you say the Crown – whatever it is – didn't delegate its duty to consult."[15] In two follow-up questions, she again said, "The Crown, whatever it is…" and "the Crown, the Attorney General of Canada or whatever."[16] This line of questioning foreshadowed the Court's interest in function rather than form.

In its decision, rather than trying to parse the meaning of "the Crown," the Supreme Court took a functional approach to whether or not the duty to consult was triggered by examining whether there were potential adverse impacts upon Aboriginal and treaty rights. Once there were, it did not matter who within the executive branch of government, broadly speaking, triggered or responded to them. The Court noted that the Crown has at least three shades of meaning. It refers to "the personification in Her Majesty of the Canadian state," "denotes the sovereign in the exercise of her formal legislative role (in assenting, refusing assent to, or reserving legislative or parliamentary bills)," and represents "the head of executive authority."[17] The Court reiterated that the duty to consult is owed by the Crown, but accepted that despite the NEB, being neither the Crown nor an agent of the Crown, nevertheless acted "on behalf of the Crown when making a final decision on a project application."[18] For the Court, it was not the board's formal legal status but rather its role and function that determined whether or not it triggered and could discharge the Crown's duty to consult.

This pragmatism was similarly on display when the Mikisew Cree First Nation argued that the Crown had a duty to consult them on the development of omnibus environmental legislation that had the potential to adversely affect their treaty rights.[19] The case was appealed to the Supreme Court of Canada, which found that ministers of the Crown are not subject to judicial review when they are acting in a legislative capacity. Despite ministers obviously being Crown agents, the Court again focused on the function that they were carrying out. When acting in a legislative capacity, ministers did not trigger the duty to consult, which was limited to executive government action.

While these two cases are contemporary illustrations of the conceptualization of the Crown depending on the context and circumstances, pragmatism concerning the Crown is not new or unique to Canada. Maitland gives the sixteenth-century example of Elizabeth I using the royal style "Queen of England, France and Ireland, Defender of the Faith, etc." The "etc." was added in response to ambiguity over the Queen's role in relation to the Church of England and Ireland. He observed,

> No doubt she is Defender of the Faith, though we cannot be sure what faith she will defend. But is that all? Is she or is she not Supreme Head upon earth of the Church of England and Ireland?... It was a difficult problem. On both sides there were men with extreme opinions, who, however, agreed in holding that the solution was not to be found in any earthly statute book.... Then a happy thought occurs. Let her highness etceterate herself. This will leave her hands free, and then afterwards she can explain the etceteration as occasion may require.[20]

The Queen is the stone that ripples the pond that is the Crown. The contradictions inherent in the Crown are part and parcel of how the "English conception of the Crown was the ambivalent institutional outcome – a corporation arguably both aggregate and sole, both progressive and retrospective, open to the evolution of representative government and attractive to royal interests and sensibilities."[21] The Queen is a visible and tangible representation of half the equation, while the Crown as an institution is more nebulous, but pervasive beneath the surface.

Hereditary and Democratic

The hereditary principle has been a feature of the monarchy for nearly a thousand years, subject to occasional disruption by revolution or intervention by Act of Parliament. The rules governing the succession to the throne used to be based on the same common law principles that governed the inheritance of land, including the rule favouring male heirs. Following the purported abdication of James II in 1688, the British Parliament provided that William III and Mary II would assume the Crown jointly. The *Act of Settlement* of 1701 ensured the Protestant line of succession by settling it on James I's granddaughter, Sophia of Hanover, and her Protestant heirs.

In 2011, the heads of the sixteen Commonwealth realms that recognize the Queen as head of state agreed to two changes to the law of the succession to the throne. The first was to remove the preference for male heirs, whereby an elder daughter could be displaced by a younger male sibling. The second was to put an end to the marrying of a Roman Catholic as a disqualification for acceding to the throne. The United Kingdom's *Succession to the Crown Act 2013* made these changes in 2015.[22] In accordance with the constitutional convention recorded in the preamble to the *Statute of Westminster, 1931*, the Parliament of Canada enacted the *Succession to the Throne Act, 2013* assenting to the changes being made in the United Kingdom.[23]

The hereditary principle has resulted in the long reign of three sovereigns: from 1763 to the diamond jubilee of Queen Elizabeth II in 2012, three monarchs have reigned for a combined total of 184 years. This has provided stability and predictability and has made the Crown a moderating influence in Canadian government and politics. Of course, the personal rule by sovereigns is a practice of the past. In the West, monarchy has long been both constitutional and democratic. The principle of responsible government requires that the Queen and her representatives act, in nearly all cases, on the advice of the ministers of the Crown. The House of Commons, provincial legislative assemblies, and the electorate are tempering influences on ministers, holding them to account and withdrawing confidence in the House or assembly or at the ballot box when they disapprove of the policies or decisions of the government. Canada's elected representatives provide democratic legitimacy to the legislative bodies to which they belong and, through them, to the Crown. Canada has retained a monarchical form of government, but one where ministers take responsibility and are held accountable for acts that are formally taken by or in the name of the Queen, the governor general, or the lieutenant governors (the vice-regals).

Since the British system of government developed incrementally and not by grand design, the role of the Crown rests on a sometimes amorphous combination of legal rules, constitutional conventions, historical practices, and tacit understandings and arrangements. In his 1947 presidential address to the Canadian Political Science Association, Robert MacGregor Dawson observed, "Cabinet government was the product of a series of historical accidents, experiments, and temporary expedients, so haphazard in its origin and development that no one could have planned it in advance, or, even if this had been possible, would have been so rash as to suggest that it could ever have been made to work."[24]

How to characterize the role of a constitutional monarch and her representatives has been an enduring dilemma. The expedient approach is to explain it away, as the *New York Times* did in relation to the Queen's role in the Brexit prorogation: "Britain's Queen Is a Figurehead, but She Just Got Dragged into Brexit Politics."[25] Similarly, a Canadian lawyer and scholar has suggested that "in political reality, the focus of power is in the Cabinet, with the governor general retaining a role as a legally necessary figurehead."[26] At the other extreme are those who suggest that vice-regal officers should exercise their formal powers in accordance with their own or someone else's views to thwart the will of a prime minister or premier. This occurred in 2019, when Rachel Notley, former premier of Alberta, urged the province's lieutenant governor to deny royal assent to a legislative initiative of the government with which she disagreed as leader of the opposition.[27] These extremes miss the mark. The Queen and her representatives are more than automatons but less than free agents.

The Queen, the governor general, and the lieutenant governors play a central role in formalizing decisions taken by ministers and by ensuring that Canada always has a prime minister and each province a premier. The public sees the outcome of the interplay between the political actors who tender advice and the vice-regal officers who approve it. The vice-regals lend dignity and solemnity through the issuance of proclamations, commissions, orders in council, and other formal documents often affixed with the symbols of the state, as will be examined in chapter 5. This formalism camouflages and obscures what happens beneath the surface. Their outward facing roles are formal, yet their inward facing influence can, in appropriate circumstances, be subtle but significant.

The vice-regals are often appointed following significant experience and distinguished service to Canada and can therefore provide an informed confidential perspective to a first minister within the framework of the three "rights" formulated by Walter Bagehot in relation to the Crown: the right to be consulted, the right to encourage, and the right to warn.[28] The Crown's representatives can be counted on to be discreet sounding boards for first ministers who may otherwise be surrounded by political rivals.

A vice-regal can, in appropriate circumstances, question, inquire, and at times delay acting on advice in order to give the government the opportunity to reflect on its course of action and for the political actors to resolve disagreements among themselves. This is what happened in December 2008 when Prime Minister Stephen Harper asked Governor General Michaëlle Jean to prorogue Parliament shortly after an election and before any laws had been enacted in order to avoid a vote of non-confidence. The governor general agreed, but only after a meeting with the prime minister that lasted over two hours, where they reportedly discussed "the state of Canada's economy, the viability of an alternative coalition government, and the mood of Parliament and the country," and where the governor general confidentially consulted her constitutional advisor, Peter Hogg.[29]

Similarly, a vice-regal can avoid explicitly rejecting formal constitutional advice by questioning government policy that would undermine the structure of the Canadian system of government. Adrienne Clarkson recounts resisting "three entreaties from the Prime Minister's Office, including one from Mr. Martin himself" for her to swear in the Martin government in Centre Block's Hall of Honour instead of at Rideau Hall. Clarkson observed that every other swearing in had taken place at Rideau Hall and that the governor general only attends the Parliament buildings in the Senate Chamber. She further thought that she was being asked to participate in a "presidential-type installation" that was inconsistent with Canada's form of government.[30]

Furthermore, the mere presence of a vice-regal officer can affect the way that the political actors behave. The necessity of securing the formal approval of a non-partisan actor can restrain a first minister from acting controversially. The Crown's role in government formation often affects how the political actors behave following an uncertain election outcome. Although the Crown must formally appoint the first minister, the Queen and her representatives must not become involved in any deal-making following an election. Bogdanor in *The Coalition and the Constitution*, which examined the formation of Britain's 2010 coalition government, noted that the party leaders must "ensure that the Queen is not brought into the negotiations or caused political embarrassment."[31] It is exceedingly rare for a representative of the Crown to refuse to act on the advice of a first minister, with the best-known Canadian examples being Governor General Lord Byng's refusal of a dissolution to Prime Minister William Lyon Mackenzie King in 1926, and Lord Aberdeen's refusal to make appointments after Prime Minster Sir Charles Tupper had been defeated in 1896. Canada's dispersed monarchy has experienced a few other experiments and aberrations, particularly at the provincial level. When Norman Ward reviewed John Saywell's *The Office of the Lieutenant Governor*, he insightfully noted the greater latitude afforded to the provincial Crown's representatives throughout Canada's post-Confederation history: "As representatives of the monarch, Lieutenant-Governors have selected premiers under trying circumstances, dismissed ministries, refused dissolutions, vetoed bills, all on a grander scale than would have been tolerated from either the governor general or the monarch during the same period."[32]

Despite these occasional examples to the contrary, the modern view in Canada is that a vice-regal officer cannot thwart the express will of a first minister who enjoys the democratic legitimacy of the confidence of a legislative body. To do so would invite constitutional tension. Nevertheless, the Queen and her representatives are the ultimate check – or constitutional "fire extinguishers," to borrow an analogy from Frank McKinnon – in the event political actors behave entirely outside of accepted norms. In these rare circumstances, a representative of the Crown might be justified in refusing to act on advice or in taking personal initiative in order to preserve or protect a fundamental constitutional value.

In the *Patriation Reference*, the Supreme Court speculated that if an incumbent prime minister "clung to office" after another political party had received a majority of seats in the House of Commons at a general election, the governor general would be entitled to dismiss the ministry.[33]

Andrew Heard also suggests that there are some occasions where a vice-regal might refuse to act on clearly unconstitutional advice: "Some harms cannot be undone after the fact, either by the courts or by an election. Some injuries to property, to lives or even to the political system have to be prevented before they occur, since no remedy can undo the damage. Certainly, the governor general [and lieutenant governors] should leave most constitutional problems to either the courts or the electoral system to sort out. Yet there are still some matters that are perhaps dealt with by the governor general refusing to act on unconstitutional advice."[34] Unfortunately, for the political observer these occasions invariably transpire behind the scenes and are rarely revealed until many years after the fact.

The requirement that the Queen and her representatives act on advice originally emerged as a method of curbing the "arbitrary use of royal power."[35] However, the requirement to act upon advice now also functions as a way of insulating the sovereign and the vice-regals from political involvement. It protects the Queen and her representatives from criticism if they have no policy independent from that of their ministers. In Canada, this does not prevent the governor general and the lieutenant governors from taking an interest in certain issues, but it does require that the issues be scrupulously non-partisan. The Canadian representatives of the Queen tend to personalize their time in office by emphasizing certain themes and have championed initiatives such as the arts and letters, science, journalism, sports, the family, youth, volunteerism, philanthropy, innovation, and outer space. Under Governor General David Johnston's leadership, the Rideau Hall Foundation was established as a charitable organization to promote learning, leadership, innovation, and giving initiatives.[36]

In contrast to the Queen, the vice-regals in Canada are not hereditary, and the full ambit of their vice-regal role concludes upon departure from office, as does a significant degree of their public notoriety. The distance from court, a concept that will be examined in chapter 5, along with the rotating cadre of eleven representatives, as members of what has become known as the "vice-regal family," makes the Canadian Crown and its representatives accessible and relatable to citizens. This allows Canada to retain the advantages of the Royal Family, whose members take an interest in Canada through regular royal tours, the acceptance of patronages, and championing of Canadian activities and initiatives, while allowing Canadian society to remain egalitarian without the emergence of an elite ruling class of vice-regals.

Unlike the Queen, who began preparing to become monarch following her father's accession, her Canadian representatives are often not as aware of or conversant with the role of the Crown. In recommending the appointment of a vice-regal, the prime minister makes a calculated choice in deciding what type of experience and qualities will best suit the circumstances. As discussed below, the trend since 1999 has generally been to choose candidates who have not previously been involved in party politics. When this is combined with a lack of diplomatic, military, or senior public service experience, vice-regals will be at a disadvantage in the sense that they "will have to learn everything" about their role and the functions of government "no matter how brilliant or successful the candidate's previous career may have been."[37] The former lieutenant governor of British Columbia, Steven Point, candidly admitted that he "knew nothing about the role" when he was appointed in 2007.[38] Adrienne Clarkson described how she and her husband made daily visits to a Toronto library to read about the role of the governor general, after she had been offered the position by Prime Minister Jean Chrétien but before it had been officially announced – attempting to disguise her pursuit with "a pile of books about the American Constitution and South American land problems."[39]

The democratic legitimacy of the Canadian Crown flows from the fact that it nearly always acts on the advice of democratically accountable ministers. In this regard, the chief minister, be it a prime minister or a premier, occupies a privileged position.

Largely unknown to the statute book, the prime minister's leadership of the Cabinet provides an opportunity for the prime minister to influence the exercise of powers of the Crown and of other ministers. In some cases, the prime minister is the conventional actor who tenders advice to the Queen or to the governor general, which is then approved and formalized in a legal instrument. At other times, the prime minister influences the advice given to the governor general by ministers collectively, or the powers that are exercised by other ministers individually.

A "memorandum regarding certain of the functions of the Prime Minister" that was first circulated under Prime Minister Tupper in 1896 and that was last issued under Prime Minister Mackenzie King in 1935 records the longstanding practice governing the inner workings of the federal government at the highest levels.[40] In particular, it sets out the matters upon which the prime minister expects to take the initiative by listing several recommendations as the "special prerogative" of the prime minister. This document does not confer legal powers on the prime minister; rather, it describes the matters upon which the prime minister expects to be the conventional actor who recommends the exercise of legal powers to the legal decision maker (usually either the Queen, the governor general, or the governor in council). These matters include the meeting of the Privy Council and the quorum for tendering advice to the governor in council as well as the exercise of constitutional, statutory, and prerogative powers, such as the summoning and dissolution of Parliament and the appointment of privy councillors, senators, and the chief justices of all courts, among others. The prime minister also controls the machinery of government, by approving any changes to the structure and apparatus of the federal public administration and any transfers of responsibilities between ministers. In this regard, the prime minister is the "architect and umpire" of Canada's system of cabinet government.[41]

Symbol of Colonialism and of Independence

In chapter 1, we examined the Crown as a symbol and metaphor by emphasizing the Crown as a unifying force providing a source of identity for Canadians. But there are strands of Canadian history that are less jubilant about the Crown. Both historically and in some contemporary quarters, the Crown is seen as a symbol of colonialism. The preamble to the *Constitution Act, 1867* recorded the desire of the provinces to be federally united under the Crown and acknowledged that confederation promoted the "Interests of the British Empire." Section 56 exemplified the colonial nature of the Act by requiring the governor general to send Acts of the Parliament of Canada to the United Kingdom to allow for the possibility of the British government advising the Queen to disallow them (a practice since abandoned following the 1929 Report of the Conference on the Operation of Dominion Legislation and Merchant Shipping Legislation).[42] The charge of colonialism resonates particularly strongly from North America's original inhabitants. Aboriginal law scholar Brian Slattery has written that "many indigenous people take the view that the Crown's acquisition of control over their territories was an illegitimate act, consummated without their consent."[43]

Despite being associated with Canada's colonial past, the Crown was also the principal means through which Canada achieved independence. The colonial character of Canada's Constitution conceals how Canada achieved independence. In contrast to the United States, which had a revolutionary break with the British Crown, Canada retained and embraced the Crown, achieving independence through agreements about how the Crown would behave, rather than casting it off in favour of a republican form of government. Canada's independence from the United Kingdom, along with the other self-governing dominions, was characterized in an oft-cited passage from the 1926 Balfour Report: "They are autonomous Communities within the British Empire, equal in status, in no way subordinate one to another in any aspect of their domestic or external affairs, though united by a common allegiance to the Crown, and freely associated as members of the British Commonwealth of Nations."[44] In 1926 and 1930, Commonwealth first ministers agreed that the governor general would no longer act as an agent of the British government and that both the governor general and the sovereign would act exclusively on the advice of domestic rather than imperial ministers. Independence from the United Kingdom was formalized in the *Statute of Westminster, 1931*, where the UK Parliament provided that it would not legislate for a dominion without the dominion's request and consent. In Canada's case, the final formal link to the United Kingdom was severed by the *Canada Act 1982*, which specified that no future British statute would form part of the law of Canada. This formalized the practice that had endured since 1931. The reason for the delay was not the United Kingdom clinging to colonial attachment to Canada, but rather that the Canadian federal government and the provinces had been unable to agree on a formula for constitutional amendment.[45] This final act of independence was also achieved under the auspices of the Crown when the Queen proclaimed the *Constitution Act, 1982* in force in a ceremony on Parliament Hill on 17 April 1982. Through negotiation and compromise, Canada employed the Crown to achieve independence within a colonial constitutional framework. The Canadianizing of the Crown has resulted in the establishment of an independent realm, linked through the person of the sovereign, but no longer a subsidiary of the United Kingdom.

The Crown may also hold out promise for reconciling with the Indigenous population. The courts have developed a body of Aboriginal law that seeks to accommodate prior Aboriginal occupation of much of Canada with the reality of Crown sovereignty by elaborating a duty whereby the Crown must act honourably in relation to Aboriginal peoples. In *Haida Nation v British Columbia (Minister of Forests)*, the Supreme Court explained the constitutional source of what it termed the "honour of the Crown":

> Put simply, Canada's Aboriginal peoples were here when Europeans came, and were never conquered. Many bands reconciled their claims with the sovereignty of the Crown through negotiated treaties. Others, notably in British Columbia, have yet to do so. The potential rights embedded in these claims are protected by s. 35 of the *Constitution Act, 1982*. The honour of the Crown requires that these rights be determined,

recognized and respected. This, in turn, requires the Crown, acting honourably, to participate in processes of negotiation. While this process continues, the honour of the Crown may require it to consult and, where indicated, accommodate Aboriginal interests.[46]

That reconciliation with the Aboriginal peoples of Canada depends on Crown action was also recognized by the Truth and Reconciliation Commission's calls to action, which included the development of a reconciliation proclamation to be issued by the Crown and the reconciliation of Aboriginal and Crown constitutional legal orders to recognize and integrate Indigenous laws and legal traditions within Canada's legal framework.[47]

By adapting, the Crown allowed Canada to achieve independence within the continuity of a constitutional framework that was originally designed to promote the interests of the British Empire but that now sustains Canada as an independent country, within the Commonwealth.[48] Her Majesty in Right of Canada is now, both in form and in substance, a symbol of Canadian independence.

British and Canadian

The House of Windsor is a British institution. Andrew Heard summed up the practical reality of the situation by observing that the "Queen *visits* Canada and *resides* in the United Kingdom."[49] Although the Royal Family presents as British, the Queen is shared among the sixteen countries that recognize her as head of state. To those who criticize the Canadian head of state for being "foreign," Norman Ward replied that "while technically correct, it is also true in reverse: the head of state in the United Kingdom is the monarch of another country, Canada – and Australia, and New Zealand."[50] The person of the sovereign is shared among sixteen different realms.

While clearly British in its origins and in relation to its role in the United Kingdom, the Crown is also formally and symbolically Canadian. Using the Crown to achieve independence also afforded the opportunity to Canadianize the monarchy to reflect Canadian conditions and values. This was accomplished through changes to the law, the evolution of constitutional conventions and practices, and the adoption of Canadian procedures and symbols.

A major step towards Canadianizing the Crown was the common understanding reached in the 1920s that the governor general was no longer to be a representative of the British government, but was to represent the Crown and have the same relationship with the Canadian government as the King had with the British government. Further, both the governor general and the sovereign would act, in Canadian matters, only on the advice of Canadians.[51] Although initially denounced as a "constitutional monstrosity," this practice endured.[52] The relationship between the British government and the governor general mirrored the relationship between the federal government and the lieutenant governors, which had been settled by the judges several years earlier. In 1892, the Judicial Committee of the Privy Council held that a lieutenant governor "is as much the representative of Her Majesty for all purposes of provincial government" as the governor general is for the federal government.[53] These arrangements planted the seeds for the emergence of a Canadian Crown, which would be instrumental in establishing federal and provincial autonomy within the constitutional framework. Proclaiming Elizabeth II as "Queen of Canada," as authorized by the *Royal Style and Titles Act* in 1953, brought the Queen's formal title into line with the reality of the established constitutional position that there is a distinct Canadian Crown by including an element of the royal style and title specific to Canada.

In retrospect, the appointment of Vincent Massey as the first Canadian-born governor general in 1952 was also a major step in Canadianizing the Crown, but at the time Prime Minister Louis St. Laurent was concerned that it would be perceived as a weakening of Canada's connection to Britain by a French-Canadian prime minister.[54] When Massey's appointment was announced, St. Laurent was asked whether only Canadians would be subsequently appointed as governor general and tactfully replied that he "would not like to admit that Canadians, alone among His Majesty's subjects, should be considered unworthy to represent the

King in their own country."[55] Massey's appointment demonstrated that the Crown could not only act on the advice of Canadians, but could itself be represented by a Canadian. Since Massey, only Canadians have served as governor general.[56] Following Massey's appointment, the Crown's Canadian attributes have matured both formally and symbolically, culminating in the emergence of the Canadian realm. The Queen continues to act exclusively on the advice of Canadian ministers, many of her functions have been assumed by the governor general, and, as discussed in chapter 6, the Crown has reinforced its Canadian identity through the development of Canadian symbols and practices.[57] The governor general has also represented the Queen of Canada on the international stage. Beginning in the 1960s, governors general took a more active role promoting Canadian interests outside of Canada. Roland Michener carried out state visits to the Caribbean and Europe, after being encouraged to do so by the Queen, and the governor general continues to represent Canada abroad at the request of the Government of Canada and in accordance with Canada's foreign policy as established by the prime minister and the minister of foreign affairs.[58]

A series of incremental changes have seen the governor general carry out many of the formal matters that used to be submitted to the Queen. The changes to the Letters Patent Constituting the Office of Governor General in 1947 provided the formal legal mechanism for the governor general to assume the sovereign's powers, duties, and functions in relation to Canada. Despite authorizing the governor general to exercise "all powers and authorities" in respect of Canada, the Letters Patent were not intended to change existing practices, and there was an understanding that matters that traditionally had been submitted to the King "would not be transferred to the Governor General without the consent of the Palace."[59]

Over time, the governor general gradually assumed increased responsibilities. In 1966, the Queen agreed that the governor general could approve changes to the table of titles for Canada.[60] In 1975, the governor general began to appoint Canadian ambassadors and high commissioners to foreign and Commonwealth countries and to grant *agrément* (acceptance) to the appointment of foreign representatives to Canada. In 1977, the governor general assumed responsibility for additional diplomatic functions, such as signing letters of credence and recall for Canadian ambassadors, letters of commission and recall for Canadian high commissioners (on behalf of the Queen and in the Queen's name); authorizing declarations of war and treaties of peace; and granting full powers to authorize the signing of an international treaty in head of state form, and authorizing the ratification of such treaties. Beginning in 2004, letters of credence and recall were issued in the name of the governor general, instead of the Queen. Similarly, letters of credence and recall presented by foreign ambassadors and high commissioners began to be addressed to the governor general instead of the Queen.

The matters where the Queen remains personally involved are now normally limited to matters directly affecting the Sovereign, such as: (a) appointment of the governor general; (b) amendments to the letters patent constituting the office of the governor general and the issuance of supplementary letters patent; (c) alteration of what matters will be referred directly to the sovereign, commonly referred to as changes to the "existing practice"; (d) alterations in the royal style and title; (e) granting of honours (including the creation of); (f) granting of royal patronage; (g) appointment of colonels-in-chief of Canadian regiments; (h) appointment of the Canadian secretary to the Queen; (i) designs for Canadian coinage; (j) permission for the inclusion of the crown in Canadian grants of arms and badges; and (k) the use of royal seals.[61]

Given the Canadianizing of the monarchy, and more profoundly the establishment of Canada as an independent realm with all the symbols, functions, and institutions of other independent countries, it is startling to see the assertion, from some quarters, that Queen Elizabeth II is the "first and last 'Queen of Canada'" and that "Canada's independence is at stake" on the basis of the decisions of the Superior Court of Quebec and the Quebec Court of Appeal in the litigation surrounding the succession to the throne.[62] As noted above, the law touching the succession to the throne was modernized by the United Kingdom Parliament in 2013 and was, in accordance with the convention recorded in a recital in the preamble to the *Statute of Westminster, 1931*, assented to by the Parliament of Canada in the *Succession to the Throne Act, 2013*. As the then minister of justice, Rob Nicholson, explained, the provisions and structure of the Constitution of Canada provide that "whoever, at any given period is the Queen or King of the United Kingdom is, at the same time, the Queen or King of Canada."[63] When the United Kingdom Parliament modernized the law of the succession to the throne, it was not legislating for Canada, but rather was amending the United Kingdom laws that determine who is the sovereign of the United Kingdom. Canada takes the sovereign as we find him or her, as determined by the United Kingdom Parliament. To change this basic rule of symmetry would require resort to the unanimous consent amending procedure in section 41 of the *Constitution Act, 1982*, but maintaining it does not require any Canadian action. By constitutional convention, the Parliament of Canada assents to changes to the law touching the succession to the throne, as it did in the *Succession to the Throne Act, 2013*. This position was accepted by both the Superior Court and the Court of Appeal, and the Supreme Court refused the application for leave to appeal.

Neither the outcome of these cases nor the reasoning contained in the judgments of the Superior Court and the Court of Appeal call into question Canada's formal legal independence from the United Kingdom. The United Kingdom Parliament cannot and does not legislate in relation to Canada, the Queen and her representatives continue to act exclusively on the advice of Canadian ministers in Canadian matters, the governor general continues to carry out nearly all of the Queen's functions in relation to Canada, the Queen and her successors will continue to be styled as the Queen or King of Canada, and they will continue to use a comprehensive set of Canadian seals, symbols, and practices. Furthermore, the "office of the Queen," which includes its constitutional status and royal powers, is firmly entrenched. To alter the rule that the Queen of Canada is the same person as the Queen of the United Kingdom would require a constitutional amendment, but to maintain it does not. To suggest that the outcome to the succession to the throne litigation has changed any of this might make for flashy headlines, but it does more to confuse than to promote understanding of the Crown in Canada. As Andrew Heard has noted, requiring Canada to enact mirror legislation imitating the United Kingdom's law touching the succession to the throne would "contradict both constitutional history and common sense."[64] The Canadian rule, as now affirmed by the courts, "does not undermine a real and positive relationship between Canada and the Queen."[65]

Enables and Prevents Constitutional Change

The dual nature of executive power, whereby the representatives of the Crown act on the advice of responsible ministers, has enabled organic and incremental constitutional development that has been cumulatively significant since Confederation. At the same time, the Crown's place in the Canadian constitutional framework, in particular the entrenchment of the offices of the Queen, the governor general, and the lieutenant governors, prevents precipitous or radical constitutional change in the absence of formal constitutional amendment. Canadian independence was secured, in part, by having Canadian ministers advise the Crown on matters relating to Canada. This allowed for Canadians to control the formal mechanisms of government. Since the role of the political actors in tendering advice to the Queen and her representatives is governed by unwritten constitutional conventions, the Constitution provides flexibility for the political actors to experiment with different ways of advising the formal legal representatives of the Crown. This has allowed Canada's system of government to keep pace with contemporary constitutional values and has permitted a certain amount of innovation and experimentation, while still preserving the essential characteristics of Canada's system of government.

The Crown's protective characteristics were illustrated by the lieutenant governor's role in the legislative process preventing Manitoba's early twentieth-century experiment with direct democracy that would have empowered voters – directly, by referendum – to enact legislation. Viscount Haldane, writing for the Judicial Committee of the Privy Council in 1919, found this initiative inconsistent with the Constitution on the basis that it impermissibly removed the lieutenant governor from the legislative process.[66] More recently, in 2014, the Supreme Court of Canada determined that the Harper government's proposal to legislate a framework for consultative elections to inform the prime minister's choice of candidates to recommend to the governor general for appointment to the Senate required resort to the general constitutional amending procedure and could not be established through ordinary federal legislation.[67] The Court reasoned that the governor general's power to appoint senators included not just their formal appointment, but also the entire process through which they are selected. According to the Court, consultative elections would imbue senators with the imprimatur of a popular mandate, which would be inconsistent with the Senate's role as a complementary chamber, rather than a rival, to the elected House of Commons.

Prime Minister Stephen Harper's innovation in the appointment of the governor general and lieutenant governors was more successful. At the end of Michaëlle Jean's time as governor general, the prime minister established the Governor General Expert Advisory Committee, an ad-hoc committee to advise him on her successor.[68] It was chaired by the secretary to the governor general and included the Canadian secretary to the Queen, prominent academics, and experts on the Crown. The committee carried out extensive consultations in order to develop a short list from which David Johnston was selected by the prime minister to recommend to the Queen for appointment. The use of a committee to produce the list from which the governor general was selected was so successful that it was formalized in 2012, to advise on the appointment of the lieutenant governors and territorial commissioners – the Committee on Vice-Regal Appointments, which was chaired by the Canadian Secretary to the Queen. The committee's terms of reference specified that it was to provide nonpartisan advice to the prime minister. In practice, this continued the trend that had begun informally at the federal level, with the appointment of Adrienne Clarkson in 1999, of choosing governors general who had not been involved in party politics. Five of six of Clarkson's predecessors had been active in federal politics prior to being appointed governor general.

When Prime Minister Justin Trudeau took office in 2015, he ceased to rely on an advisory body for vice-regal appointments, but he established similar advisory bodies to provide him with shortlists of individuals to recommend for appointment to the Senate and to the Supreme Court of Canada.[69] The board tasked with vetting candidates or appointment to the Senate is mandated to assess whether individuals can provide an independent and non-partisan contribution to the work of the Senate. The appointment of such individuals, who since 2015 have not sat with any of the political caucuses in the Senate, has transformed the nature of the upper house from one organized around government and opposition groups to one that is now dominated by independent senators. Similarly, the advisory board for Supreme Court appointments has been tasked with recommending three to five candidates for each vacancy on the court, with a view to advancing the government's commitments on diversity and bilingualism.

The Crown's constitutional role has also allowed Canada to experiment with so-called fixed-date elections legislation, while preserving the flexibility necessary in a Westminster system of government to have elections outside of this framework. In 2006, the Conservative Party of Canada was elected on a platform that included a commitment to "introduce legislation modelled on the BC and Ontario laws requiring fixed election dates every four years, except when a government loses the confidence of the House (in which case an election would be held immediately, and the subsequent election would follow four years later)."[70] In 2007, this commitment was implemented through amendments to the *Canada Elections Act*, which created an expectation that federal general elections would be held every four years on the fourth Monday in October. The amendments expressly preserved the powers of the governor general, "including the power to dissolve Parliament at the Governor General's discretion."[71] Most of the provinces have enacted similar regimes.

The governor general's power to dissolve Parliament was preserved for at least two reasons. First, the royal prerogative to dissolve Parliament, which is mentioned parenthetically in section 50 of the *Constitution Act, 1867*, is one of the key royal prerogative powers that is constitutionally entrenched and can be amended only by proclamation authorized by resolutions of the Senate and the House of Commons and all of the provincial legislative assemblies.[72] Second, under our system of responsible government, ministers must maintain the confidence of the House of Commons. A government that does not have the confidence of the House of Commons must either resign, to allow the governor general to invite another prime minister to assemble a ministry that will attempt to secure the confidence of the House of Commons, or it must advise the governor general to dissolve Parliament in order to see whether a general election will return a House of Commons that will have confidence in the government. A government, particularly in a minority Parliament, cannot always expect to maintain the confidence of the House of Commons for four years. The possibility of defeat on a confidence matter requires that the governor general retain the discretion to dissolve Parliament at any time.

The amendments to the *Canada Elections Act* created a statutory framework for fixed-date elections, should the prime minister wish to use it. This has allowed prime ministers and Canadians to experience fixed-date elections in 2015 and 2019, while accommodating snap elections in 2008 and 2011. The 2008 election, held two years after the 2006 election, was challenged in the Federal Courts, where both the Federal Court and the Federal Court of Appeal confirmed that the *Canada Elections Act* amendments preserved both the governor general's discretion to dissolve Parliament and the prime minister's ability to advise the governor on when dissolution should occur.[73] The amendments were interpreted as indicating Parliament's view on when dissolution should ordinarily occur, but leaving the governor general and the prime minister free to take a different view on the timing of a general election. Time will tell whether fixed-date elections become the rule rather than the exception. The ability to establish statutory expectations about the timing of elections allows for incremental or gradual experiments with democracy, while preserving the governor general's formal powers. It also creates an expectation about the timing of federal elections, from which a prime minister may need to explain or justify any departures.

The Canadian experience with fixed-date elections can be contrasted with the approach taken in the United Kingdom, where the *Fixed-term Parliaments Act 2011* provides for the dissolution of Parliament by operation of law every five years. Elections may be held earlier only if the government loses the confidence of the House of Commons, or if at least two-thirds of the members of the House support a resolution for early elections. Unlike the Canadian statute, which expressly preserved the powers of the governor general, the British statute explicitly provides that "Parliament cannot otherwise be dissolved." This example shows how the Crown is more vulnerable to legislation in the United Kingdom, where there is no rigid or formal constitutional protection for the Crown.

3

The Dispersal of Power

Appointments are made, acts of Parliament are proclaimed, mails are carried, crimi-nal prosecutions are instituted, war is declared, treaties are negotiated and ratified, in the name of the King or of the Governor-General, although the Prime Minister and the Cabinet are in fact the ones who make the selections and decide the policies which lie behind all these activities. Pomp, ceremony, and the external symbols of power and high regard are lavished on the one executive, while the other must rest content with an occasional expression of popular confidence moderated at all times by systematic opposition and carping criticism.

R. MacGregor Dawson, *The Government of Canada*, 1947

This chapter moves beyond the abstraction of the Crown as a sym-bol to address its underlying role in dispersing power throughout Canada's system of government. Those who find the trappings of the monarchy anachronistic often overlook the constitutional, statutory, prerogative, and common law powers of the Crown through which Canada is governed. Attributing executive power to the Queen has allowed for authority to be disseminated among federal and provincial jurisdictions and the individuals and enti-ties who act on behalf of the Crown.

The Crown's constitutional and statutory powers are relatively straightforward to identify since they are expressed in writing. Throughout the statute books, the "Crown" remains convenient shorthand. When Parliament wishes to empower the cabinet to make an appointment or to make regulations, it gives the power to the governor in council, on the understanding that the governor general or lieutenant governor will act only on the advice of members of the incumbent ministry.

In addition to the powers that are conferred on those who act for the Crown, certain powers are inherent in the Queen as a natural person and in the Crown as an institution. These find their source not in the Constitution or in legislation, but in the royal prerogative and the common law. The identification of these inherent aspects of the Crown's authority can be challenging, because it requires an investigation into constitutional history and practice to determine what powers, privileges, and immunities are intrinsic in the Crown and an analysis of whether they have survived to the present day and whether they have been overtaken by legislation. While the preponderance of executive powers are statutory, the Crown's non-statutory powers are among the most enduring but least studied and they are therefore the focus of this chapter.

The Crown itself was dispersed, first throughout the empire and then throughout the Commonwealth, so an appreciation of the Crown's authority often requires an examination of important developments in other jurisdictions. Although they may not appear to have an obvious connection to Canada today, they are an important part of the shared inheritance of executive authority. This is not merely antiquated attachment to a map with one-third of the surface tinted in pink; rather, it is a practical acknowledgment that the system of Westminster government we enjoy today as a constitutional monarchy was developed and refined not just in Canada and the United Kingdom, but also as the result of events in other jurisdictions that were at one time under the Crown's authority.

In *The Oxford Handbook of the Canadian Constitution*, Craig Forcese observes that the "royal prerogative is the preserve of specialists, a reflection of its irrelevance to most Canadians most of the time."[1] Focused study of the prerogative may indeed remain in the preserve of specialists, with attention often focused on the "reserve powers," but the assertion of irrelevance is more difficult to sustain. The prerogative might appear to be irrelevant because it tends to come to public attention only during moments of constitutional tension, such as the controversial decision in 2019 to prorogue the

United Kingdom Parliament prior to Brexit, a similarly contentious Canadian prorogation to avoid a vote of non-confidence in
2008, or the rejected request for a dissolution by a premier who
had lost the confidence of the legislative assembly fifty-two days
after an election in British Columbia in 2017.[2] These high-profile
exercises (or refusal to exercise) the prerogative demonstrate how
it is part of the legal fabric that is central to the operation of our
democratic institutions.

Much more often, the powers vested in the Crown are exercised
routinely without fanfare or attention. This frequency demonstrates that the prerogative is directly relevant to Canadians more
often than one might assume. Behind the scenes, prerogative powers facilitate, sustain, and nourish many aspects of government
action.[3] While there are only a handful of historical court cases
dealing with the prerogative, there is a robust and growing corpus
of modern case law in which individuals have challenged the exercise of prerogative authority. These cases arise in areas as varied as
the issuance of passports,[4] refugee health care,[5] the conferral and
revocation of honours,[6] the seeking of clemency for a Canadian on
death row abroad,[7] the ratification of an international treaty,[8] the
repatriation of a Canadian citizen detained abroad,[9] the deploy-
ment of the Canadian Armed Forces,[10] the visit of foreign naval
vessels to Canadian ports,[11] the expulsion of a foreign diplomat,[12]
the prorogation of Parliament,[13] the dissolution of Parliament,[14]
the appointment and dismissal of ministers,[15] and the granting of
mercy.[16] In these varied contexts, individuals have asked the courts
to examine the lawfulness of the exercise of prerogative authority.
The courts have recognized the prerogative as a viable source of
legal authority for government action and have gradually come to
treat the exercise of prerogative authority similarly to other sources
of executive authority, thereby unifying the legal approach to the
exercise of public power.

If irrelevance occupies one extreme of the spectrum, it is important not to overemphasize or exaggerate the role of the prerogative. In order to appreciate the prerogative, one must have a sense
of proportion, moderation, historical context, and jurisprudential
awareness. The prerogative is not a freestanding general authority

to do anything that is not expressly prohibited, nor is it an invitation to mystify or obscure the exercise of state power. Rather, the royal prerogative consists of a limited class of powers, privileges, and immunities that history has left in the hands of the Crown until or unless Parliament or the legislatures displace or otherwise affect them by statute.

The Royal Prerogative in Historical Perspective

The present-day royal prerogative is the outcome of centuries of historical development, first in the United Kingdom, and later in Canada and throughout the Commonwealth. The royal prerogative has its roots in the time when the sovereign was the sole repository of all governmental power, whether executive, legislative, or judicial.

The constitutional history of the United Kingdom reveals ebbs and flows of sovereign power: "In fact although the king was an essential part of the mechanism of state, though he enacted laws in Parliament, issued writs, granted patents, commanded armies, the part he played might be real or formal as the king might be strong or weak, the council vigorous or disunited, the parliament interested or apathetic."[17] According to Maitland, "The line between what the king could do without a parliament, and what he could only do with the aid of parliament, was only drawn very gradually, and it fluctuated from time to time."[18] If sovereignty ebbed and flowed in the past, its whereabouts are clearer today. Parliament ultimately triumphed in wresting sovereign power from the Crown, with the consequence that the non-statutory powers of the Crown are limited to those that survived the revolutionary settlement in 1689.

Canada did not experience the same struggle for parliamentary sovereignty as the United Kingdom. The pre-Confederation colonies in British North America attained representative and responsible government according to local conditions, and the transformation of personal rule by the sovereign into the vesting of executive authority in the Crown was complete by the time that

Canada was established in 1867. It was a supreme imperial Parliament that enacted the *Constitution Act, 1867*, which constituted the Parliament of Canada as sovereign within the framework of the Constitution of Canada.

A recital in the preamble of the *Constitution Act, 1867* recorded that the Province of Canada, Nova Scotia, and New Brunswick were to be "federally united into One Dominion under the Crown of the United Kingdom of Great Britain and Ireland, with a Constitution similar in Principle to that of the United Kingdom." Another recital declared that it is expedient "that the Nature of the Executive Government therein be declared." Section 9 of the *Constitution Act, 1867* so declared that executive government and authority of and over Canada continued to be vested in the Queen.

The Queen in question in 1867 was Victoria – who never visited Canada – and the *Constitution Act, 1867* was drafted to accommodate a non-resident sovereign. Although the Constitution vested executive government in the Queen, she was personally given few responsibilities. Instead, the Constitution contemplates the existence of a governor general and lieutenant governors who will perform many formal executive powers, duties and functions "in the Queen's name."[19]

In 1867, Queen Victoria was a constitutional monarch, in the modern sense of that expression, and Canada was to have a system of representative government "similar in principle" to that of the United Kingdom.[20] The Supreme Court has acknowledged that this embraces "responsible government and some common law aspects of the United Kingdom's unitary constitutionalism, such as the rule of law and Crown prerogatives and immunities."[21]

The royal prerogative stems from centuries of legal traditions in the United Kingdom, so it is understandable that it is often challenging to identify those aspects of the prerogative that remain available to the Canadian Crown in contemporary times. The framework for identifying whether or not the prerogative exists was set out by the House of Lords in a case arising out of events that took place during the Second World War in what is now Myanmar. In 1942, the British Army ordered the destruction of facilities for producing petroleum belonging to the Burmah Oil Company, among others, in order to deny them to the advancing Japanese forces. It was accepted that the destruction of the facilities was a lawful exercise of the royal prerogative to wage war in defence of the realm. The question was whether the British government must compensate the company for the property destroyed.[22]

The law lords struggled to identify the scope of the war prerogative. Lord Reid remarked, "It is not easy to discover and decide the law regarding the royal prerogative and the consequences of its exercise."[23] Viscount Radcliffe commented on the vagueness of the prerogative and said that, as the case progressed, he had "become more and more uncertain what it is that we are really talking about."[24] One reason that aspects of the prerogative are not readily ascertainable is because it is based largely on custom and usage. As discussed below, when it is cast in statutory form, the prerogative is displaced. Only in those cases where a conflict has reached the courts have the contours of certain aspects of the prerogative been conclusively settled by judicial decision. When *Burmah Oil* was argued, there were only two modern cases upon which the House of Lords could rely.[25] Lord Reid observed that there was "practically no authority" between the glorious revolution of 1688 and the beginning of the twentieth century. He also noted that "*obiter dicta* and the views of institutional writers and text writers are not always very helpful."[26]

Nevertheless, Lord Reid proposed a historical approach to the prerogative. In order to rely on prerogative authority, it is necessary first to examine the traditional or historical extent of the Crown's powers, next to search for the contemporary scope of those powers in modern usage, and finally to examine the extent to which any limitations have been imposed by statute. Lord Reid concluded that there was no prerogative to take or destroy property without compensation because the parties could point to no modern instance of taking or interfering with property without payment.[27]

When applying Lord Reid's framework, one has to be sensitive to whether and how the prerogative has been adapted to the Canadian context. Although Canada has a constitution "similar in principle" to that of the United Kingdom, there are some aspects of the prerogative that may be suitable for the United Kingdom, but not for Canada. Many historical prerogatives, such as a Queen's property interest in sturgeon, swans, and whales have never been asserted in Canada.[28] Similarly, the prerogatives in relation to the established Church of England obviously do not extend to the Canadian context.

The most common prerogatives can be divided into five main groups, presented in no particular order in a list that is necessarily illustrative rather than exhaustive. First are the prerogatives that relate to the executive and legislative branches of government. These include the appointment and dismissal of ministers; the prorogation and dissolution of Parliament; the conferral of honours, and the establishment of offices and appointment of certain office holders. Second are the administration of justice prerogatives, such as the Crown's historic immunity from being liable in tort (now largely eliminated by statute), immunity from statute (now a rebuttable presumption provided for in the interpretation acts), and the power to grant pardons. Third are the property prerogatives, such as escheat and power to set aside lands for use as Indian reserves. Fourth is the defence prerogative, which includes the declaration of war and peace and certain powers linked to the defence of Canada. Fifth are the foreign affairs prerogatives, such as entering into treaties, the appointment and accreditation of high commissioners and ambassadors, and the conduct of official communications with foreign governments, including the issuance of passports.[29]

Defining the Prerogative

The prerogative is subject to duelling definitions, and there remains an enduring debate about how to describe the non-statutory powers of the Crown. There are two leading definitions, the broader of which is that of British constitutional theorist A.V. Dicey. Dicey defined the prerogative as "the residue of the discretionary authority which at any given time is legally left in the hands of the Crown."[30] He claimed that "every Act which the executive government can lawfully do without the authority of an Act of

Parliament is done in virtue of this prerogative."[31] This definition captures the sources of authority that are unique to the Crown as well as those that all legal persons possess at common law. The former encompasses things that the state alone can do, such as declare war and dissolve Parliament, while the latter includes the power to enter into binding legal obligations, the power to hold and dispose of property, the power to make gifts, and the capacity to sue and be sued.

British jurist Sir William Blackstone, on the other hand, provided a narrower definition of the prerogative and confined it to those inherent legal attributes that are unique to the Crown.[32] Blackstone suggested that where any of these powers or privileges are made available to another legal person, they cease to be part of the prerogative. There is variation in academic and judicial opinion as to which definition is preferable.[33]

Among the most fervent and persistent adherents to the Blackstonian definition of the prerogative was Sir William Wade. When delivering the Hamlyn lectures on "constitutional fundamentals," he argued that, in establishing the Criminal Injuries Compensation Board to distribute public money to victims of crime, the British government was "merely doing what Miss Hamlyn did when founding this lectureship and what any of us could do if we had the money ready to hand."[34] Similarly, he compared the appointment of ministers to the power "which all legal persons have at common law to employ servants or agents."[35] He also took issue with the publication of a government pamphlet being described as a prerogative power of the Crown to issue information as a "choice example of a non-prerogative."[36]

Martin Loughlin has cogently criticized Wade's "ostensible objective" of promoting clear thinking for reducing too many of the Crown's unique attributes to the status of an ordinary person.[37] Loughlin questions whether equating a passport issued by the foreign secretary to a letter of introduction from a colleague, or the appointment of a secretary of state with the issuance of a contract of employment to a management consultant is a fair characterization of the Crown's powers.[38] Wade later acknowledged that his "comments were made purely for purposes of terminological accuracy, without any suggestion that they had legal consequences."[39] In the Canadian context, Peter Hogg has arrived at the same conclusion, noting, "Nothing practical turns on the distinction between the Crown's 'true prerogative' powers and the Crown's natural-person powers, because the exercise of both kinds of powers is reviewable by the courts."[40] This has been confirmed by the courts of the United Kingdom and of Canada.[41]

However, from an analytical perspective, there is much to recommend the Blackstonian approach as a way to differentiate between what only the Crown can do and what an ordinary person can do, because there is greater consensus about the nature and scope of the capacities and powers that the common law ascribes to a natural person than there is about the extent of the powers, privileges, and immunities of the Crown. For this reason, it can be advantageous, from a conceptual point of view, to distinguish between the capacities and powers that the Crown enjoys with its subjects and those powers, privileges, and immunities that it possesses alone.

Conversely, while the Blackstonian approach can assist in isolating those powers that are unique to the Crown, the Diceyan approach avoids the question of whether the Crown's powers as a natural person flow from a "third source" of authority that is found neither in statutes nor in the prerogative. This theory of authority was described by Stephen Sedley in lectures he delivered following his retirement from the Court of Appeal for England and Wales as "a jurisprudential version of the emperor's new clothes."[42] Attributing to the Crown the capacities of a natural person has attracted some controversy in the United Kingdom, but not in Canada.[43] The Supreme Court of Canada has expressly rejected the proposition that a Crown agent seeking to enter into a contract on behalf of the Queen must be specifically authorized to do so by statute or order in council. The Court acknowledged that "Her Majesty is clearly a physical person," and that she can, like any other person, act through agents.[44]

Sedley's objection to the Crown's powers being assimilated to those of a natural person is that the Crown "may have the capacities, and even the liberties, of a natural person," but it does not "have their powers."[45] He points out that the "Crown and the individual share the capacity to dispense their money or property stupidly, maliciously, or capriciously; but where the individual is also legally free to do so, the Crown is not."[46] His real objection is that the Crown, whatever the source of its powers, must be "constrained by ordinary principles of public law."[47] Although decrying the third source of power as "a theory of government outside the law," he nevertheless acknowledges that both the high (Blackstonian) and broad (Diceyan) prerogative powers must be "exercised within the law."[48] Once one accepts that the exercise of public power, whatever its source, is subject to the same principles of public law, any objection to whether or not the prerogative includes the powers and capacities of a natural person would seem to fall away.[49]

In reality, the word "prerogative" readily admits several shades of meaning. In its legal sense, the royal prerogative is a source of lawful authority, which encompasses powers, privileges, and immunities of the executive branch of government. In its colloquial sense, the word simply means a course of action that one is able to determine for oneself to the exclusion of others. In order to properly understand the non-statutory powers of the Crown, it is necessary to keep this distinction in mind.[50] Many constitutional or statutory grants of authority provide a power to be exercised according to the discretion of the legal or conventional actor, but the existence of such a choice is not determinative of the source of legal authority that is being exercised. In elaborating or elucidating aspects of the prerogative, analytical rigour is crucial. Maitland was not being facetious when he cautioned against the use of the term "Crown." The following paragraph from his lectures followed immediately from his observation that executive power is no longer held by the Crown exclusively, but is conferred on a variety of governmental actors. Therefore, it was natural for him to counsel that

> there is one term against which I wish to warn you, and that term is "the crown." You will certainly read that the crown does this and the crown does that. As a matter of fact we know that the crown does nothing but lie in the Tower of London to be gazed at by sight-seers. No, the crown

is a convenient cover for ignorance: it saves us from asking difficult questions, questions which can only be answered by study of the statute book. I do not deny that it is a convenient term and you may have to use it; but I do say that you should never be content with it. If you are told that the crown has this power or that power, do not be content until you know who legally has the power – is it the king, is it one of his secretaries: is this power a prerogative power or is it the outcome of statute? This question is often an extremely difficult question.[51]

Two contemporary authors have either overstated or understated the royal prerogative by extending it in areas where it clearly does not exist or denied it by defining it out of areas where it certainly does exist. Philippe Lagassé writes that the "Canadian Crown retains many prerogative powers in areas ranging from appointments to national security."[52] He adds that the "appointment prerogative allows the prime minister and ministers to name senior civil servants to key roles throughout the government, including deputy ministers and advisory positions within the Privy Council Office" and that "even when appointments are specified by statute, the appointment prerogative ensures that many senior officials occupy their positions at the pleasure of the prime minister and cabinet."[53]

Lagassé confuses and conflates the two meanings of the word "prerogative" when only one of them is appropriate in this context. Authority to appoint individuals to senior positions in the federal public administration is provided by statute. For example, a standard such provision is found in section 3 of the *Department of the Environment Act*: "The Governor in Council may appoint an officer called the Deputy Minister of the Environment to hold office during pleasure and to be the deputy head of the Department."[54] Furthermore, there is a general appointing authority in the *Public Service Employment Act*, which authorizes the governor in council to appoint other deputy ministers and other senior officials.[55] The source of authority for these appointments has been provided to the executive by Parliament in statute.

Similarly, the tenure of these appointments is also determined by statute, not by prerogative. The quality of the tenure of deputy ministers appointed under departmental statutes is specified in those acts as being at pleasure. Appointments made pursuant to the general power in the *Public Service Employment Act* are subject to the default rule in the federal *Interpretation Act* that they are at pleasure unless otherwise specified.[56] By constitutional convention, the prime minister (and premiers in the provinces) takes the initiative in recommending the appointment of deputy ministers and senior officials to the governor in council and of recommending their dismissal or replacement, but the appointments are quite clearly the exercise of statutory powers. To use the term "prerogative" in this context is to comingle the colloquial meaning with the legal one. Of course, there is a royal prerogative appointment power, which may be used only in circumstances not covered by statute.[57] However, where a statute expressly provides the authority to make an appointment, it is statutory – not prerogative – authority that is at issue, regardless of whether the prime minister takes the initiative in recommending the appointments to the governor in council.

In the other direction, Craig Forcese denies what certainly must still be a prerogative power by defining it out of existence. Forcese writes, "Another classic prerogative – the Governor General's appointment and dismissal of prime ministers – may have its origins in prerogative but is now more properly regarded in contemporary Canadian law as a constitutional convention."[58] Forcese similarly calls into question the source of authority for the appointment of ministers, writing that the appointment of ministers "may be best described not as the residue of royal authority recognized by the common law, but as rules that determine which executive official may instruct the Governor General in the exercise of his or her prerogative or constitutional powers."[59]

With respect, these statements confuse the identification of the source of legal authority for the appointment of the prime minister and ministers with the way in which such authority is exercised. Under the Constitution of Canada, there are no constitutional conventions that *provide* a source of legal authority for government action. Rather, constitutional conventions *constrain* or *condition* the manner or extent to which legal powers may be exercised. The convention that determines who may advise the governor general is found in conventions that support the operation of the principle of responsible government, which tells us that it is ministers of the Crown who have the confidence of the House of Commons. As the Supreme Court of Canada explained in the *Patriation Reference*, as a matter of convention, the governor general is not obliged to take the advice of a government attempting to cling to office after another political party has received a majority of seats at a general election and would be justified in dismissing the ministry under such circumstances.[60] However, any actions taken by ministers before being dismissed would be unimpeachable as a matter of law:

> An order or a regulation passed by a minister under statutory authority and otherwise valid could not be invalidated on the ground that, by convention, the minister ought no longer be a minister. A writ of *quo warranto* aimed at ministers, assuming that *quo warranto* lies against a minister of the Crown, which is very doubtful, would be of no avail to remove them from office. Required to say by what warrant they occupy their ministerial office, they would answer that they occupy it by the pleasure of the Crown under a commission issued by the Crown and this answer would be a complete one at law, for at law the government is in office by the pleasure of the Crown although by convention it is there by the will of the people.[61]

The prime minister and other ministers must be legally appointed to their positions.[62] This is one of the prerogative authorities that the governor general is expressly authorized to exercise under the 1947 Letters Patent, and it is done formally.[63] When there is a change of government in Canada, the governor general invites an individual to become prime minister and to form a government, then appoints that person as prime minister by commission under the Great Seal of Canada. The prime minister tenders an instrument of advice advising the governor general of which individuals the prime minister wishes to be summoned to the Privy Council, if they are not already privy councillors, and appointed as ministers. Once the governor general approves the instrument of advice, commissions issue to the ministers under the Great Seal of Canada appointing them to their positions. This situation is replicated in each of the provinces with little variation other than with respect to the style accorded to certain offices.

The foregoing fine distinctions may seem nitpicky and pedantic, but whether a power is sourced in prerogative or in statute has implications for how to determine the scope of the power, whether there are any conditions on its exercise, and how it may be limited or altered. J.A. Corry once cautioned that "if a search for the essential elements of a constitution is not to lose itself in a welter of confusing materials, some categories of classification and analysis will have to be adopted."[64] He continued by noting, "Just as the amateur botanist, lacking a principle of classification, wanders among the flowers and gets only the impression that nature is wonderful, so the student of government without categories for sorting out his material decides that the subject is incomprehensible."[65] Classifying the types of executive power allows us to appreciate the continuing role of the royal prerogative in the governance of Canada.[66]

Limits on the Royal Prerogative

There are certain limits on the extent to which the prerogative can disperse power throughout the government. The residual nature of the prerogative accounts for a significant limit: it cannot be expanded. When the British Broadcasting Corporation attempted to claim Crown immunity from taxation as a modern development of the prerogative, Lord Diplock remarked, "It is 350 years and a civil war too late for the Queen's courts to broaden the [royal] prerogative."[67]

In Canada, the *Canadian Charter of Rights and Freedoms* also limits the way the prerogative can be exercised, as it did when the Federal Court found that it was an unjustified violation of an individual's mobility rights to refuse to issue an emergency passport to allow him to return to Canada from abroad.[68] However, importantly, the prerogative has been recognized as a sufficient authority to constitute a "reasonable limit prescribed by law" for the purposes of limiting rights under section 1 of the *Charter*.[69]

The prerogative is also subject to developments in the common law concerning the exercise of executive powers. For example, those who exercise the prerogative in a way that affect the rights, privileges, or interests of an individual are subject to a common law duty to act fairly, which emerged in the last century and continues to be refined in the administrative law jurisprudence.[70]

Grounding government action in the prerogative has implications for the nature of the power that may be exercised. The Supreme Court has emphasized that the constitutional principle of the rule of law requires that "the exercise of all public power must find its ultimate source in a legal rule."[71] In this regard, the royal prerogative is a viable but often limited source of authority. There are two broad types of lawful authority for government action, which have been labelled as *imperium* and *dominium*.[72] The former is the coercive power of the state to affect the rights and interests of individuals, while the latter is the power to "employ the government's resources of wealth or property," including "those legal devices of the common law, such as contracts, gifts and other transfers, through which the wealth of the government may be deployed."[73]

While a statute, through clear language, can justifiably interfere with legal rights, the prerogative usually provides a more limited type of lawful authority and is generally not a viable source of authority to override or restrict the legal rights of individuals.[74] Nevertheless, Sir William Wade and Christopher Forsyth noted, "There are still a few prerogative powers which can have unwelcome legal effects on individuals."[75] This includes, for example, declarations of war, which by their nature contemplate armed conflict and the taking or destruction of property.[76] Exercises of the prerogative can also have pleasant effects. Consider the exercise of the royal prerogative of mercy, which provides a reprieve from the otherwise ordinary effects of the law. Each aspect of the prerogative must be examined on its own merits in order to determine its scope and the extent to which it authorizes interference with rights. These tend to be narrow aspects integral to particular prerogatives.[77]

However, despite its limits, the prerogative is still a viable source of lawful authority and is particularly relevant in terms of *dominium* authority. The usual sources of *dominium* authority are the annual and supplementary appropriation acts, which authorize the spending of public money from the consolidated revenue fund for, among other things, the "operating expenditures" of government departments. The salaries of public servants are paid out of these operating expenditures, and the payment of their salaries will be lawful charges against the appropriations only if the public servants are engaged in the business and operations of the relevant department. The main business of a department is to support the minister who presides over it, so the operations of the department consist of supporting the mandate of the minister. A minister's mandate is derived from many sources, including the minister's ability to act for the Crown under the prerogative where the subject matter in question has not been assigned to another minister or entity by statute.

The Office of the Federal Interlocutor for Métis and Non-Status Indians is a prime example of the prerogative being used to confer mandate on a minister. This role was created in 1985 to provide a point of contact between the Government of Canada and the Métis and non-status Indians. Over the years, this role has been held by the minister of justice, the minister of natural resources, the minister of public works and government services, the minister of Indian affairs and northern development, and the minister of Crown-Indigenous relations. Each of these ministers was authorized by prerogative order in council to act as federal interlocutor and to enter into contribution agreements with organizations representing Métis and off-reserve Aboriginal peoples.[78] The governor in council could act under the prerogative because the role of interacting with Métis and non-status Indians was not dealt with by statute. The mandate conferred under the prerogative resulted in a unit being created in the department to support the minister's work as federal interlocutor. In this way, the prerogative was used to broaden the purposes for which the department's appropriation could be used in support of the minister.

Parliament and the Prerogative

Parliament and the legislatures have occasionally acted to constrain the Crown's non-statutory powers but have more often left the Crown a margin of manoeuvre in their exercise. In this regard, the prerogative has been a resilient source of executive authority. Nevertheless, Parliament and the legislatures are sovereign and may legislate in relation to the prerogative within their constitutional limits. As Lord Reid remarked in *Burmah Oil*, "The prerogative is really a relic of a past age, not lost by disuse, but only available for a case not covered by statute."[79] This was echoed by the Supreme Court of Canada, which has affirmed the approach to take when analysing the impact of statute on prerogative authority: "Once a statute has occupied the ground formerly occupied by the prerogative, the Crown [has to] comply with the terms of the statute."[80] The Supreme Court summarized the impact of statute on the prerogative as follows: "As statute law expands and encroaches upon the purview of the royal prerogative, to that extent the royal prerogative contracts." The court added, "This displacement occurs only to the extent that the statute does so explicitly or by necessary implication."[81]

These apparently straightforward rules can be challenging to apply in practice. However, it is possible to make some general observations. Statutes may have three types of effects on the prerogative. First, except for those aspects of the prerogative that fall within the ambit of the multilateral constitutional amending procedures, prerogative authority can be abolished by express statutory language. The offices of the Queen, the governor general, and the lieutenant governors are constitutionally entrenched by virtue of section 41 of the *Constitution Act, 1982*. This includes the constitutional status and powers of those offices, including the central prerogative powers. However, outside of these key royal prerogatives, legislation on the prerogative – including express abolition – is possible.[82]

Second, a statute dealing with an aspect of prerogative authority may nevertheless make it clear that it intends to leave the prerogative authority applicable to the same subject matter intact. Many statutes make it clear that prerogative authority remains, despite legislation on the same subject matter. Amendments made in 2007 to the *Canada Elections Act* created the expectation that elections would occur at four-year intervals on a "fixed date" in October, but expressly preserved the governor general's discretion to dissolve Parliament at any time.[83] Similarly, the *Criminal Code* authorizes the governor in council to grant a free pardon or a conditional pardon to any person who has been convicted of an offence and to order the remission of a fine. However, Parliament specified that nothing in the act "in any manner limits or affects Her Majesty's royal prerogative of mercy."[84] The *Criminal Code* sets out a detailed scheme for dealing with wrongful convictions, but does not otherwise constrain the prerogative of mercy. Therefore, the governor in council may act pursuant to the statutory authority of the *Criminal Code*, or the governor general may act under prerogative authority as authorized by the *Letters Patent, 1947*, as he did in 2012 when a number of farmers who had been convicted of violating the Canadian Wheat Board monopoly were pardoned under the prerogative.[85]

The third category of statutes is one that maintains the royal prerogative as the source of legal authority, but structures the way in which such authority is to be exercised or provide consequences for the exercise of the prerogative. Consider subsection 7(2) of the *Official Languages Act*, which provides that "all instruments made in the exercise of a prerogative or other executive power that are of a public and general nature shall be made in both official languages and, if printed and published, shall be printed and published in both official languages."[86] This provision does not call into question the authority to make an instrument under the prerogative, but it does impose a requirement that a certain class of such instruments must be made in both official languages.[87]

Other times, a statute will supplement or augment prerogative authority. The *Criminal Records Act* states that it does not limit or affect the royal prerogative of mercy, but it provides that two sections of the Act apply to any pardon granted pursuant to the royal prerogative.[88] The first provision requires that the criminal record of an individual who is granted a pardon be kept separate and apart from other criminal records and be disclosed only with the consent of the minister of public safety and emergency preparedness. The second prevents any federal public sector employer or any employer in a work, undertaking, or business that is within the legislative authority of Parliament from asking job applicants to disclose a conviction for which they have been granted a pardon. It was necessary to set out these obligations in statute because the prerogative is not a viable source of authority to impose them. The result is that Parliament has left the prerogative of mercy intact, but has provided statutory consequences attendant upon its exercise.

The fourth and more challenging scenario is where a statute relates to a matter where there is prerogative authority, but is silent on the intended effect on the prerogative. The courts have generally accepted that, to the extent that a statue overlaps with the prerogative, the prerogative is displaced, abridged, or placed in abeyance.[89] Finally, we must recall that – although having pride of place in the Constitution of Canada – the *Constitution Act, 1867* originated as an enactment of the United Kingdom Parliament. The *Constitution Act, 1867* must be read with care in order to determine its impact on the royal prerogative. Some powers, such as the power of dissolution, are mentioned parenthetically in the *Constitution Act, 1867* (see section 50), but remain exercises of the prerogative. Other powers, such as the power to grant royal assent (section 55) are expressly conferred by the *Constitution Act, 1867*, even though – at one time – they may have found their source in the prerogative.[90]

When a statute genuinely occupies the same subject area as the prerogative, it would be an affront to parliamentary sovereignty and the rule of law to allow prerogative authority to somehow continue to operate as a parallel source of legal authority. However, absent clear legislative intent to permanently extinguish or abolish an aspect of the prerogative, prerogative authority will likely be revived should a statute that merely overlaps with a prerogative be repealed.

The Courts and the Prerogative

The courts have recognized the royal prerogative authority as a source of lawful authority, but have also modernized their approach to cases involving the prerogative by treating them similarly to cases dealing with other sources of executive authority. The prerogative survives, but must be exercised in accordance with contemporary legal values. In some ways, the prerogative shares similarities with the common law, since both embrace the aspect of Westminster constitutionalism that abstains from codification or the need to otherwise reduce everything to writing. The courts have afforded the government a degree of flexibility and adaptability by allowing the prerogative to be exercised as the circumstances require.

The courts used to approach prerogative questions quite narrowly. A court would determine the existence and scope of a prerogative power but would not review its exercise. This approach was premised on the assumption that the source of the power precluded judicial scrutiny of its exercise, since exercises of the prerogative ordinarily raised questions that courts were not qualified or competent to answer. Now, however, the source of the power will not be determinative of its reviewability. Even when government action is based on the prerogative, courts will proceed to consider several factors to determine the justiciability of exercises of prerogative power: whether the decision in question has a sufficient legal component to warrant an assertion of expertise by the courts; whether it is based on a delicate balancing of competing policy, ideological, political, social, and moral factors, making it more suitable for decision by political actors than by the courts; and perhaps most critical in recent decisions, whether it affects an important individual right, interest, or legitimate expectation.[91]

The courts acknowledge that the exercise of prerogative powers can raise a spectrum of issues ranging from purely political questions to important questions of legal rights. At the political end are matters of high policy, such as the decisions to enter into an international treaty, to declare war, or to dissolve Parliament, where public policy and public interest considerations far outweigh the rights of individuals or their legitimate expectations. These decisions are generally not amenable to judicial review. At the other end of the spectrum lie administrative decisions such as the refusal of a passport, where the mobility rights of a specific individual are affected.

There have never been serious calls to codify the prerogative in Canada, but a desire for deference is no impediment to legislating in relation to the royal prerogative. Whether the source of a power is prerogative or statutory, the courts will examine the context in which it is exercised to determine the degree of deference owed to the decision maker. Take, for example, the *Kyoto Protocol Implementation Act*, which was a private member's bill enacted in a minority Parliament after Prime Minister Harper's government had announced that Canada would not meet the targets set out in the Kyoto Protocol for greenhouse gas emissions. The Act required the minister of the environment to table in the Houses of Parliament an annual report describing the "measures to be taken to ensure that Canada meets its obligations" under the Kyoto Protocol. The minister reported that the Government of Canada had no intention of meeting its Kyoto Protocol commitments. When this was challenged in Federal Court, the Court held that the Act merely required the minister to report on how Canada was implementing the Kyoto Protocol and did not require the government to implement the protocol. The court also found that the extensive mechanisms for public and parliamentary accountability were a "substitute for judicial review," such that the reasonableness of the government's response to Canada's Kyoto commitments was not justiciable.[92] The case illustrates how the source of a public law power is not determinative of whether or not it is justiciable.

The manner in which the prerogative is exercised can have implications for how it is treated by the courts, including whether or not it is subject to judicial review. For example, the courts have held that where a scheme is established for the exercise of the royal prerogative, individuals will have a legitimate expectation that such a scheme will be followed.[93] This does not guarantee any particular outcome or result, but it does mean that certain procedural rights may be enforceable – even if the ultimate decision is not justiciable. For example, it is well settled that the conferral of honours is not a matter suitable for judicial determination. However, the Federal Court of Appeal has held that, if a procedure is set out for the award of an honour, that procedure must be followed. In *Chiasson v Canada*, Justice Strayer held that the *Canadian Bravery Decorations Regulations* created a legitimate expectation of the process that would be followed for the award of the Canadian Bravery Decoration, and that the regulations – even though adopted pursuant to the royal prerogative in relation to a matter that is substantively not justiciable – provide a set of rules sufficient for the court to determine compliance.[94] Similarly, the Federal Court of Appeal assumed, without deciding the matter, that a policy on the steps that would be taken before an individual's appointment to the Order of Canada is terminated could create legitimate expectations enforceable on judicial review.[95]

In 2019, the United Kingdom Supreme Court issued a momentous decision in the context of the United Kingdom exiting the European Union. The UK government had failed to secure a withdrawal agreement acceptable to Parliament, and the prime minister advised the Queen to prorogue Parliament in circumstances making it more likely that the United Kingdom would exit the European Union without any withdrawal agreement. The lawfulness of the decision to prorogue Parliament was challenged, and the Supreme Court found that the prime minister's advice to the Queen was unlawful because it had the effect, without reasonable justification, of preventing Parliament from carrying out its constitutional responsibilities of legislating and holding the government to account.[96] The Court opened its decision by remarking that the circumstances of the case "have never arisen before and are unlikely ever to arise again" and that its decision was to be considered as an "on off."[97]

We anticipate that the exceptional circumstances surrounding Brexit will confine this decision to its particular facts. Whether or not one agrees with the outcome in the case, the decision is constitutional innovation disguised as legal orthodoxy. The Court says it is doing no more than "performing its proper function under our constitution"[98] by defining the scope or extent of the prerogative, but there are at least two novel features to the decision. First, the court overlooked the legal decision maker and focused on the conventional actor, in this case the prime minister. Until now, the conventional actor was unknown to the law of the Constitution, or at least his or her advice was subsumed by the actions of the person in whom legal authority was formally vested.[99] Second, the Court blurred the line between the considerations relevant to the scope and exercise of the prerogative by purporting to examine neither the particular scope nor the precise exercise, but rather the "extent" of the prerogative of prorogation. This allowed the Court to articulate two limits, based on parliamentary sovereignty and responsible government, against which to evaluate the prime minister's advice. Although based on legal principles, the meaning given to them by the court – that it was unlawful for a prime minister to use prorogation to frustrate Parliament – is hardly an objective legal criterion to be applied dispassionately by judges. Rather, it amounts to a formula for finding a prorogation unlawful whenever it is thought to be undesirable. After all, every prorogation frustrates Parliament. In the face of the monumental implications of Brexit for the United Kingdom, we take to heart the caution of H.V. Evatt, who worried that the "spot diagnosis" of constitutional infirmities might not be reliable on account of "the physician being ten thousand miles away from the spot."[100] Nevertheless, the Brexit litigation demonstrates how the prerogative remains central to the operation of the institutions of Westminster government and shows that the courts are willing to innovate in order to protect what are seen as important constitutional principles or values relating to democratic institutions.

4

Beyond All That Glitters: Reassessing Bagehot's Efficient and Dignified Crown

Canada possesses a governmental system whose principal institutions comprise a constitutional monarchy, a bicameral federal parliament, and ten unicameral provincial legislatures. While at a glance this statement appears straightforward enough, in fact the words disguise a subject of considerable complexity. It is generally accepted that English law failed "to develop a coherent concept of the modern state" and that the explanation for the failure lay in "the incremental formation of the English State, which has been primarily a political rather than a legal achievement."[1] One might ask, in a book devoted to examining Canada's Deep Crown, Why then are we talking about the English state? The reply is that when it comes to the *constitution*, it is impossible to separate Canada from its English (not British) heritage. As with the English state, Canadian-English relations in the realm of the constitution are subject to evolution – no ruptures, no explanations of governmental structures. It is against this apparently seamless backdrop that Walter Bagehot, the author of *The English Constitution* appears.[2]

Although *The English Constitution* first appeared over 150 years ago, its author remains a pre-eminent scholar of the Westminster constitution, whether the variant of that constitution is found on the banks of the Thames or the Ottawa Rivers, in Canberra or in Wellington. K.C. Wheare, himself a universally acknowledged author and teacher in the fields of federalism and the constitution, went so far as to credit Bagehot with "inventing" the English constitution, one that people had failed to "recognize or apprehend," before he wrote about it.[3] More to the point, says Ferdinand Mount, author of *The British Constitution Now*, Bagehot "*invented a career* for British monarchs."[4] Bagehot was unusual among political theorists for not being a theorist. He wrote for periodicals, was editor of the *Economist* (1861–1877), and possessed a journalist's talent for perception along with a capacity for communicating his insights through accessible prose. It is these qualities that explain the influence and longevity of his work and have won him a place alongside the Mills and Alfred Marshall, among others, in the Victorian pantheon of politics.[5]

Yet that reputation, in recent years, has encountered scepticism. Vernon Bogdanor, has gone so far as to say that "the evolutionary constitution, the constitution of Burke and Bagehot, is dead and can never be revived."[6] Part of the reason for the eclipse of Bagehot's stature as a theorist, Bogdanor believes, is that people have lost interest in the constitution, because "there is no narrow [i.e., understandable] sense" of what the term means. Placing to one side the *Constitution Act, 1867*, and subsequent amendments to that Act, one might argue that, when it comes to constitutional questions, associated, for instance, with minority government, conventions, or even the composition of the Senate of Canada, Canadians have not demonstrated an acumen or attentiveness much greater than their counterparts in the United Kingdom on comparable matters. It is in the context of "reputational slippage" (at home) that the continuing relevance, if such is the case, of Bagehot's thought to twenty-first century Canada must be examined.

As befitted the mid-Victorian passion for organizing facts, Bagehot sought to impose order on the accretion of institutions and practices that comprised Britain's constitution. For this purpose he employed categories derived from a series of dichotomies, the best known of which is the division of the constitution into dignified and efficient parts (that is, parts that hold authority and use authority). In this approach Bagehot was prompted by more than a desire for rational ordering, although his reasons are largely tangential to the concerns addressed here. Let it be said that they originated in an awareness of the British class structure and especially in the rise of an urban working class, which Bagehot saw as a threat to middle-class (but minority) control of Parliament. He believed that the lower classes must be excluded from active governing, and that it was the function of the dignified parts of the constitution to legitimate that exclusion. That Bagehot was politically elitist, or more, a social snob, is immaterial to the study of the influence of his writings. Certainly, it did not dissuade Prime Minister Sir John A. Macdonald in 1884 from citing his work as an authority to guide the behaviour of lieutenant governors, nor did it prevent another Father of Confederation, Alexander Campbell, from using the leisure that appointments as senator and, later, lieutenant governor, gave him to turn, "naturally," he said, to Bagehot. Campbell, nonetheless, had reservations about the great work stemming in part, it would appear, from its social preoccupations. As he wrote to Macdonald, "You must have experience in a colony to enable you fully to appreciate the inapplicability of much of the book."[7]

There is another explanation for monarchy's influence, which becomes clearer when the focus shifts from the monarch (or his or her surrogate) to the Crown as an organizing principle of government. (By the way, Bagehot was not consistent in his use of terms, although he favoured the personal reference, a usage that over time has imparted to his framework a distinctly un-Canadian flavour). The argument goes like this: because the parts of a dichotomy are interdependent, contraction of one necessitates expansion of the other. Confinement of Bagehot's Crown to the dignified sphere cleared the way for the House of Commons to occupy without hindrance the efficient sphere of government. In fact, says M.J.C. Vile, conferment of absolute authority on Parliament was Bagehot's purpose.[8] By awarding the legislature a monopoly of power, he destroyed rival claims based on the older doctrine of separation of powers. So interpreted, Bagehot thus becomes the father of the Westminster model of government, whose distinctiveness he (and a legion of subsequent writers) attributed to the fusion of executive and legislative power. Political Science 101 teaches that under this system the executive sits in the legislature, its members come from the legislature, and it is accountable to the legislature for its actions. Students are also taught that these cardinal features of parliamentary-cabinet government originate not in law but by convention. That is, there is no *legal* requirement that the executive sit in the legislature, or its members come from that body or that they be held responsible to it.

Convention, not law, then, is the issue, and Bagehot more than any modern authority did an admirable job of conflating the two. The legal basis of the executive derives from the Crown (see Part III of the 1867 Act), but in Bagehot's scheme of things this singular fact is ignored or treated as irrelevant. Most modern texts follow his lead, even though by so doing they perpetuate a serious misunderstanding of the comparative powers of the executive and the legislature. Writing more than a century ago, constitutional scholar Sydney Low declared that "our constitution was based not on codified rules but tacit understandings," although, as he ruefully remarked, "the understandings are not always understood."[9] The more accurate depiction might be summarized as follows: "The constitutional obligation imposed on the executive to seek (for some of its actions) the consent of parliament no longer confers on parliament a power of control, but only a right to be consulted."[10]

As a result, the study of government in Canada and other countries where the Westminster model prevails is exclusively a study of politics. The reason for the bias is obvious: it does not conform to democratic theory to demonstrate the executive's autonomy from the people's representatives. On the rare occasions when government has been incautious enough to deny that its authority is "delegated by the House of Commons," criticism has been swift and sharp. Reflecting on one of these rare occasions, Prime Minister Louis St. Laurent observed that "it is well to have the truth as one's inspiration but it is sometimes wise to express only as much of it as one's supporters can be expected to accept."[11] The long arm of history has had a role to play in promoting the study of politics over law as well. In the Whig view, the struggle for responsible government was but an early stage of a journey along the road from colony to nation. In the course of this progress the Crown had to be vanquished twice; first, when executive power succumbed to legislative oversight, and second, when imperial power receded as local self-government grew. For Prime Minster William Lyon

Mackenzie King, Canada's chief Whig, dominion autonomy was symbolized in the subservience of the monarchical Crown to the local political Crown (that is, the Canadian cabinet). Insistence on this relationship after 1926 forced the Crown's representative into "the humiliating position" of total ignorance of governmental affairs, an arrangement King defended on characteristic (if Pinteresque) grounds that "it is always important to remember the significance of the things the Governor General did not do."[12]

It is time to reclaim the Crown from the dignified limbo to which Bagehot and a succession of practising politicians have condemned it. Because of Bagehot's finesse, political scientists have invariably limited their references to the Crown to its symbolic, ceremonial, or emergency (reserve power) role. And not just political scientists! According to British politician and writer Tony Benn, "Here is the secret of the modern system: although the person of the monarch has no political power, the Crown has great powers and these powers are exercised in practice by the prime minister. This explains why every prime minister ends up supporting the Crown."[13] By contrast, the concept of the Crown as agency, permeating the political system and empowering the political executive, receives no attention. The Crown is an integral part of a practical form of government, and proof for this proposition lies in three areas of Crown influence: representation, information, and participation. Other areas, for example, administration ("the secret garden of the Crown") and law, could be discussed as well, except for the limitation of space.[14]

To modern ears there is a dissonance in joining the concepts of representation and the Crown. The impetus to self-government is fundamental in the Anglo-American political tradition, and in British territories that has meant submitting the powers of the Crown to political control. Submission was not the same thing as abolition, however; and for that reason the appointment power might still encroach on and even, in some cases, supplant the mechanisms of popular representation. Appointments flow from the use of the Crown's patronage power. The media and the public have long criticized patronage appointments on the grounds that they are distributed by the governing party for partisan purposes.

Dispute over these matters has tended to disguise the reality that appointments emanate from the Crown and not from the party in the first place.

Whether proportionately more appointments are made at the national level in Canada than in other countries is a subject to be determined at another time. In any case it is not the numbers that matter but the centrality to the political system of those who are appointed. Indeed, the preservation of the political system could be said to depend upon it, since the prevailing theory of Canadian politics – elite accommodation – could not function without the use of the power. Because appointments are at the initiative of the Crown, their numbers may not be limited, nor their determination shared. The prerogative of choice is the political executive's alone, since it alone monopolizes access to the Crown's representative. Unrestrained by a confirmation process, the potential for action is limited only by the self-restraint of the Crown's advisers. For this reason, and because the prerogative power of the Crown itself is imprecise, it is at the very least misleading to describe the Crown as nothing more than "the authority … [of] the reigning monarch."[15]

The federalization of the cabinet, which began with Macdonald's first government, and labyrinth of boards and commissions created in response to the demands of the positive state, all embrace the idea of appointments being used for accommodative purposes. Appointments to take account of claims of language, religion, region, race, and gender are now so familiar as not to occasion comment, but in the context of a study of the Crown they should – for they present the good (or at least acceptable) face of patronage. The attraction of appointments is that once the principle is adopted, the object sought is easily secured. Certainly there is none of the uncertainty that comes with competitive elections.

The importance of information to the conduct of government is unquestioned, or so it would appear in Canada, where, aside from the literature on copyright, social scientists pay it scant attention. And yet, if Americans are, as one U.S. historian has labelled them, "a calculating people," then Canadians are an inquiring people.[16] Canadian governments have, with great frequency made use of royal commissions to inquire into narrow and broad areas of public policy. Of the latter, some of the best known are the Royal Commission on Dominion-Provincial Relations (Rowell-Sirois, which reported in 1941), the Royal Commission on National Development in the Arts, Letters and Sciences (Massey, 1951), and the Royal Commission on Bilingualism and Biculturalism (Laurendeau-Dunton, beginning in 1967). To these might be added, as examples of commissions with a more specific focus, inquiries into the automotive industry, health services, and banking. These are commissions appointed at the national level, but there is an extensive array of provincial commissions too. Between 1867 and 1982, there were 767 provincial royal commissions and commissions of inquiry with either a narrow or a broad focus.[17]

The number and breadth of inquiries are impressive, yet those data scarcely indicate the extent of the investigations undertaken, for many of these bodies in turn commissioned comprehensive research studies on specific topics as well. The details of each of these endeavours is beyond the scope of this discussion, but they all share the common feature that they are "predominantly concerned with knowing."[18] What is significant about Canadian practice is that so many public inquiries are conducted and, from the perspective of this study, that these inquiries "take [their] formal origin in the legal centre of authority, the Crown."[19] Whether or not governments use the information provided or follow the proposals made is unimportant from the perspective of the royal commission as an instrument of executive choice. But it is important to note that royal commissions have the secondary effect of focusing interest upon their own subject matter, as witness the Rowell-Sirois Commission, most of whose recommendations in 1940 were not immediately implemented, but that, through the precedence it awarded to central rather than to provincial government questions, exerted an impact on social science scholarship for a generation. Indeed, that report reinforced a bias against "parochial" provincial concerns, which had largely been responsible for the commission's creation in the first place.

Royal commissions are one, but not the only, way of knowing. In the first Parliament, the plea for an initial "personal census" was soon heard, for "on that," said Alexander Mackenzie, "depended the political relations of the several Provinces under the *Union Act* towards each other."[20] All governments depend upon statistics, but federations even more so. Until provinces began to establish their own executive agencies, such as the CCF government's innovative Budget Bureau and Planning Board in Saskatchewan in the mid-1940s, federal data prevailed for the reason the dominion statistician (as he then was) told the Rowell-Sirois Commission: "The federal government under the *British North America Act* has no powers in certain fields but it has the right to know all about those fields."[21] That right rests in "the Crown prerogative [whose goal] is to ensure the quality, accuracy and credibility of ... information."[22]

If the Crown exerts a formative influence (directly and indirectly) over appointments and information, the same could be said about democratic participation. It can be argued that the weakness of the concept of constituent power in Canada is a consequence of the principle that the Crown is the source of authority. In history and in practice, the inviolate Crown acts as a visible check on campaigns for direct democracy. Less obvious but equally effective restraints by the Crown on the transmission of voter preferences into public policy exist as well. Arguably the best example reaches back to the era of the struggle for responsible government. Lord Durham believed that "good government [was] not attainable" unless there was central control over expenditure, and no adviser to the Crown since 1839 has dissented from that judgment. The executive monopoly on spending is a cardinal feature of responsible government, and one with extensive ramifications: it denies to the legislative branch a policy-making function and, as a consequence, assigns to the member of Parliament a very different role from that played, for example, by a member of the United States Congress. The job of the Canadian member of Parliament is "to monitor, evaluate, judge and decide on the [government's] proposals."[23] It is not, contrary to the view of critics, to legislate. At the same time, "ministerial responsibility has a narrow statutory base. Its operation is principally derived from convention."[24]

The dignified-efficient dichotomy, with which Bagehot and *The English Constitution* are so indelibly associated, is both a ruse and false. It is a ruse because the object of the contrast is to justify the acquisition of power: "Every constitution must first gain authority and then use authority; it must first win the loyalty and confidence of mankind, and then employ that homage in the work of government."[25] It is false because the duality implies that the categories are exclusive when, in fact, they are complementary. The legislative process is linear, a sequence of stages at the conclusion of which stands (or sits) the Crown, prepared to grant or withhold assent. While Bagehot's division appears to offer mental clarification, in fact it compounds confusion. If theorists such as Bogdanor and Loughlin are correct when they say that the Crown today is enigmatic and poorly understood, perhaps *The English Constitution* helps explain why. The dichotomous approach of the nineteenth century is perpetuated in the twenty-first by what might be called the sporting metaphor and the Crown: "The Crown's role [the "Royal Prerogative"] remains part of our constitution to ensure that the rules of the game are always followed."[26] Or in support of cabinet manuals, already in use in other Westminster systems, which set out "agreed-upon practices of parliamentary and cabinet government and the principles that underlie them."[27] In fact, the two subjects may be joined, as constitutional theorist Peter Russell has demonstrated: "The political consensus on fundamental principles," which a manual would embody, is desirable, he maintains, because otherwise "the governor general [is placed] in the position of refereeing a game without an agreed-upon set of principles."[28]

Notwithstanding first impressions, it is neither impossible nor even rare to discover a symbiosis between persons or outlooks that initially may be treated as opposites. For instance, it is not infrequent to have the Crown (whether in the person of the sovereign, governor general, or lieutenant governor) and the respective prime minister or premier viewed in this manner. Yet it may be argued that, paradoxically or not, a unity exists in the form of an essential reciprocity between the Crown and elected advisors, and that this union is well-established: "The fact that acute controversy concerning the role of the Crown has consistently been avoided in the United Kingdom for more than a century is evidence, not that the Sovereign has been bound by convention invariably to follow the advice of a government to dissolve Parliament, instead of seeking an alternative ministry, but that ... all ministers have been particularly scrupulous to shield the Sovereign from the necessity of making any debatable use of the royal discretion."[29] The foregoing comment appeared in a London newspaper, although its author was a political scientist of long standing in Canada. Moreover, the thesis of the piece – that politicians choose to keep the Crown out of politics – applies equally to Canada, and has done so for a long period of time, notwithstanding rare interventions, such as that of Lord Aberdeen in the 1890s during the Manitoba schools controversy. Nor is it the first counsel to guide Canadian governors in the fulfilment of their duties. Consider the following comments from Lord Elgin, governor general of the Province of Canada (1847–54) to Lord Grey, colonial secretary: "A Governor General by acting upon them with tact and firmness may hope to establish a moral influence in the Province which will go far to compensate for the loss of power consequent on the surrender of patronage to an Executive responsible to the local Parliament"; and "Our system depends a great deal more on the discretion with which it is worked than the American where each power in the State goes habitually the full length of its tether."[30]

That disposition toward "discretion," noted so long ago, was not unique to that period. Indeed, another governor general, Vincent Massey, observed that "Canadian contributions at meetings of international bodies are said to be marked always by moderation and impartiality."[31] Contrary to the quick summary that governments are active and the Crown passive, or in Bagehot's terminology, the first efficient and the second dignified, the gubernatorial assessment appears more perceptive. The Crown contributes to the efficiency of the constitution and by so doing promotes consensus and indirectly allows Bagehot's dignified part to prosper. It helps enforce consistency and coherence in Canadian politics, as well as attaining the real goal of a political system: harmony. While it completes the political act, its effect is, at the same time, dialectical in that its presence makes Canadians aware of government, political parties, and Parliament (among other actors), which in turn raises awareness of the Crown. Thus the hidden meaning of the Crown is more than aesthetic: it survives not as shadow but as substance, although one whose real influence is seldom apparent.

As previously noted, there is an agreement – unwritten, certainly, but unarticulated, as well – that the Crown should be shielded from making "any debatable use of the royal discretion."[32] Thus disagreements must be resolved by the parliamentary parties before the Crown's participation, at the last stage of the legislative process, is sought. The presence of the Crown, in short, acts as a moderating influence in Canadian federal and provincial politics. This may be one explanation why, no matter how controversial proposed legislation might be – for example, legalizing gay marriage or abortion, or ending capital punishment – once such bills pass through the legislature the controversy that preceded them disappears from the public forum in Canada. In the American republic, law-making is apportioned among a score of institutions and groups; in a constitutional monarchy such as Canada, it is monopolized by government. That is why representation is central in a republic and why participation as partnership with the Crown is at the heart of politics in a monarchy. Similarly, notwithstanding Bagehot's famous book and the dichotomy of constitutional "parts" that it presents, it is important to emphasize that the dignified part is efficient in its influence – very efficient.

5

The Vice-Regal Family: Canadian Surrogates of the Sovereign

The absence of the person of the sovereign and members of the Royal Family from Canadian soil – other than on an infrequent basis – has allowed for the development of an institution that, although linked by history to the Crown in the United Kingdom, has come to embody a distinct and separate group of representatives of the Crown in Canada. A symbol of cohesion and consistency, deeply rooted in civil society and government in an unobtrusive manner, this institution, with a uniquely Canadian character and function, is embodied not solely through the office of the monarch or the ubiquitous "Crown-in-Right of Canada," but also in a reflective manner, through the sovereign's representatives: the governor general and lieutenant governors. The transient nature of these distant surrogates, members of what David Johnston referred to as the "vice-regal family,"[1] coupled with Canada's federal structure, have afforded the Crown a dynamic outlook and presence in Canada. The Crown's compound character in Canada exists by virtue of this cadre of eleven representatives – what we have is a dispersed Crown with a shared function and multiple personalities.[2] So often royalty, and the star status of the sovereign and her family, what is ably described as the "celebrity monarchy,"[3] deflect from the quality and nature of the government that Canada possesses. The flippant comment made by Charles Dickens while attending a speech from the throne in Nova Scotia, "at which ceremonial the forms observed on the commencement of a new Session of Parliament in England were so closely copied, and so gravely presented on a small scale, that it was like looking at Westminster through the wrong end of a telescope,"[4] failed to appreciate the nuances of Crown's uniquely Canadian function and presence, even in the British North America of 180 years ago.[5] That the monarchy, as it has evolved in Canada, is not an identical reflection of its British counterpart is evidenced by the fact that such shared institutions transported across the seas "did not always result in a seamless or predictable adoption of British institutions or practices."[6]

An examination of Canada's constitutional monarchy in the broadest sense would be incomplete without dissecting the evolving functions of the Crown's representatives: the governor general and the lieutenant governors. These positions embody our oldest state offices, and their influence over the evolution of the Crown in Canada extends beyond the confines of their constitutional roles, as outlined in the *Constitution Acts 1867 to 1982*, the *Letters Patent Constituting the Office of the Governor General 1947* or the *Instructions for Lieutenant Governors 1976*. This chapter will delve into the flexible nature of the Crown's representatives and how this rotating cast of vice-regals has shaped the broader institution, beyond the constitutional and conventional aspects of the authority exercised by those at the formal apex of Canada's political system.

Canada's first prime minister, Sir John A. Macdonald, held the Queen, the Crown, and the position of the governor general in high esteem.[7] Nevertheless, he intended for the role of the provincial lieutenant governors to fade into the scenery – reduced to federal agents, occasionally directed to carry out the will of the central government.[8] It should not be forgotten that Macdonald correspondingly viewed the provincial legislatures as "big county councils."[9] The redoubtable Goldwin Smith felt that the office of lieutenant governor was little more than a sinecure that deserved to disappear, providing nothing more than "a decent retirement for those who have spent their energies in public life but on whom the public refuse to bestow pensions."[10] Several prominent political scientists of the mid-twentieth century traced the fading role of the lieutenant governors.[11] Often discussions on the vice-regal role focus chiefly on the function and office of the governor general in the national sphere.[12] Nevertheless the role of the lieutenant governors constitutes a central aspect of the Crown in Canada, and the ten disparate offices, which are closer to the citizenry than the governor general, have helped to serve as a bulwark against the tendency for residents of Rideau Hall and successive federal governments, to subdue the reflective nature of the governor general's position as the representative of the Queen of Canada,[13] and attempt to elevate the office to the presidential personification of the Canadian state.[14] Relations between specific governors general and their provincial counterparts have not always been treated as *primus inter pares* – or in the vein of the "vice-regal family," as articulated and executed by David Johnston during his tenure at Rideau Hall. The collegial and collaborative nature of the vice-regal family has ebbed and flowed, invariably dictated by the personalities involved. From the closing days of Roland Michener's term when all the lieutenant governors came to Rideau Hall for a vice-regal conference and the gathering evolved into a long weekend family get away in the country, to the more infamous episode of a certain governor general insisting on being addressed as "Your Excellency" and for lieutenant governors to rise whenever she and her husband entered the room.

In particular it has been observed that lieutenant governors have done much to preserve and enhance the Crown in their respective jurisdictions, as the "defence of the Crown was left to an *ad hoc* group of provincial lieutenant governors' offices (notably those of Ontario, Saskatchewan, and Newfoundland)."[15] Writing more than sixty years ago, J.T. Saywell, in his comprehensive study of the vice-regal role in the provinces, *The Office of the Lieutenant Governor*, adroitly observed that the offices "will continue to evolve"[16] and that during periods of constitutional crisis "the public momentarily awakened will ask where the Lieutenant-Governor comes from and where he goes."[17] This has indeed been the case.

Against the backdrop of limited resources, positions occasionally filled by patronage-seeking partisans,[18] and a series of federal governments that were "steadily chipping away at such manifestations of the traditional royal connection as can be dispensed with quietly,"[19] the Crown and vice-regal offices have somehow survived beyond serving as perfunctory constitutional cyphers. Indeed, the vice-regals in both the federal and provincial spheres have actually expanded the role played by the sovereign's representatives in civil society – past the traditional legal and constitutional functions of the offices, or the staid, protocol-driven formal events of state once closely associated with life in Government Houses.[20] Borrowing from Walter Bagehot's well-worn dichotomy, the efficient role of the Crown in Canada has remained largely static, while the dignified presence has expanded greatly. We must also accept that the "role and function of monarchy in Canada has never been so categorical as Bagehot had suggested."[21] There has been an inherent flexibility and practicality to the system as it came to develop and evolve in this country. Somehow Canada's "distant and abstract monarchy"[22] has outlived the soothsayers who predicted the marginalization of the lieutenant governors in particular.

An aspect of Canada's development in the post-war period that has greatly aided the gradual growth of a dynamic and innovative approach by the vice-regal family is the manner in which the Crown came to shed significant elements of its British character, both legal and symbolic. Given the dispersed and multi-jurisdictional composition of the Crown, it is difficult to precisely identify when this change commenced. Although it was not until 1952 that a Canadian was appointed as governor general, lieutenant governors positions had been filled, almost invariably, by a person born in Canada since shortly after Confederation.[23] Despite initial negative public reaction to the appointment of Vincent Massey as governor general in 1952,[24] the ascension of a Canadian to the highest appointed post in the land did not bring about drastic changes to the office of the governor general. In many ways Massey continued with the traditional pattern of service and tours that was well established by his predecessors going back to Lord Dufferin.[25] With this in mind, it would be misleading to view the appointment of Canadians as the moment of transition for Canadian vice-regals. Rather, the development of a more dynamic function of the vice-regal offices was gradual beginning in the late 1960s, extending into the 1990s.

As in England, much of Canada's political development has been "one of slow adaption of ancient forms in response to shifts in power relations,"[26] and this is a theme that touches directly upon the durability of the Crown in its Canadian incarnation. During the Diamond Jubilee of Confederation in 1927, a committee of eminent historians noted that "the free institutions which are our pride were not created at any special moment,"[27] and this too is true of the Crown's metamorphosis. This has been demonstrated with the vice-regal role as it has evolved for the governor general and lieutenant governors over the past forty years in particular.

An incremental change was linked, at least in part, to what is referred to as the "Canadianization of the Crown" – a term first popularized by F.R. Scott in "The End of Dominion Status," an article that appeared in the *American Journal of International Law* more than seventy years ago.[28] This is what scholars of the decline of the British Empire have come to call "de-dominionization" when examining the changing character of the Crown and relationship with the United Kingdom in relation to Australia, New Zealand, and in the other self-governing dominions.[29] In the Canadian context, this is more accurately reflected by the term "realmization" – whereby Canada moved from being a British dominion to becoming an independent realm itself with a sovereign shared with a number of Commonwealth countries, where the Crown came to be represented by local symbols, customs, traditions, and office holders. This was much more than simply removing Union Jacks and replacing them with maple leaves, or discontinuing use of the term "dominion." On a national scale this change included shifting the focus from the historic British connection,[30] the adoption of new symbols and modification of protocols and traditions, and the adoption of bilingual and multicultural policies. Obviously, these changes were not limited to the vice-regal offices alone, yet they did touch upon the role of the Canadian Crown in a very distinctive manner. While retaining some of the earlier elements of the vice-regal role such as speeches from the throne, levées, and patronage of royal organizations, the push to Canadianize foundational institutions, while becoming involved with other civic and volunteer organizations, allowed for the vice-regal offices to step beyond the confines of the duties of Victorian vice-regals. Government Houses, and their residents, moved from being the gathering place of the social elite, as observed by Sam Slick who noted that the governor "was the fountain of honour and the distributor of patronage and rank,"[31] to a place where citizens from a broad cross section of society are brought together to be recognized, celebrated, and honoured.

In some jurisdictions, notably the Australian states, the change has been much more recent and gradual. This was in part a result the appointment of British citizens as governors of some states up until 1980.[32] In New Zealand as well, the attachment to a British elements of the vice-regal office persisted longer than in Canada – with the appointment of the first New Zealand–born citizen, Sir Arthur Porritt, only in 1967,[33] the continuance of wigs for lawyers and judges, and the adoption of a distinctive governor general's flag only in 2008. Yet in other areas, notably Indigenous relations, New Zealand has been the leader amongst all of the Queen's realms.[34]

The Non-Resident Sovereign

Although the sovereign has been physically absent, "the Sovereign's role in Canada has been constitutional, legal, symbolic and psychological"[35] throughout our modern history. If the Crown has been a permanent fixture of Canadian life since the settlement of the first Europeans, for much of that history there has been a temporal permanence to the sovereigns themselves. Over the quarter-millennia since the accession of George III, what is modern-day Canada has been reigned over principally by three monarchs: George III, Victoria, and Elizabeth II. For more than two and a half centuries since George III's coronation, the throne has been occupied by a triumvirate of monarchs for 190 years – during which entire generations lived and died under the same head of state. Canada's array of jurisdictions have seen 467 governors general, governors, and lieutenant governors come and go over the same period.[36] While the sovereigns have embodied stability and longevity, the vice-regals represent a rotating cadre of representatives who, during the reign of Queen Elizabeth II, have helped to imbue the Crown with a degree of flexibility and innovation that defies the otherwise nearly permanent imagery of the present Queen. The crux of this corollary is that the monarchy in its Canadian context is versatile and able to embody continuity while also allowing for broader change to the institution apace with the civil society it serves.

Canada has always had a non-resident sovereign. Consequently, members of the Royal Family have typically had a greater symbolic, rather than physical, presence, appearing on currency and postage stamps and for royal tours – being in the country for only a few weeks at a time. There have been notable exceptions. Although he did not serve as a governor, Queen Victoria's father, Prince Edward Duke of Kent, served as commander-in-chief of British North America at the turn of the eighteenth century. His close friendship with the lieutenant governor of Nova Scotia (and his wife) imbued the lieutenant governor and his suite with a star-like social status in the fledgling colony.[37] By the time of his departure from North America in 1800, he had spent more than six years in what would become the four founding provinces. Later, the appointment of the Marquis of Lorne as governor general in 1878, accompanied by his consort, Princess Louise, fourth daughter of Queen Victoria, added a royal splendour to social life in Ottawa. One of Queen Victoria's sons, the Duke of Connaught would serve as governor general from 1910 to 1916; however, his approach to vice-regal life was more soldier-like than as a precious prince of the realm.[38] Finally, there was Princess Alice, Countess of Athlone, wife of the Earl of Athlone who served as governor general from 1940 to 1946 – who was himself the younger brother of Queen Mary. A granddaughter of Queen Victoria, Princess Alice came with the cachet of a distinguished family lineage, previous vice-regal service as consort, and a royal style and title, yet a practical approach when it came to rationing, military service, and the overall war effort. Her many involvements, personal demeanour, casual approachability and deep interest in Canadians endeared her to the public in ways that are rare for a vice-regal consort.[39]

Since the appointment of Edward Schreyer as governor general in 1979, every five years, when speculation about the governor general designate reaches a crescendo, members of the Monarchist League of Canada, or occasionally columnists, propose the idea that one of the Queen's children or grandchildren should be appointed as the next occupant of Rideau Hall.[40] The Queen Mother was routinely suggested in the press as a candidate for governor general in both Canada and Australia throughout the 1970s, and Charles, Prince of Wales, was similarly proposed to serve as his mother's representative.[41] In late 2019, during a period of heightened criticism of the then governor general, Julie Payette, the *Ottawa Citizen* ran a piece calling for the Duke of Sussex to be appointed as Canada's next governor general.[42] Such ideas are fanciful at best and incongruous with the role and function that has come to be attached to the Canadian vice-regal offices and the Crown in the federal and provincial spheres since the beginning of the present reign. While anecdotal evidence indicates that members of the Royal Family have a decent knowledge of Canada – better than a number of post-1952 governors general – the importation of an international celebrity and the optics of returning to a non-Canadian vice-regal, albeit a direct relation of the Queen, would be problematic. To some such an appointment would be viewed as a regressive measure: a British prince born into wealth and status supplanting an accomplished Canadian would, at the very least, run counter to the broad character of vice-regal office holders of the last half a century. In the short term, such an appointment would elevate the presence of the institution in the eye of the public, but it would also be accompanied by the more challenging alteration of a position that has been held for generations by a temporary office holder who, at the end of service, returns to being a regular citizen.[43] Members of the Royal Family on the other hand never cease to be associated with the monarchy, even if they are occasionally marginalized.[44] Unlike in the United Kingdom or the United States, an aspect of Canadian public life is that almost regardless of what high office citizens rise to, within a relatively short period of time after leaving office, they merge back into the society they once served. They may depart office with a few more postnominals but the aura and trappings of vice-regal office evaporates and there is no lingering status other than a permanent place on the table of precedence.

Prior to Vincent Massey's retirement from office in 1959, it had been the practice for governors general to return to the United Kingdom and largely fade from Canadian life, other than infrequent returns. In 1965, following the conclusion of the Canadian Conference on the Family, which was held at Rideau Hall under the patronage of Georges and Pauline Vanier, the Vanier Institute of the Family was established with significant financial support from the Government of Canada.[45] Since Vanier, upon departing office, nearly all governors generals have, with significant financial support from the Government of Canada, headed up the establishment of a foundation that focuses upon an aspect of their vice-regal mandate.[46] In addition to the creation of these foundations, the provision of federal funding to reimburse former governors general for certain expense related to duties carried out in relation to their previous role as a vice-regal has aided in keeping some former governors general involved in causes and charities that they had focused on during their mandate.[47] Nevertheless, the financial support that endures after a governor general has departed Rideau Hall plays only a modest role in keeping the former office holder in the public eye – something that is far more dependent on the personality of the individual than the amount of government funding afforded. Lieutenant governors, given their more subdued status, typically recede from public duties after leaving office. There is no analogous funding program or practice of establishing foundations for former lieutenant governors.

Senior members of the Royal Family are trained from birth into service and understand that they are expected to have a public role into old age. Vice-regals are, with a few months' notice, thrown into representing the sovereign in their jurisdiction with little more than a briefing by federal and provincial officials and several weighty binders laden with laconic language about the right to be consulted, to advise, and to warn – accompanied by the more mundane details of protocol, precedence, patronage organizations, and living arrangements.[48] No one is trained to become a governor general or lieutenant governor, nor is there a finishing school for vice-regal aspirants. Only a few office holders in modern Canadian history could be said to have overtly desired to be governor general or lieutenant governor. The most notable was Vincent Massey.[49]

Canada is served by the Queen, along with eleven vice-regals, drawn from the broader society, each exercising constitutional and ceremonial functions. As of 2021, Her Majesty has had more than 125 Canadian representatives since the beginning of her reign. The situation in the United Kingdom is rather different. In place of the vice-regal family, the United Kingdom has the Royal Family, which has almost no formal role in the government of the nation, aside from the four senior members who are councillors of state.[50] While there are the lords lieutenant, they are only vaguely akin to a Canadian lieutenant governor, possessing exclusively ceremonial duties. The vice-regals routinely encounter matters touching upon the operation of government. Aside from the Queen, there are no such analogous positions in Britain. Of course, the eleven vice-regals lack the celebrity status that senior members of the Royal Family have come to be identified with, but in place of this most have presented an approachability and familiarity that has rarely been associated with members of the Royal Family.

The regular rotation of vice-regals in Canada means that the public does not become attached to them in the same manner that attachment grows towards the sovereign and to some members of the Royal Family. A by-product of the impermanence of vice-regal office holders is that the public, in addition to feeling a greater connection with the sovereign, clings more tightly to the symbols closely associated with the Crown. The impermanence of vice-regals leads to a natural affinity towards the permanent elements of the Crown under which the vice-regals serve. Therefore, the changing cast makes us more attached to the sovereign and the symbols of the Crown, as they remain constant on the proverbial stage in the play that is Canada's constitutional monarchy.

Another facet of the non-resident sovereign is the absence of a "court" and the long-serving courtiers who are associated with monarchies. By contrast, Canada's vice-regals serve five to six years on average[51] and are advised by a private secretary (chief of staff) who is usually a career civil servant who carries out the dual role of serving as principal advisor and interlocutor with the broader bureaucracy – although with a more pronounced degree of independence than most similarly ranked senior bureaucrats.[52] Occasionally a vice-regal will also be advised by a personally appointed assistant, but this has been rare in the provinces, although more common in the office of the secretary to the governor general with the hiring of term-specific personnel known as "exempt staff."[53] This can be a source of some problems, especially when "the lack of experienced advisors can make it very difficult for a new governor general to learn the role quickly."[54]

Since Confederation, secretaries to the governor general, with three notable exceptions, have served for the duration of a single governor general's term, normally with a brief overlap for a successor to acclimatize to the post.[55] The situation in the provinces is different, with the private secretaries serving an average of eight years in their positions, and usually under two or three different lieutenant governors. The tenure of the vice-regal secretaries contrasts with that of the Queen's private secretaries, of which there have been nine since the beginning of her reign, with a median of nine years of service in the post.[56] This figure is misleading unless one considers the long household careers of the Queen's private secretaries who typically entered the private secretary's department as an assistant private secretary, being promoted into the deputy role, and eventually rising to the senior-most position in the private secretary's office.[57] The median total period of service in the royal household for private secretaries has been 23 ½ years. This contrasts significantly with the vice-regal secretaries, who have rarely been promoted through the ranks of the vice-regal offices, which in the provinces are quite modest in size.[58]

While it may seem only of cursory importance to the evolution and durability of the Crown in Canada, a key component of the vice-regal offices that ends up projecting the Crown to the citizenry daily is the small group of officials who support the offices of the governor general and the lieutenant governors. These civil servants, by virtue of the length of their service, provide continuity for the rotation of vice-regals. However, unlike the royal courtiers, the vice-regal private secretaries rarely remain in the posts for decades. The slow transience of these officials combined with the quinquennial cycle of vice-regals, has allowed for a greater flexibility and willingness to experiment with the role of the governor general and lieutenant governor in reaching beyond traditional events and functions. The transitory nature of vice-regal office holders means that the private secretaries end up serving as the institutional memory, whereas at Buckingham Palace the Queen is the undisputed curator of the institutional memory, well supported by long-serving experienced senior staff.

Duality of Reflection

The absence of the physical person of the head of state, who has only a vicarious presence, via a team of eleven vice-regals, has helped the monarchy in Canada to evolve in "ways reflecting Canada's own political and cultural development, and with a range of disparate goals."[59] That the monarchy's Canadian iteration has a persona different from its counterpart in the United Kingdom is a direct by-product of the vice-regal family, its accessibility, its propensity to engage in innovative ways of interacting with citizens, and the fact that its symbolic capital is borrowed from the sovereign. Furthermore, the governor general and lieutenant governors are not imbued with all the symbolic authority of the sovereign.[60] The legal and symbolic reality that there is an office superior to that of the chief executives in the federal and provincial spheres, who is the ersatz living embodiment of the Canadian state, and by extension the institution that the vice-regals serve, helps to further illuminate the reflective nature of the interplay between the sovereign and her surrogates. This permits the ubiquitous institution of the Crown to take on multiple personalities and to be tailored for the realities and requirements of each of the jurisdictions over which it holds sovereignty.

While the vice-regals represent the head of state and are, in the protocol sense, accorded similar honours and recognition, they are separate reflections of the sovereign and have a routine physical presence in the broader civil society that is different from the symbolic presence of the sovereign. To borrow from an astronomical analogy, there can be no moon without the sun that shines upon it, making the celestial body visible to terrestrial life. Similarly, the vice-regal offices would lack their lustre and symbolic capital were they not directly associated with the sovereign and the trappings of the monarchy.[61] The vice-regals represent but are not the head of state, hence the vicarious nature of the roles discharged by the governor general and lieutenant governors.

Those appointed to vice-regal office have been drawn from a reasonably broad cross section of Canadian society over the past forty years. They come to office with no formal training, are often well known within their home communities and professional fields and seem "more like us," with the gold cording and red velvet of the monarchy thrown in to add flair and a sense of grandeur. They are citizens who come to assume an office, not elected into a role, nor have they been born into a position or been trained for a lifetime on how to serve the public. The paradox of having regular citizens represent the sovereign is not an impossible one to overcome through the simple fact that the vice-regals are the part of Canada's monarchy that people come into contact with much more frequently than the sovereign or her family.

Governors general and lieutenant governors cannot depend solely on their professional achievements, personal prestige, or the status of the prime minister who recommended their appointment. They do, however, rely on the position, patrimony, and aura of the monarchy – both the sovereign and the symbolic trappings of the Canadian Crown. The reality that the vice-regals constitute a reflection of the sovereign means that the vice-regal role is exercised, with certain limitations, as the surrogates are the representatives of the sovereign and not the personification of the entire institution of the Crown. If the vice-regals borrow from the status of the sovereign and more broadly from the stability of the Crown and its associated symbols, the vice-regals in turn help to make the Crown local, reflecting the society it serves, and yet simultaneously is part of a broader institution. While the Crown itself is seen as "being and not doing," it is the vice-regals who look after the

"doing" element of the Crown's work, most often at the local level –
they are not impersonators of the sovereign.

This also comes with a peripheral level of risk, in that ill-behaved
vice-regals could tarnish the image of the office they hold, or the
Crown as an institution. Such occasions have been infrequent in
Canada's history, the most notable resulting from the 2015 conviction of the former lieutenant governor of Quebec, Lise Thibault,
of fraud in the amount of $300,000, who was sentenced to eigh-
teen months in prison. On 22 January 2021, Governor General Julie
Payette and her secretary, Assunta di Lorenzo, resigned following a workplace review that revealed a "toxic" and "poisoned"
work environment that included allegations of yelling, screaming,
aggressive conduct, demeaning comments, and public humilia-
tion.[62] These cases highlight the reality that there is an expectation
that vice-regals will not only follow the law, but also be exemplary
citizens discharging their constitutional and ceremonial duties
with the highest degree of probity.

Just as the vice-regals are a reflection of the sovereign in their
duties and function, the office holders have in turn become a
reflection of Canadian society. The gradual transition to a cadre
of vice-regals who were more reflective of the population can be
traced to Nova Scotia and the appointment of Sir Malachy Bows
Daly as the first Roman Catholic lieutenant governor in 1890 by Sir
John A. Macdonald's administration. This was a highly unusual
choice, given the level of anti-Catholic sentiment that had been
prevalent in Nova Scotia during the first half of the nineteenth century, which was only "gradual[ly] cooling."[63] Protestants gradually
accepted Catholics as "bona fide Nova Scotians, a group whose
loyalty could be trusted."[64]

Since the end of the Second World War, with an increasing trend,
the increasingly diverse nature of office holders has been followed
by the appointment of other members of historically marginalized
communities. Several observers have noted that "having individuals from these groups serve as head of state is an excellent
means of making a symbolic statement that the members of their
group are equal partners in the Canadian political community."[65]
In the fall of 2019 an open member of the LGBTQ2+ community

Table 5.1. Initial Appointment of Individuals from Historically Marginalized
            Communities to Vice-Regal Office

Community	Jurisdiction	Office holder	Appointment
Acadian	Prince Edward Island	Joseph Bernard	1945–50
Disabled (amputee)	New Brunswick	David MacLaren	1945–58
French-Canadian	Canada	Georges Vanier	1959–67
Ukrainian-Canadian	Saskatchewan	Stephen Worobetz	1970–6
Female	Ontario	Pauline McGibbon	1974–80
Indigenous	Alberta	Ralph Steinhauer	1974–9
African-Canadian	Ontario	Lincoln Alexander	1985–91
Chinese-Canadian	British Columbia	David Lam	1988–95
Métis	Manitoba	Yvon Dumont	1993–9
Disabled (paraplegic)	Quebec	Lise Thibault	1997–2007
Jewish-Canadian	Nova Scotia	Myra Freeman	2000–6
LGBTQ2+	New Brunswick	Brenda Murphy	2019–
Muslim-Canadian	Alberta	Salma Lakhani	2020–
Indigenous-Canadian	Canada	Mary May Simon	2021–

was appointed for the first time as lieutenant governor of New Brunswick.[66] This being the exception, vice-regal appointments of individuals from historically marginalized communities have invariably been in advance of members of the same community being elected head of government, either provincially or federally. As of September 2021, eight of eleven vice-regals and all three territorial commissioners are women.[67] This is the first time that women have outnumbered men in these roles. It has been noted by at least one scholar that the appointment of women in particular "has helped to transform both the image and the priorities of the lieutenant governor."[68]

The age of vice-regals at the time of their appointment in real terms has remained almost entirely static since Confederation; appointments have been made at the end of a career, with retirement from full-time employment often following the conclusion of vice-regal service. Nevertheless, in relation to the average lifespan of Canadian adults, which has improved by nearly a quarter century over the period 1921–2011,[69] the cohort of vice-regals has been getting younger and closer to the median age of the overall

Canadian population. For the first hundred years following Confederation the average age of appointees has been 61.9 years, while the median was 62 years. Over the entire course of Canada's post-Confederation history, the average age of appointees has been 62 years while the median has been 63 years of age. When examining the appointments made since 1967, there remains only a modest change: the average age of those appointed to vice-regal office from 1967 to 2019 has been 57.8 years, while the median age of appointees has been 64 years of age.[70] Relative to the improvement in lifespan of Canadian adults, the vice-regal cohort has been getting younger. This is especially true when considering that the average lifespan in 1921 was 57.1 years – by 1967 this had improved to 71.2 years, and by 2011 it rose further to 81.7.[71] Thus over the period 1921–2011, the lifespan of a Canadian adult gained 24.6 years. A lieutenant governor appointed in 1921 with the average age of 60.9 years was already on borrowed time, statistically speaking, having exceeded the average life expectancy by 3.8 years, and being considerably older than most Canadians – the median age at the time being 23.8 years of age.[72] Lieutenant governors in this period were nearly three times the age of the citizens they served. By 2011, when the average age of a lieutenant governor was 62, they could statistically expect to live for another 19.7 years and were much closer in age to more than half the Canadian population than in 1921 – which had a median age of 40 years by 2011. The overall improvement in lifespan and health determinants means that the vice-regals have been getting younger in relative terms to their lifespan, even though their average and median age at the time of appointment have experienced only modest changes.

Practical Dynamism

This chapter opened with the contention that the vice-regal offices, certainly in the provincial sphere, were never intended to survive beyond serving as perfunctory officers of the federal government. In spite of limited resources and the periodic closure of Government Houses,[73] these offices have endured and expanded well

beyond their constitutional role or the "time-honoured functions,"[74] such as levées and socialite events once deeply associated
with vice-regal life in Canada.[75] There has been a practical and
dynamic approach taken by the vice-regal representatives over the
past forty years in particular, and this has helped to ensure the
continued presence, growth, and success of the Crown's position
in Canada.

The sovereign and her eleven Canadian representatives have
long embodied the ethos and outlook of the Scandinavian monarchies. Characterized by a modest degree of formality and limited budgetary resources, and juxtaposed to a high degree of civic
engagement and public access, the Crown in Canada can be considered *monarchy light* – a typology aided by a physical distance
from the person of the sovereign and her court. While there has
long been a penchant for royal tours and the involvement of the
Royal Family[76] in the signal moments of the nation's life, public tolerance for routine lavish spending on entertaining, complex state
ceremonial, ostentatious official residences, and frequent travel –
for any public officer, whether appointed or elected – have always
been slight. No longer are the vice-regal offices characterized by
the "full panoply of proconsular aggrandizement and mimetic
monarchy,"[77] which was observed in the late eighteenth and early
nineteenth centuries. These offices and their holders needed to
find other ways to give purpose and relevance to their function. As
the cast of vice-regal office holders diversified over the past forty
years to become more representative of an increasingly multicultural Canadian demographic, the ability for citizens to interact and
connect with the eleven vice-regal offices and their involvement
in patron organizations has increased more than threefold.[78] This
dynamic and innovative aspect in part helps to explain the longevity of offices that, through a literal reading of our Constitution,
could be replaced by an auto-pen or rubber stamp.

While approximately two-thirds of the vice-regal role is prede-
termined, made up of constitutional duties, investitures, awards
ceremonies, travel, diplomatic engagements, standing patronages,
and long-established events such as New Year levées and garden
parties, one-third of the role is left for each incumbent to define.

The definition of the individual vice-regal role, or mandate of a new governor general or lieutenant governor, is most often outlined in the installation speech, where a number of themes or interests are articulated broadly, leaving ample room for them to be refined and precisely tuned to meet operational and budgetary realities, as well as the personal expectations of the office holder.

Some newly installed vice-regals have approached the seemingly restrictive and traditional barrage of official events and patronages with an overt desire to "banish the four olds": old customs, old culture, old habits, and old ideas.[79] This has ranged from Edward Schreyer's famous comment after being announced as the next governor general to "just call me Ed"[80] and Jules Léger's discontinuation to the wearing of white tie and tails, to Jeanne Sauvé's replacement of all senior staff at Rideau Hall within the first year of her mandate.[81] This is by no means a novel reaction on the part of newly appointed vice-regals. Lord Sydenham, governor general from 1839 to 1841, was one of the most notable early dissenters: "He had abandoned traditional customs such as meeting members of the assembly and the new speaker at the bar of the Legislative Council. Instead, he met them outside while seated on a horse."[82] Members of the legislature found this an unbecoming approach for the Queen's representative, and he was promptly satirized.[83] There is a certain irony in the fact that Sydenham's untimely death was an indirect result of his disdain for ceremony and tradition.[84] Most often the gubernatorial revolution is aimed at loosening protocol and formality in an effort to give the office a more folksy appearance. The inward desire of a new vice-regal to change processes, fully grasp their role, and gain a sense of ownership is natural, while the outward one can, when executed with vision and forethought, result in increasing the public profile and a positive image of the vice-regal office, as was the case for Adrienne Clarkson and David Johnston.

The other constraint upon a wholesale remaking of a particular vice-regal office, or figurative banishing of the "four olds," is the reality that there is never enough time or sufficient resources to achieve pervasive change – with the average office holder spending five and a half years in the position. The temporal constraint forces the incumbent to set goals and develop a specific set of themes at the beginning of the mandate. As a by-product, this allows for the periodic refreshing of the vice-regal offices at the national and sub-national level, without resulting in revolutionary change to the institution, its purpose, or its outlook. With eleven jurisdictions of varying sizes and scopes of involvement, it is possible for vice-regal offices to experiment with different programs and types of engagements that can aid in the development of best practices. Additionally, there is the moderating influence of the institutional inertia of the Westminster system, which provides an element of stability, and this too extends to the vice-regal offices and the institution of the Canadian monarchy. The Queen's popularity and the well-entrenched presence of the Crown in Canada can only shield vice-regals so much from criticism in the event they attempt to make drastic changes, decisions, or excessive expenditures. Over the course of a "long reign a sagacious king would acquire an experience which few Ministers could contend,"[85] and well beyond the traditional three rights to be consulted, to encourage, and to warn. The nature of this experience cannot be emulated by a governor general or lieutenant governor. The nature of vice-regal appointments emanating from the prime minister, coupled with the necessity for the governor general and lieutenant governors to remain politically neutral actors during their time in office, naturally requires a degree of forethought and caution that is not required of most politicians. Being unable to defend themselves publicly – that role is left to the prime minister federally or the premiers in the provinces – also normally militates against taking on contentious causes. As demonstrated by James Bartleman, who served as lieutenant governor of Ontario from 2002 to 2007, it is possible to approach highly sensitive and prescient matters of public concern, where the major political parties are supportive of action – in the case of Bartleman on matters related to Indigenous suicide and accessibility to literacy – but such interventions are unusual.

One of the more significant influences on the vice-regal offices has been the convening of regular meetings of the governor general and lieutenant governors and their chiefs of staff – the private secretaries.[86] This tradition commenced in 1967 during the Centennial celebrations when Michener brought together his ten vice-regal colleagues to meet the Queen, which was followed by a meeting to discuss the challenges and opportunities of vice-regal service. A more formal format was adopted in 1973 when Michener brought together his ten vice-regal colleagues at Rideau Hall to discuss common constitutional and ceremonial matters. These meetings became biennial and extended over several days, where vice-regals discussed a broad range of constitutional, ceremonial, and operational matters. Experts from the Privy Council Office, the Secretary of State's Office (now the Department of Canadian Heritage), and noted scholars such as Eugene Forsey, J.R. Mallory, and Norman Ward also presented papers and offered advice.[87] This sharing of best practices has had a multiplier effect in creating a support network for vice-regals and their senior staff, which had hitherto consisted almost solely of the Department of the Secretary of State. By 1995, the vice-regal conclaves became annual, with the addition of a separate gathering of private secretaries commencing in 2010. The sharing of best practices has seen provincial projects being borrowed by the governor general, and those from the governor general's office being scaled down and imported to the provinces. This has been particularly reciprocal in the adoption of email, electronic invitations, and social media, and the development of official websites. Another area where practices first employed in one province would spread to other provinces and then to the office of the governor general is in the field of Indigenous relations.

A few examples that demonstrate the sharing of best practices and dissemination of ideas first tested in one jurisdiction and transplanted to another can be found in the awards given by the governor general and lieutenant governors. One of the more recent developments was the establishment of a lieutenant governor's award for excellence in wines. First established in British Columbia in 2003, it would be replicated in Ontario in 2011, and then a similar award program was launched in Nova Scotia in 2014. In each jurisdiction, partnerships have been struck between professional associations that represent the industry and the lieutenant governor's office. These partnerships have ventured outside the traditional pattern of vice-regal involvement, tend to be locally focused, and are tailored to the specific jurisdiction. Another development relates to the internet. Canada's vice-regals entered the World Wide Web in the late 1990s, with the Office of the Secretary to the Governor General and Office of the Lieutenant Governor of Ontario being the first to launch websites. The lieutenant governor of Ontario's debut in the electronic world was almost simultaneous with Rideau Hall, with Manitoba and Alberta following in 2000. Best practices were shared among the vice-regal secretaries, which accounts for the very similar look and feel of these early webpages. All of them focused on the role of the Crown and a particular vice-regal, including a short biography of office holder and spouse. The explanatory role of the vice-regal online presence has remained and become more robust, coupled with routine updates of activities, photos, and postings of upcoming and recent events.

As will be examined in chapter 6, during the past forty years, the vice-regals have also assumed a robust role in promoting federal and provincial honours. This is but one example of the accretion of the institution and practices associated with the Crown's representatives and their work. The establishment of the Order of Canada in 1967 was followed by every province adopting its own jurisdiction-specific order of merit between 1978 and 2001.[88] Vice-regals play a direct role in the recognition of thousands of exemplary citizens annually. The historic position of the Crown as the "fount of all honour"[89] has been revolutionized into a grass roots–driven and non-partisan system of recognition. Although the conferral of Crown honours is an ancient aspect of the sovereign's role, it was only in 1967 that it was fully patriated and retooled for the recognition of outstanding contributions to community, province, and country rather than the old pattern of honours as a patronage tool.[90] Given the intermittent nature of honours conferral in Canada from 1918 to 1967, which included only six years where civilian honours were presented,[91] the opportunities for the governor general and lieutenant governors to participate in the honours system, or to be seen as champions of exemplary citizenship, were infrequent. Today, in every jurisdiction aside from Quebec, all vice-regals serve as chancellor of their jurisdiction's order. They preside over investitures, promote nominations, recognize excellence, and periodically assemble members of orders for provincial and national events of importance. The growth of awards given out by the governor general and lieutenant governors, from 23 different awards in 1967 to 127 in 2019, has expanded the Crown's largely forgotten role as promotor of excellence in specific fields and service to society in the broader sense. While the post-1967 Canadian honours system was devised largely at the direction of the federal and provincial governments, vice-regal involvement has been deep and constant as each vice-regal has adopted the mantle of "promoter-in-chief"[92] of each jurisdiction and its peoples.

Like the sovereign, the vice-regals have always had the power to convene people – indeed in the most formal and occasional sense, the power to summon an individual – but this had largely gone into abeyance and was limited to calling the premier to account for a particular action. Following passage of the revised *Citizenship Act* in 1977, the vice-regal convening power extended to welcoming new citizens into the Canadian family. This was and continues to be achieved through citizenship ceremonies. There is a unique symbolism to having the Queen's representatives administer the oath of allegiance that all new citizens swear to the Queen of Canada. The oath itself, which is an oath of allegiance to the Queen, has been brought before the courts on a number of occasions. In *McAteer v Attorney General of Canada*, 2014, it was found that the "reference to the Queen of Canada is a symbolic reference to our form of government, a democratic constitutional monarchy, which promotes *Charter* values."[93] The Queen remains the personification of the Canadian state, and the symbolism remains highly relevant, especially to new citizens from non-democratic states.

One of the more monumental moments of a vice-regal convening politicians was brought about by Ontario's lieutenant governor, James Bartleman, who, in addition to working to destigmatize those living with mental health issues, embarked upon an ambitious program to provide books to libraries in remote Indigenous communities. Bartleman spoke to a sitting of the Ontario Legislature on this very topic and garnered unanimous support for his program, which sought to reduce youth suicide amongst Northern Ontario's Indigenous population.[94] While Indigenous rights, reconciliation, and inclusion of Indigenous peoples in society are very much at the forefront of public policy discussion today, they were only on the periphery when Bartleman addressed the legislature.

The concept of the convening power of the Crown was reinvigorated and regularly promoted and practised by David Johnston during his tenure as governor general.[95] Johnston viewed the viceregal office as not only a neutral place for diverse parties to meet to discuss contentious issues, but also as a safe place, free of partisan machinations, where ideas and the good offices of the Crown could be extended to allow the development of dialogue and constructive discourse. This was dramatically demonstrated in January 2013 when Johnston welcomed members of the Indigenous protest phenomenon known as Idle No More into Rideau Hall. Johnston encouraged members of the group to discuss their grievances. The convening function could take place under the auspices of the governor general without expectation of participants that he was seeking a vote, support, or affirmation of a particular position. While in office, the lieutenant governor of Ontario, Elizabeth Dowdswell, viewed the convening power as exceedingly important, noting that "one thing the lieutenant governor can do is model dignity and civility."[96]

The ability for the vice-regals to gather people together in a nonpartisan and collegial manner well predates Johnston. Dating back to the emergence of party politics in British North America, "the governor's ceremonial presences had removed men from their political factions, and brought them together in a show of peace and unity."[97] As we traipse through the history of Canada, we find the governor's first convening role was exercised in a meeting with Indigenous peoples to make treaty and negotiate the use of the land and their resources – establishing that first of relationships. In the more recent past, the convening function was reinvigorated in Vincent Massey's routine gathering of elements of the arts and culture community together at Rideau Hall, Roland Michener's role in championing physical activity through the ParticipACTION program, or Michaëlle Jean's bringing together of youth leaders with members of the Order of Canada to discuss an array of issues. None of the aforementioned initiatives have fallen within the traditional concept of the vice-regal role, nor are they necessarily initiatives that one could picture the sovereign being directly involved in – although supportive from a distance she most certainly is.

6

Yet Symbols Still Matter

We are symbols, and inhabit symbols.

Herman Hesse

The symbols and ceremonies of the state might seem incidental to an examination of the monarchy in Canada, yet there is a ubiquitous presence to the sovereign and Crown beyond those matters of interest to the numismatist and philatelist. The Crown's symbolic presence is woven deeply into the Canadian state and society, often in a subtle manner. In monarchies and a number of republics, the head of state is the paramount personification of the state, while in many presidential republics it is the Constitution that is the accepted personification of the state. Every state possesses an official outward identity that is intended to serve simultaneously as an image of authority and of belonging. The Queen is the personification of the Canadian state, yet the importance of this personification goes beyond a single person or office – extending to a suite of associated and interconnected symbols. In the broadest context these symbols are made up of ceremonies, customs/rituals, flags, coats of arms/emblems, honours, and the overall imagery used to represent the state itself. These are adaptable mediums through which the sovereign, governor general, lieutenant governors and institution of the monarchy come to be viewed and experienced. As we will see, many of these elements are often discretely intertwined – as in such central parts of the Canadian identity as the national flag – yet are more pronounced in such ceremonies as the swearing in of new citizens.[1]

Ceremonies, customs, and symbols play a number of roles in government and civil society, including the fostering of a national community. They aid in creating a shared identity: "Hegemony cannot be asserted; it must be negotiated between citizens and elites through the creation and manipulation of symbols. The instruments of nation-making are most notably flags, anthems, idols, monuments, and civic architecture."[2] Symbols as objects are the furniture of the state, just as ceremonies, which invariably include the same symbols, result in a form of interactive state theatre involving government actors (officialdom), the citizenry, and members of the broader civil society. Furthermore, symbols are the proverbial veneer atop the state, which provides it with an identity beyond the mechanics of government or individual participants in the wider system. In a constitutional monarchy, it is natural that the symbols associated with the Crown and person of the sovereign are plentiful – be they the effigy on coins or stamps, coats of arms, the national flag, portraits, oaths, or official documents. While this work has focused largely on the method and theory of how constitutional monarchy has functioned in the Canadian context, omitting a discussion of the role of symbols would ignore the important multidirectional and reinforcing relationship between symbols and the monarchy in Canada. The trappings of ceremonies and symbols have little meaning if they are not explained,[3] and this chapter will examine how symbols support the constitutional monarchy, and how symbols, ceremonies, and the Crown have come to be deeply symbiotically connected. This has afforded flexibility to the constitutional monarchy in Canada and an ability to adapt and remain relevant. Given the diversity of symbols and ceremonies across jurisdictions, an exhaustive study of this topic would furnish material for several volumes; therefore, this chapter will provide an illustrative overview and is not a complete accounting of every aspect of the symbols and state ceremonial in Canada past and present.

"National symbols are so much a naturalized part of our everyday experience that it always seems to come as a shock when we are suddenly forced to take a step back and remind ourselves that symbols are not natural, but conventional signs."[4] Indeed, Canadian history is particularly replete with debates about symbols, and this helps to illustrate their importance. If symbols were of only incidental importance to Canada, why then was Parliament paralyzed for six months in 1964 debating a new national flag?[5] Why did Sir Robert Borden almost allow his wartime government to collapse over the issue of titular honours in 1918?[6] Why did it take until 1980 for the country to adopt "O Canada" as the national anthem?[7] Why did the announcement that the Government of Canada was to cease providing printed portraits of the Queen become a lead story in the nation's largest media outlets for several days in May 2019?[8]

The ability to manipulate symbolic representations is a rare trait that helps distinguish humans from other creatures.[9] Symbols and ceremonies cross all time periods and cultures and are ubiquitous in every society and system of government. Nevertheless, there is an inherent difficulty in quantifying the role that ceremonies, in particular, have to play in public perception of institutions. Such "information is quite rare because the whole point of a ceremony was that it was a visual demonstration of authority, not a defence of it."[10] In Clifford Geertz's examination of ceremonial life in nineteenth-century Bali, he found that "court ceremonialism was the driving force.... [M]ass ritual was not a device to shore up the state, but rather the state ... was a device for the enactment of mass ritual."[11] While the same cannot be said of the Canadian state, Geertz's work does demonstrate the centrality of ceremonies in the public life of a state. The performance of "ritual in public can be seen as an attempted display of power. So long as the ritual is accomplished unchallenged, the greater the display of power. The ceremony is a public expression of power of the individuals and collectivities to display the significance of the beliefs and objects that they value."[12] Those who witness ceremonial in person are more than mere spectators. They are an integral part of the event without whom the display of authority, transition, or historic moment would itself lack influences over anyone other than a small cadre of courtiers or officials.

Scholars have examined in detail the traditions, ceremonies, and symbols that came to be associated with the monarchy in Britain, most notably Eric Hobsbawm and David Cannadine.[13] The study in Canada has focused on royal tours, notably Philip Buckner and Ian Radforth who undertook highly informative examinations of Canadian royal tours, while H.V. Nelles ably chronicled the commemorations of Quebec's tercentenary.[14] Cecilia Morgan wrote a survey of Canadian commemorations from the 1850s to 1990s, but this was not specifically focused on the Crown.[15] In *Celebrating Canada*, editors Matthew Hayday and Raymond Blake examine national holidays and the adoption of "O Canada" as the official national anthem. Despite these significant works, little has been written on what Frank MacKinnon referred to forty years ago in what today is in a very limited sense the "decorative function"[16] of the Canadian state. The absence of the decorative function similarly can send a message, as there can be no vacuum of symbolic authority – someone or some office ultimately takes on this mantle. MacKinnon noted that these functions consist of symbols and ceremonies, which aid the non-partisan conduct of civil society. They have also arguably supported the durability of the constitutional monarchy in Canada. MacKinnon's nuanced understanding of the decorative function, beyond Bagehot's "dignified and efficient" dichotomy, is useful to our present study, as much for its ambit as for the period during which it was written. Although his study of the Crown was directed towards a popular audience, it was released in the mid-1970s, at a time when elements of Canada's constitutional monarchy were being quietly reduced.[17] The symbols and ceremonies of the state are much more than just buttons, ribbons, and bows that amuse or annoy the citizenry – they simultaneously provide legitimacy to the existing order. MacKinnon's reflection on the decorative function, when married to John Maynard Keynes's observation of the rise of fascism in the 1930s – that "the failure of the twentieth-century democracies … is in part attributable to their failure to invest the state with ceremonial"[18] – provides a more meaningful lens through which to view the flummery of the state. Obviously, symbols and ceremonies are not associated with monarchies alone, but with those at the apex of authority in any state. They can be used to convene and encourage inclusion. Conversely, they can serve as mechanisms of exclusion, marginalization, and oppression – witness the rallies of Nazi Germany and other totalitarian regimes. Elements of the ceremonies and symbols associated with the Crown in Canada, and the authority of the state in Canada, trace their origin back to the meeting of the first elected legislative assemblies in British North America, and now have become "the supreme moment of our country's political life. [They exemplify] Canada's status as a united, independent sovereign state."[19] Overall these ceremonies remain similar in structure in each jurisdiction, with nuanced and jurisdiction-specific augmentations that have been made over many years.[20]

Canadian humourist Thomas Chandler Haliburton's iconic character Sam Slick commented,

> When a custom can and ought to be fullered, foller it.
>   When it can't, set your own compass and steer your own course.[21]

Indeed, this has been the Canadian approach to symbols and the monarchy overall. While elements of Canada's symbolic lexicon are borrowed from Britain, France, and Indigenous sources, they have been augmented and remade with the passage of time. Most notably, the relatively recent inclusion of Indigenous components in state ceremonial, such as territorial acknowledgment, smudging, and drumming, reflect the dynamic nature of the symbols used by the state.[22] The concept of the "grand vice-regal regime,"[23] which was established by Lord Dufferin during his time as governor general, 1872–8, was never simply the importation of the Court of St. James to Canada. As governor general, Lord Dufferin "established a precedent for those who would follow and as the office evolved, a collection of 'invented traditions' began."[24] New symbols and ceremonies had to be established: things such as a ceremony for the grant of royal assent, the inclusion of Roman Catholic clergy in some ceremonies and the tables of precedence,[25] release of documents in two languages, to name a few of the innovations. The strict rules of court were untransferable to a society with very modest social gradation,[26] and Canada had to forge its own path in many respects by borrowing, augmenting, and inventing tradition.

Canada has been at the vanguard of these changes amongst the old dominions – especially in relation to Australia and New Zealand.[27] It is during the present Queen's reign that Canada's symbolic lexicon has undergone the greatest transformation – just as the country underwent the process of realmization – the transition from being a British dominion to an independent Commonwealth realm. These were actions that "sought to give constitutional and symbolic expression to their independence from Great Britain."[28] The creation of the style and title of "Queen of Canada,"[29] the establishment of Canadian citizenship, a distinctive national flag, a national honours system, and the associated ceremonies and celebrations that have accompanied many of the signal events in the life of the country, have seen Canada at the forefront of shedding its mantle as a British dominion and evolution into a mature independent country. The augmentation of symbols such as flags, anthems, and citizenship, and the invention of ceremonies such as the 1953 Coronation celebrations held on Parliament Hill, the 1967 Centennial celebrations, and the patriation of the Constitution in 1982, must "be seen as part of a wider process of material and ideological change beginning in the mid-1950s."[30] The Crown has played a central role in all these events as the vector through which these moments were convened – presided over by the sovereign or a vice-regal – carried out before members of the citizenry, both live and electronically. We have been able to debate symbols and even the Canadian identity under the permanence of the Crown.

The following section examines the relationship between Canada's constitutional monarchy and central symbols. This will be followed by consideration of ceremonies that are relevant to this discussion of the sovereign, Crown, and monarchy in Canada. Finally, officially sanctioned forms of recognition – be they honours or awards – will be examined, as there is an important interplay between the offering of recognition, acceptance of it, and the sorts of activities being recognized by the state – in this case through the Crown and its function as the "font of all honour."[31]

Symbols

Every country and most sub-national jurisdictions have physical symbols that are meant to embody the identity and authority of a particular place. In Canada these are often the subtle elements of the Crown that remain ubiquitous throughout officialdom: the effigy on a coin, banknote, or stamp, the coat of arms on the front of the passport and citizenship certificate, or references to the sovereign in a document, oath, or commissions of appointment. One of the most potent symbols of a country is its flag, and the national flag of Canada illustrates how the Crown and the role of the sovereign were woven into the adoption of a new national symbol in 1964–5, and its subsequent broad acceptance.[32] Of course there other national symbols that are less tangible: hockey and lacrosse as national sports, the coffee and doughnut chain Tim Hortons, and such government programs as publicly funded hospitals and health care services. These other symbols are less permanent; we should not forget that at one time cricket was the national sport, Eaton's was the national department store, and Macdonald's National Policy was seen as essential to the Canadian identity.

The replacement of the Canadian Red Ensign in 1965 with a national flag of Canada (maple leaf flag) brought Parliament to a near standstill for the last six months of 1964. The final choice was revealing, not for its now iconic design, but on account of how it came about. It is one of those elements of Canada's symbolic lexicon that eschewed the British connection and managed to retain a deep connection to the Crown.

The colours red and white were chosen as the colours for the new flag because they are the national colours, which had originally been assigned to the country in 1921 by King George V, shortly after the end of the First World War.[33] The new flag was not formalized through an Act of the Parliament of Canada – arguably the most profound exercise of the will of the representatives of the people. Rather its adoption was authorized via a joint resolution of both houses of Parliament. Proclaimed in the Queen's name under the Great Seal of Canada and her signature, the elaborate ceremony on Parliament Hill, held on 15 February 1965, saw the Canadian Red

Ensign respectfully retired and the national flag formally inaugurated. Nevertheless, in the Canadian context, the national flag has never been the sole symbol of the state. It is not the personification of the state; we do not swear allegiance to the flag, and there are other flags that rank ahead of the national flag,[34] and we are permitted legally to desecrate the flag – it is a central symbol but not a holy or unassailable one of paramount importance.

While the retirement of the Canadian Red Ensign was a significant step in setting aside symbols that overtly displayed Canada's connection to the United Kingdom, the adoption of the maple leaf flag fully embraced the sovereign's role as Canada's head of state, in assenting to the symbols of the state that functions in her name. A similar approach was made when the Order of Canada was established in 1967, whereby the new honours system was created through letters patent issued by the Queen, and not an Act of Parliament. For more than fifty years, Canadian honours policy, which had been greatly restricted following passage of what became known as the Nickle Resolution by the House of Commons in 1918, almost brought the conferral of honours upon civilians to a complete stop.[35]

The physical design too brought together elements of the new national flag and the symbolism of the Crown itself.[36] Like the adoption of the flag, the sovereign and symbols of the Crown played a direct role. Given Canada's previous experience with honours, some innovations to the traditional selection mechanisms were included; most notably the adoption of a grass roots nomination model and the exclusion of politicians from the new system – either as decision makers or recipients during their time in office.

A less well-known example of this transformation of a central national symbol is the Great Seal of Canada, and its symbolic transformation as part of Canada's realmization. Following the death of George VI, a new seal was adopted. This was the first seal to carry its inscription in English and French, for previous versions had been in Latin, and to carry the title QUEEN OF CANADA – REINE DU CANADA.[37] The design, the first undertaken by a Canadian and engraved in Canada was also shorn of its gothic decoration and had a simple background with the sovereign seated and the Royal Arms of Canada.[38]

Ceremonies and Ritual

Often discussion of the sovereign, her representatives, and the Crown focus upon who has what specific power, how it may be exercised, and under what circumstances. This is done within the framework of how governments function and the legal constitutional aspects of the executive authorities, which, in constitutional monarchies like Canada, are left in the hands of the sovereign, the governor general, or lieutenant governors. While "power is like the wind: we cannot see it, but we feel its force. Ceremonial is like the snow: an insubstantial pageant, soon melted into thin air … but this conceals, more than it indicates, their real importance."[39] Ceremonial and the public display of the flummery of the state, be it a coronation, inauguration, swearing-in, legislative opening, national day celebration, state funeral, or investiture, are practised throughout the globe in myriad different forms and are an essential element of officialdom in every country. Ceremonies, custom, and ritual are "the warp that holds together the many stiches in the rich tapestry of civilized life, which we are still weaving."[40] Ritual and symbols "help to enforce respect for authority and for existing institutions"[41] and thereby create an appearance of stability, and also usually continuity.[42] Historically, when it comes to projecting the power and presence of the state, amongst the most significant such displays has been the coronation of a new monarch.[43] Canadian participation in the four coronations of the twentieth century was steadily enhanced from 1902 to 1952, reflecting an increasing presence and official role.[44] In a softer manner, official visits by the head of state or representatives convey a similar sense of authority, connection and sense of belonging, attachment, and fealty. These occasions also provide citizens with a direct connection to the state at the highest level, well beyond the vote-seeking politician or non-partisan civil servant, who tends to be the most frequent point of official contact for Canadians. All ceremonies are invented and augmented over time to suit the image that the people putting on the proverbial show wish to project.[45] In the Canadian setting, this is the government of the day. Nevertheless information about how ceremonies are perceived and accepted by the general public is "quite rare because the whole point of a ceremony ... [is that it is] a visual demonstration of authority, not a written defence of it."[46] An element of public attitude towards ceremony can be discerned from media reports; however, such reports tend to be narrow in focus and lacking defined methodology.

The presence of these symbols and ceremonies plays into what has been characterized as a "banal awareness of the monarchy,"[47] which seems "to be a significant influence that constantly reinforces knowledge and acceptance of the institution."[48] Ceremonies in Canada have never taken on the spectre of Kremlinology, where every minute detail of state ceremonial and public display was dissected to discern changes or augmentation in the popularity of the regime or influence of its key actors. Where the level of examination has entered the public realms has been on account of the absence of specific officials, not where they were seated or what they were wearing. One example was the absence of the Queen for the opening of the 1988 Calgary Winter Olympics, which were presided over by then Governor General Jeanne Sauvé.[49] The absence of the Queen was widely noted, given that it was she who opened the 1976 Montreal Summer Olympics, alongside Jules Léger, then the governor general. That being said, a ceremony by its very nature requires methodical planning and a guiding logic. For significant national events, this has required an element of creativity and placement of symbols, participants, and the sequence of events that goes beyond simply adhering to a protocol-driven table of precedence.

Canada's symbolic path to becoming an independent realm has been realized largely by having the Queen exercising her function as head of state in the country – not through having a member of her family presiding over an independence ceremony or "goodbye" moment. The development of a distinctive Canadian Crown, through the Canadian sovereign and her representatives, has been achieved in the form and function of Canada's constitutional monarchy – both in its legal and constitutional function and its symbolic, ceremonial, and convening role, which constitute some responsibilities of the head of state – be it direct or vicarious through representatives. It is worthwhile noting the prominent role that the sovereign and her representatives continue to play in state ceremonial in relation to the symbols of the Canadian state, both federally and provincially.[50]

Nevertheless, it is entirely possible to marginalize the figures and symbols associated with the Crown, as was ably demonstrated by the Irish Free State between 1922 and 1937, in part through the *Executive Authority (External Relations) Act 1936*, but more pervasively through the systematic removal of symbols and the decorative functions of the Crown.[51] South Africa followed a similar route in the period following the election of the National Party in 1948, accompanied by the formal adoption of apartheid.[52] While on the surface we can find some similarities with the Irish example in Quebec, following the Quiet Revolution and restyling of the Legislature of Quebec as the "Assemblée Nationale" in 1968, there remain significant differences. The lieutenant governor still gives an annual address to the legislature (in place of a speech from the throne), the office of the lieutenant governor remains funded by the provincial government, oaths of office are still sworn or affirmed in the name of the Queen, the executive functions of the lieutenant governor remain intact, and bills and orders in council still require the assent of the Crown's representative. Even the table of precedence still affords the lieutenant governor primacy over all other dignitaries. Conversely the lieutenant governor, unlike vice-regal counterparts in every other part of the country, does not serve as chancellor of the provincial order, and within the province the vice-regal flag is treated as subordinate to the provincial flag, but this has also periodically been the case for the national flag of Canada within Quebec's provincial institutions.[53]

Beginning in the 1950s, various British governments struggled with the handover of overseas territories, and just how the Crown and members of the Royal Family would be represented at these signal events in the development of new nations.[54] While a parade of royals headed off across the seas to witness the lowering of the

Union Jack and the symbolic birth of more than forty new nations, neither the Queen nor Queen Elizabeth the Queen Mother attended any of these ceremonies. The undersecretary of state for the Colonial Office, Sir Hilton Poynton, commented, "Queens – even former Queens – do not give things away."[55] Conversely, during the same period, Canada played host to a record number visits by the Queen and members of the Royal Family, who participated in a wide variety of events throughout the country.[56]

Despite the iconography of independence through "freedoms at midnight,"[57] the instant transition from colony to nation is firmly identified with a new country coming of age.[58] Canada's transition was realized through a series of events and new symbols, not by a single occasion that could be defined as the instant of independence. This makes for poor myth making, but it produces a nuanced, multifaceted narrative and is not limited to a single moment of national crystallization. Cannadine notes that the old dominions of Canada, Australia, and New Zealand took a "non ceremonial path to independence."[59] While this was certainly true in relation to there being no single ceremony that encapsulated the realization of Canadian independence, there was no lack of ceremony surrounding the adoption of new symbols and the realization of Canadian constitutional independence. All of these signal moments have included symbols associated with the Crown and the sovereign or their representative. The Canadian example of achieving independence has not been duplicated by many other countries that attained independence in the post-colonial era.

In place of the "independence/goodbye" episodes, Canada held "welcome to the family" moments such as the 1949 accession of Newfoundland to Confederation, which was held in the governor general's study with Lord Alexander and Prime Minister Louis St. Laurent at Rideau Hall, prior to the national celebrations on Parliament Hill. Then there was the 1999 ceremony to mark the partitioning of the Northwest Territory and establishment of Inuit self-government in the new territory of Nunavut. The ceremony held in Nunavut was presided over by Governor General Romeo LeBlanc and included artistic and cultural performances, along with more formal elements such as the inauguration of the new territorial flag and coat of arms. As part of the event it was indicated that the sovereign would be visiting in the near future.[60] The involvement of the sovereign's representatives, officialdom, symbols, symbolism, and legal instruments, as well as the encouragement of the general public to partake in the celebrations were common throughout.

The adoption of the national flag in 1965 was significant because of its design and method of selection, but also for the inauguration ceremony, which saw it raised for the first time. This ceremony in February 1965 held on Parliament Hill was itself high state theatre, bringing together Canadian officialdom and military along with the general public, who were encouraged to attend the ceremony. "O Canada" and "God Save the Queen" were sung, and the event was presided over by the Queen's representative. It was unlike any of the ceremonies held in the newly independent countries where the Royal Union Flag was lowered, a new flag was raised, and the independence leader offered a rousing speech about the winning of independence. Many of the signal Canadian events have been non-tropical, taking place during the winter/spring months. The Canadian flag raising in 1965 was an honestly contrived ceremony marking the adoption of a new national symbol – one that, despite its newness, retained deep linkages to history and tradition, most notably the use of colours assigned by King George V, and formalization of the new symbol through the most traditional of instruments, a royal proclamation.

The 1982 ceremony that brought about the proclamation of the *Constitution Act, 1982*, including the *Charter of Rights and Freedoms* and the constitutional amending procedures, provides another relevant window into how ceremonial and the sovereign have provided a sense of stability in the midst of significant change –constitutional and symbolic. The sovereign and symbols of the Crown were the constant in the pageant of ceremonial that brought about the proclamation of the amended Constitution. While the words in the document had been adapted since 1867 – along with all the political actors, the very building where Parliament sat, and the complexion of the country itself – the sovereign remained paramount and intact, surrounded by symbols of the Crown, as part of a new ceremony that took place on a stage constructed to appear like the interior of the Senate Chamber.[61] It is worthwhile recalling that the Constitution was amended by resolutions adopted by each house, asking the Crown to request that the Parliament of the United Kingdom make amendments to what was then the *British North America Act*.

As in 1867, political leaders chose that Canada would remain a constitutional monarchy. Although not quite as overt a decision as Norway's 1905 referendum on whether to remain a monarchy following the dissolution of the United Kingdoms of Sweden and Norway, it was still a signal moment. The 1982 ceremony on Parliament Hill witnessed the Queen, wearing her Canadian orders, and her consort, wearing the unification green Canadian Forces uniform as the colonel-in-chief of the Royal Canadian Regiment, presiding over another Canadian moment of transition. The event helped to articulate not the transfer of authority from the United Kingdom to Canada, or the swapping of theoretical Crowns between the Queen of the United Kingdom and the Queen of Canada; rather, it was the symbolic and legal realization of the Canadian monarchy and that the Canadian realm was no longer tied to Britain, but linked through a person who shares the duties of sovereign with other countries. The event, like the inauguration of the national flag, included the senior-most representatives of the citizenry (officialdom), along with thousands of citizens who showed up to become part of the moment. The 1982 ceremony was made conspicuous by the absence of the premier of Quebec, and as if to serve as a counterbalance, the presence of so many Quebeckers in the ceremony itself. This was not some ancient ceremony unearthed from the archives, but a new state event created in part to suit the mood and moment and choreography required of a decades-long constitutional debate – one that simultaneously signalled a constitutional change and the continuity of Canada's constitutional monarchy: the sovereign, associated symbols, and the decorative function of the Crown on full display.

Rare though such state events may be, Canadians do see a purpose to them well beyond glorification of the government of the day or an antiquated attachment to the monarchy. The roles of the governor general and lieutenant governors, who, as we have seen, carry out many of the sovereign's duties, vicariously reflecting the role and function of the head of state, routinely place them at the centre of all manner of state events in their specific jurisdictions. Visits to Canada by members of the Royal Family have also served to support the symbolic presence of the Crown, albeit more periodically than what is achieved through the constant presence of vice-regals. The "promotion of monarchical symbolism and ceremony, as well as provincial sponsorship of royal visits, seems to have been well received by the citizenry."[62] In 2012 and 2019 Ipsos Global Public Affairs undertook research into Canadians' views of the role of the vice-regals. The survey found that those queried saw value in the role of the Crown's representatives: 80 per cent responded in 2019 that attending state occasions was important, up from 62 per cent in 2012; in 2019, 61 per cent responded that carrying out the Queen's constitutional duties was important, up 10 per cent from the same question in 2012. Such ceremonies, which seem like ancient rituals, "illustrate the amorphous quality of the Crown as a flexible and adaptable political system that takes up meaning appropriate to the political and social environment"[63] in which is functions.

Recognition

The recognition of good deeds, be it over an extended period of time or through the performance of a particularly deserving act, is an area where the Crown's legal and symbolic personalities converge to bring about recognition of exemplary citizenship through honours and awards. The conferring of honours and awards serve as official "thank yous" from the citizenry for services rendered, and the practices are observed nearly universally in countries and societies around the world.[64] Depending on their type and rarity, honours and awards can be very significant, such as appointment to the Order of Canada, or of more personal significance, such as being awarded the Lieutenant Governor's Education Medal for high school students in Nova Scotia. While the quality of the recognition varies, either due to the scarcity and antiquity of the award, the status of the person conferring the award, or the perceptions of the recipient, it is all part of a gift exchange, whereby someone in authority bestows recognition on behalf of a larger community for an act or acts that have been considered laudable. In accepting the recognition, recipients acknowledge the legitimacy of the authority giving the recognition and the formal tribute to their contribution. On rare occasions the honour or award is declined. In the case of an honour such as the Order of Canada, most often the refusal comes out of a sense of modesty and is infrequently due to the desire for a higher honour or on account of political views.[65]

Given the multiplicity of forms of official recognition in Canada, the role of the sovereign and her representatives in conferring honours and awards brings the Crown's representatives into direct contact with thousands of citizens each year. The Crown is the fount of all official honours, be they federal or provincial. Over the last seventy years, as Canada transitioned from being a British dominion to becoming an independent realm, there were significant changes in the modes and methods of recognition accorded – from a period where there were almost no civilian honours and very few awards, to the present where a greater array of honours and awards are conferred annually than even at the zenith of the British Empire.

Honours and awards are official symbols of recognition and come in a wide variety. Beyond serving as official tokens of gratitude from the Crown, honours and awards also reveal the sorts of contributions or acts that the state considers worthy of recognition. For instance, great importance is placed on volunteers and volunteerism: 19.4 per cent of those appointed to the Order of Canada from 1967 to 2016[66] were recognized on account of their contributions to the volunteer sector. The conversion of the Governor General's Caring Canadian Award, which had been created in 1995, into the Sovereign's Medal for Volunteers in 2015 – which elevated the award to a national honour – further demonstrates the significance and status that the state has placed on volunteerism. With official orders, decorations, and medals created by the sovereign, the state defines what deeds should be recognized, and the Crown serves as the conduit through which recognition is conferred. In the establishment and presentation of awards, and in what is being recognized, the vice-regals have more flexibility in creating their own forms of recognition in the form of awards. Although subordinate to a national or provincial honour, they are means by which citizens are formally recognized.[67]

The Canadian experience with honours, which had frequently been used as a partisan tool not always associated with merit, meant that state recognition now had to allay the suspicions and concerns of a populace that had not known a civilian honours system for nearly fifty years. This was achieved in 1967 with the establishment of the Order of Canada and eventually the broader Canadian honours system, which provides another example of the accretion of institutions and practices associated with the Crown and its representatives. The sovereign, vice-regals, and symbols of the Crown have proven to be flexible instruments through which this transformation could be realized effectively, both nationally and provincially. Successive governments, governors general, and lieutenant governors have seen the Crown as a useful conduit for according official recognition to citizens and organizations, well above party politics. The Crown has come to offer such honours and awards with legitimacy, dignity, and prestige – while the high calibre of those recognized multiplies this effect and enhances the prestige and legitimacy of the particular honour or award. In several polls, the conferral of honours and awards has been deemed important by a significant portion of the population surveyed.[68] Meanwhile, recipients become living confirmation of the Crown's legitimacy. In addition, they become ambassadors for the propagation of other good works that may also be recognized by the Crown. Governor General David Johnston noted that recognition of volunteers at the local level, with a modest honour such as the Sovereign's Medal for Volunteers, is "so very Canadian,"[69] because the it recognizes the unsung heroes and those who would otherwise most likely go unrecognized by the state.

At the time of the Centennial in 1967, Canada had no honours system, having phased out the use of British honours for civilians at the end of the Second World War. The Centennial year included the establishment of the Order of Canada and was a catalyst for the establishment of the Canadian honours system. This system has grown to include a separate order for every province and territory, along with more junior honours. In every jurisdiction, aside from Quebec, it is the vice-regal who presides over investitures and serves as the chancellor of the order. While not selecting recipients, the vice-regals, on behalf of the Crown, oversee elements of the honours systems, promoting recognition and civic engagement. Since 1967, aside from those given military honours, more than 450,000 Canadians have been recognized with a national or provincial honour of the Crown. In time, Australia and New Zealand followed the Canadian example in the establishment of realm-specific honours that no longer relied upon the status or history of the British honours system.

The Order of Canada and the broader Canadian honours system have come to derive their legitimacy and acceptance from a quartet of factors. Honours emanate from the Crown under the authority of the royal prerogative; honours lists are drafted independently from the ministry/government of the day by an arm's-length advisory council that reviews grassroots nominations from the general public; such honours are rare; and those who have been recognized by Canadian honours since 1967 are of high calibre.

Aside from honours, the Crown – through the governor general and lieutenant governors – has become patron of a wide variety of vice-regal awards, in a pattern established when Lord Dufferin created the Governor General's Academic Medal in 1873.[70] Provinces followed this example for recognizing scholastic and academic excellence; however, since 1974 the number and diversity of vice-regal awards has grown beyond the confines of schools and universities. The range and diversity of vice-regal awards reveal the varied nature of activities that are being recognized and, by extension, considered to be significant to the broader society, often helping to recognize people and contributions that would not typically be acknowledged with a national or provincial honour. In 1974 there were twenty-three vice-regal awards across Canada; as of 2019, there are 127 different awards, including:

- Governor General's Award in Visual and Media Arts
- Governor General's Performing Arts Award
- Governor General's Award in Commemoration of the Persons Case
- Governor General's Innovation Awards
- Lieutenant Governor's Award for Excellence in Wines (British Columbia, Ontario, and Nova Scotia)
- Lieutenant Governor's Respectful Citizenship Award (Nova Scotia)
- Lieutenant Governor's Seniors Medal (Quebec)
- Lieutenant Governor's Award for the Advancement of Interreligious Understanding (Manitoba)
- British Columbia Community Achievement Award
- Lieutenant Governor's Award for Outstanding Service to Rural Saskatchewan
- Lieutenant Governor's Community Volunteer Award for Students (Ontario)

Many of these awards are administered in collaboration with a government department, professional association, or well-established community organization. Use of vice-regal offices to afford the awards prestige and legitimacy and the fact that many of these awards recognize contributions to non-traditional areas is further indication of the broadening presence of the Crown, through the vice-regal offices and officeholders.

This chapter has surveyed the importance of ceremonies and symbols and their interplay with the sovereign, her representatives, and the overall constitutional monarchy as it has come to function in Canada. There has developed a multidirectional and reinforcing relationship between symbols – be they ceremonies, emblems, or other forms of recognition – and the monarchy, unobtrusively and pervasively. The symbolic presence of the Crown is deeply woven into the Canadian state and society, even if it is not always blatant or propagandistic. The corollary reinforces the decorative function of the Canadian state, which has the monarchy, including symbols of the Crown, at its centre, whether through ceremonies, physical symbols, flags, honours, or awards – all which have a Canadian persona and many of which have come into being during the present reign, adapting to the needs and realities of the Canadian state and citizenry.

7

A Moment in Transition

The phone will ring in the secretary's office at Rideau Hall, and shortly thereafter Operation London Bridge will be set into motion to inform senior officials and the country, "The Queen is dead. Long live the King." One can imagine the secretary to the governor general will pause for a moment, gaze across the mahogany desk at the 1951 Karsh portrait of the then Princess Elizabeth that hangs on the wall, and reflect on the life and reign of the longest-reigning monarch in Canadian history.

The demise of the Crown, a rather laconic, if slightly euphemistic manner of referencing the death of the sovereign, will bring about events legal and constitutional, as well as symbolic and ceremonial in their outward display. The legal and ceremonial necessities surrounding the demise of the Crown and the accession of a new sovereign will unfold as part of a highly detailed and rehearsed plan to ensure continuity of government. The theory and mechanics of the "moment in transition" that will witness the assumption of the powers and authorities of the sovereign of sixteen independent realms in an instant has the appearance and aura of antiquity. While significant elements of ancient tradition will be borne out following the death of our rightful Liege Lady Elizabeth the Second,[1] there will also be substantial newness to the succession – the perpetual invention and reinvention of tradition that has helped keep the monarchy relevant will persist. The death of the Queen of Canada will represent the full achievement of realmization, in that the country will have experienced an entire reign with a Canadian head of state at the apex of an institution that, although shared in the physical person of the sovereign, has been Canadianized from start to finish. Along with Canada, fifteen other countries will experience this transition.[2] While the catalyst for the event – the death of the Queen – is one shared element, the remaining details will vary in each of the realms over which the Crown in its various manifestations is sovereign. This concluding chapter will provide an overview of the principal aspects of the demise of the Crown as they relate to Canada.

Since the Queen's accession to the throne in 1952, officials in the United Kingdom, and to a lesser degree in other Commonwealth countries, have been preparing for the inevitable.[3] In the period immediately following the Coronation, Canadian preparations for the next succession were embryonic. From the internal release of the *Manual of Official Procedure of the Government of Canada* in 1968[4] to the present day, senior officials in the Privy Council Office have been seized with the matter in an increasingly detailed manner.[5] Other questions about what happens if the United Kingdom invokes provisions of the *Regency Act* are also of peripheral relevance to our discussion here. In broad terms, how will the demise of the Crown and accession of the heir apparent unfold?

There will be the inevitable emotion that accompanies such an international event over an individual with whom so many peoples feel a personal connection, even if they have never actually met her. The death of the sovereign will bring a flood of commentary from an endless supply of instant experts, many of whom may not have a grasp of the constitutional fundamentals. Some will claim that Canada is to become a republic if the federal government refuses to proclaim the new sovereign,[6] or that if a province or group of provinces refuse to recognize the accession of a new sovereign, Canada will by default cease to be a monarchy, with the governor general as ersatz president. There will doubtlessly also be those who will wish to "skip" Prince Charles in favour of Prince William. While none of these claims will be supported in law, history, or practice, they are certain to enter public discourse and the debate about the future of the monarchy.

The demise is likely to fuel novel or far-fetched court challenges alleging that Canada is no longer a constitutional monarchy, that the country has reverted to a colonial status as an overseas territory of the United Kingdom, or that somehow Canada was denied its moment in transition, and the country has entered a constitutional abyss in the role and function of the head of state as carried out by the sovereign of Canada. As we have seen with the litigation surrounding the modernization of the law touching on the succession to the throne, initiates and enthusiasts – along with those looking for a wedge issue to "open up" the process of constitutional amendment – are not shy about using the Crown as their target for creative legal arguments.[7] The novel idea that the "Crown-in-Right of Canada" can somehow be personified in the Constitution will arise in an attempt to forge new ground that would see Canada avoid the complex and necessary constitutional negotiations for a country to shed constitutional monarchy for another form of government. More orthodox commentary will reflect on the seamless nature of the demise of the Crown and subsequent transition, which we aim to offer here. There will also be proposals that call for downplaying the ceremonial aspects of the Crown and removing the visible elements as a way to cope with the complexities of actually abolishing the monarchy and converting Canada into a republic.[8] There will also follow thoughtful reflection and reasoned discussion of the role of the Crown in Canada, potential reforms, and republican options, with an eye to Ireland and Germany as examples of stable rights-based liberal democracies that are parliamentary republics. As discussion and debate unfold, many will come to the realization that Canada has never seriously considered adopting a republican form of government,[9] and the natural question of "why" will emerge. On a personal level, Canadians will need to acclimatize to the idea of Prince Charles as King and, on a symbolic level, to the idea of the institution now labelled the King's Privy Council for Canada and the Court of the King's Bench, along with the singing of "God Save the King." Beyond these ceremonial niceties, it is also natural to expect "some change after the reign of Elizabeth II."[10]

Media Explosion

Given the proliferation and saturated nature of electronic media that has developed since the turn of the century, the death of the Queen will be an international media event on a magnitude beyond that endured following the death of Diana Princess of Wales and the January 2020 media storm surrounding the departure of the Duke and Duchess of Sussex from the United Kingdom and temporary relocation to Canada. While the focus in this work has been on the Crown as a Canadian institution, it is important to note that other realms will experience the transition as well.[11] Around the globe, the press has been preparing for this event for decades: television, Instagram, Twitter, Facebook, and every media platform will be flooded with endless documentaries, interviews, and vignettes for the ten days between the announcement of the death, the funeral service in London, and memorial events across Canada and throughout the Commonwealth. This will certainly drive republicans and even some practical supporters of constitutional monarchy a bit loopy. There will be an interminable account of the number of royal tours, foreign visits, trees planted, distance travelled, honours conferred, bills assented to, prime ministers who have come and gone, photos taken, stamps, coins, and banknotes issued, etc. To a degree, this account of Elizabeth II's reign in its sheer density will aid in deepening the public's understanding of just how constantly persistent and pervasive the Queen's involvement has been in the life of many countries. There will also be a corresponding number of reports and documentaries offering views on the nature of the new reign and the new King. A window opened into this media explosion following the death of the Duke of Edinburgh in April 2021, just two months shy of his 100th birthday. The death of the Queen's consort resulted in a constant flow of reports, stories, and documentaries during the eight days that led up to his funeral.

Legal Mechanics

The law of the United Kingdom governs the succession to the throne.[12] Upon the demise of the Crown, Prince Charles will automatically become the King of Canada. This will be officially announced in Canada by an accession proclamation issued by the governor general on the advice of the King's Privy Council for Canada.[13]

Throughout the Constitution of Canada, as well as in statutes and regulations, the expression "Queen" shall immediately mean "King." Norman Ward described this as the operation of "constitutional alchemy."[14] In practice, the transformation is assisted by various rules of construction and interpretation. Section 2 of the *Constitution Act, 1867* originally provided that the provisions referring to "Her Majesty the Queen extend also to the Heirs and Successors of Her Majesty, Kings and Queens of the United Kingdom of Great Britain and Ireland."[15] The oath of allegiance taken by senators, members of the House of Commons, and members of provincial legislative assemblies, which is set out in the fifth schedule of the *Constitution Act, 1867*, also anticipates the accession of Kings and Queens by providing that the "Name of the King or Queen of the United Kingdom of Great Britain and Ireland for the Time being is to be substituted from Time to Time." For federal statutes, the *Interpretation Act* provides that "Her Majesty, His Majesty, the Queen, the King or the Crown means the Sovereign of the United Kingdom, Canada and Her or His other Realms and Territories, and Head of the Commonwealth."[16] The provinces all have similar rules of construction.

The demise of the Crown used to have several effects on the operations of government. Historically, Parliament dissolved on the demise, and offices under the Crown became vacant. Legal proceedings involving the Crown were also put to an end upon the demise. All of these effects have been reversed by legislation, both federally and in the provinces. For example, the *Parliament of Canada Act* provides that Parliament shall carry on "in the same manner as if that demise had not happened."[17] The federal *Interpretation Act* provides that "the demise does not affect the holding of any office under the Crown in right of Canada" and that all legal proceedings involving the Crown continue "as though there had been no such demise."[18] Although public office holders are not required to swear an oath of allegiance to the new sovereign, many do so voluntarily.

Unlike Elizabeth II's accession in 1952, none of the principal actors or officials who are responsible for the transition have experienced the demise of the Crown in their professional lifetimes. This is in stark contrast to what occurred in 1911 and 1936, upon the death of Edward VII, George V, and the abdication of Edward VIII. In Canada, the last official to have been involved in the demise of the Crown at the time of George VI's death, was Gordon Robertson, then a senior official in the Privy Council Office.[19] Robertson was involved in early Canadian plans for the death of Elizabeth II, the details of which were included in the *Manual of Official Procedure of the Government of Canada*.[20] In February 1952, he was present shortly after word was received that George VI had died, and recalled the profound sense of shock felt by everyone involved, from the administrator and prime minister[21] down to the correspondence and registry clerks.[22] Through institutional memory, Robertson's boss, Norman Robertson, then clerk of the Privy Council, had been briefed on the process by one of his predecessors, Ernest Joseph Lemaire, who served as clerk of the Privy Council from 1923 to 1940. Lemaire shepherded the government of Canada through the death of George V, the accession and abdication of Edward VIII, and the accession of George VI. He in turn had been schooled in the process by his colleague the redoubtable Sir Joseph Pope,[23] who was responsible for the plans surrounding Queen Victoria's death and accession, and also the demise of Edward VII and the accession of George V.[24] Until 1952 there was an unbroken institutional memory of how to deal with the demise of the Crown and how plans gradually changed as Canada's constitutional status evolved and matured to that of full independence.[25]

A Regency?

As the Queen ages, speculation recurs about the potential of a regency, where Prince Charles would exercise the Queen's powers as regent in the United Kingdom. Regency used to be dealt with on an ad hoc basis, such as when the British Parliament enacted a statute creating Prince George, then Prince of Wales, as Prince Regent during the incapacity of George III from 1811 until his death in 1820, when the Prince Regent ascended to the throne as George IV.[26] A series of subsequent British statutes, collectively the *Regency Acts, 1937 to 1953*, provide general rules permitting a regent to act where the sovereign is a minor, incapacitated, or unavailable for another definite cause. In addition, counsellors of state may act for the sovereign, in a limited capacity, in the event of lesser illness or absence from the United Kingdom.[27] While in office, "the Regent preforms the royal functions in the name and on behalf of the Sovereign."[28] Unless the sovereign is a minor, a regency can be proclaimed only "by reason of infirmity of mind or body incapable for the time being of performing the royal functions,"[29] or when the sovereign is "for some definite cause not available,"[30] and not simply because the Queen desires to lighten her constitutional workload.[31]

This raises the question of how the regent would relate to Canada. The *Regency Acts, 1937 to 1953* require that the Commonwealth realms be informed that a regency has been proclaimed, but they do not apply to Canada. They came into force following the enactment of the *Statute of Westminster, 1931*, and the Government of Canada did not request and consent to their extension to Canada.[32] Thus, if a regency was proclaimed in the United Kingdom, the Queen of Canada would remain in office and empowered to discharge her duties, while the Queen of the United Kingdom would find her duties being discharged by a regent. If the regency was due to incapacity, this may have implications for Canada. A Canadian prime minister could not reliably expect to advise a monarch who was in such a state as to no longer be deemed fit to discharge her duties in the United Kingdom. Whatever the multiple legal personalities of the Queen, there is only one physical person of the sovereign, and her health and disposition is uniform across all the realms. If the Queen of the United Kingdom is incapacitated for medical reasons, so too is the Queen of Canada. Canada was nearly faced with this scenario when George VI fell ill in 1951 and authorized counsellors of state to act on his behalf for certain matters in the United Kingdom. Prime Minister St. Laurent did not wish to burden the King with Canadian documents for signature during his illness and contemplated having the governor general act in the place of the King. Fortunately, the King recovered and indicated that Canadian documents "should be sent to Buckingham Palace in the usual way."[33]

It is also worth returning to the fact that Canada already lives under the aegis of a perpetual "vice-regency," as examined in chapter 5, with the governor general and lieutenant governors serving in the stead of the sovereign, dealing with almost every matter that comes before the state to be managed or dealt with. In the provinces, the lieutenant governors are complete surrogates for the sovereign and exercise all formal powers of the Crown in relation to their respective governments. It is only at the federal level, where the Queen remains personally involved in several Canadian matters, that a regency might raise challenges.

As we saw in chapter 3, the *Letters Patent Constituting the Office of Governor General, 1947* allow for the governor general to exercise almost every power of the Queen in relation to Canada. In most cases it is established practice, rather than a legal requirement, that sees certain matters continue to be submitted to the Queen. In fact, the provisions made for a regency in the United Kingdom played a direct role in the development of the Letters Patent, 1947.[34] Rather than attempt to enact Canadian regency legislation, the view at the time was that a sufficiently broad delegation to the governor general in letters patent would allow for those powers still in practice exercised personally by the sovereign to be assumed by the governor general in the event of the sovereign's incapacity; "thus paralysis of government should not arise during a Regency."[35]

Nevertheless, two areas may raise challenges during a regency. The most significant is the appointment and dismissal of the governor general. Under existing practices, the governor general is appointed by the Queen on the recommendation of the prime minister. Despite the broad wording in the *Letters Patent, 1947* authorizing the governor general to exercise "all powers and authorities" in respect of Canada, there is uncertainty about whether this authorizes the governor general to appoint a successor.[36] Prime Minister Paul Martin considered having then Governor General Adrienne Clarkson appoint Michaëlle Jean as her successor, but ultimately decided not explore this possibility because it would have required consultation with the Queen.[37] Given that the governor general is the Queen's representative in Canada, it is certainly fitting that the Queen make the appointment.

However, what would happen if the Queen was incapacitated? It seems likely that, under these special circumstances, a governor general could appoint a successor on the advice of the prime minister. The alternative would be either to force the governor general to remain in office for a potentially prolonged period, or else for the office to become vacant for an uncertain period. In this latter scenario, the governor general's powers would be assumed by the administrator of the Government of Canada whose responsibilities as chief justice of Canada would preclude him from carrying out the entirety of the governor general's program over a lengthy period. Even pared down to the bare minimum, it would not be sustainable for the chief justice to act as administrator beyond six months. Faced with the alternative of the administrator appointing a deputy administrator to act for a prolonged period, it would seem preferable for the administrator to appoint a new governor general – on the advice of the prime minister. In these exceptional circumstances, it would be prudent for the new governor general to have broad support from across party lines.

The more challenging scenario is the dismissal of the governor general. Fortunately, Canada does not have experience with "rogue" governors general, but the matter is not entirely theoretical. Two lieutenant governors have been dismissed for cause in the provinces.[38] Anne Twomey provides detailed examples from around the world where governments have dismissed, or considered dismissing, a governor general.[39] Any situation where a prime minister contemplates the dismissal of the governor general would arise in a moment of constitutional tension and would be complicated by the practical fact that, in a dispute with the prime minister, a governor general is unlikely to agree to be dismissed!

One other constitutional curiosity could potentially arise during a regency. Section 26 of the *Constitution Act, 1867* contemplates the exceptional increase of the Senate's complement beyond the usual 105 senators by the appointment of 4 or 8 additional senators. This power has only been exercised once, when 8 additional senators were appointed in 1990 to secure the passage of the Mulroney government's goods and services tax. Ordinarily, senators are appointed by the governor general. However, the additional senators may be appointed only if "the Queen thinks fit to direct" that the governor general make the appointments. The fact that the Constitution explicitly sets out a role for both the Queen and the governor general in these circumstances points away from the governor general being able to act both as governor general and on behalf of the Queen.

While a regency would cause a couple of challenges for Canada, government would otherwise carry on, with the governor general carrying out the Queen's remaining responsibilities in relation to Canada. Parliament could provide for a regent to act with respect to Canada, but such legislation would relate to the "Office of the Queen" as that expression is understood in the constitutional amending procedures and would therefore need to be preceded by a constitutional amendment authorized by resolutions of the Senate, the House of Commons, and each of the provincial legislative assemblies.

Symbols and Ceremonies

The minutia of the symbolic and ceremonial changes that will take place upon the Queen's death and the accession of her eldest son to the throne is not the primary focus of this work, however some elements of the transition do merit mention. As noted earlier, there will be a great outpouring of emotion upon The Queen's death, but it will also present an opportunity to modernize the way Canadians pay their respects. There will not be an extended six-month period of "court mourning" as was the case following the death of

Queen Victoria, nor the similarly lengthy, black crepe clad mournful tenor that characterized the deaths of Edward VII, George V and George VI. The obsession with death and mourning which emerged during the Victorian era has long since given way to a more instant and raw outpouring of emotion that is best characterized as an unregulated burst of feelings. There will still be a series of statements of condolence and loyalty from various government officials. Those working in the vice-regal, military and parliamentary world will be issued with some combination of black ties and black armbands for use during the period of mourning.

Following news of the death of George VI, a Committee of the Queen's Privy Council for Canada was convened, to recommend the issuance of a proclamation of the death of the King and the accession of Queen Elizabeth II.[40] J.W. Pickersgill, then head of the Prime Minister's Office, recalled that Prime Minister St-Laurent included Privy Councillors who were not members of the ministry in order to "emphasize the place of the Crown in the Constitution."[41] Those Privy Councillors present re-subscribed the oath of allegiance to the new Sovereign. These were symbolic gestures towards the new Queen, which were not legally required. A number of press releases containing information about the accession along with statements of condolence and loyalty from the governor general and prime minister were subsequently issued. Canada's new governor general-designate, Vincent Massey, happened to be in London at the time of the King's death and, as a member of the United Kingdom's Privy Council (then referred to as the Imperial Privy Council), attended the accession proclamation ceremony in the presence of the Queen, as he had done for her father in 1936.[42] Cabinet, after considerable discussion, decided that there should be an official national memorial service to coincide with the day of the funeral in London. Given the success of the 1939 royal tour of King George VI and Queen Elizabeth (the Queen Mother) and the more recent 1951 royal tour of then Princess Elizabeth and Prince Philip, it was gauged that there would be significant public expectation of a national ceremony.

The ceremonial surrounding the service for George VI was based on the combined elements of the 1910 and 1936 commemorations that were held for Edward VII and George V respectively, with the added elements of the laying of wreaths, firing of gun salutes, music and anthems. The Canadian memorial service was planned for 3:00 pm on 15 February 1952 at the National War Memorial, with alternate plans made for the Hall of Honour in Parliament in the event weather did not allow for an outdoor ceremony. It turned out to be -11°C on the day of the service, which was consequently held in the Hall of Honour in Parliament. The service was held late enough in the day to allow members of the government and general public to attend religious services of their choosing and then attend the national service, with crowds gathering outside the Centre Block of Parliament.

The service consisted of the laying of memorial wreaths by the Administrator, Speaker of the Senate, Speaker of the House of Commons, Leader of the Opposition and Minister of Veterans Affairs and a representative from the Royal Canadian Legion, a number of gun salutes and the playing of *God Save the Queen*. Invitations were only extended to those on the *Table of Precedence for Canada* as the King's death came suddenly with little forward planning for the legal or ceremonial aspects of the demise. The national memorial service for George VI unfolded as follows:

- The Great Bell of the carillon was tolled at one-minute intervals from 2 pm to 2:45 pm;
- 2:45 pm the ceremony commenced;
- 2:53 pm massed bands of the Royal Canadian Navy, Canadian Army, Royal Canadian Air Force and Royal Canadian Mounted Police played Chopin's *Funeral March* followed by *Abide with Me*, *God Save the Queen*, *O Canada*;
- Two-minutes of silence, the firing of a single artillery piece at 2:48 pm;
- 3 pm first gun fired off a 56-gun salute (one for each year of The King's life);
- Wreath laying commenced following the conclusion of the two-minutes of silence;
- At the 15th gun the Guard of Honour (which lined each side of the Hall of Honour) presented arms and the drummers

undraped their instruments and played the first 6 bars of *God Save the Queen;*

- Following the placement of the final wreath a piper from the Cameron Highlanders of Ottawa played *The Lament;*
- At the end of the fifty-six gun salute there was a flourish of trumpets/fanfare played followed by the playing/singing of *God Save the Queen;*

A memorial program, outlining the memorial service was printed by the Department of the Secretary of State.[43]

In light of the precedent set for her father in 1952, and the closure of the Centre Block of Parliament, which will last until at least 2029, it seems likely that the Queen's national memorial service will also take an ecumenical form and be carried out at Christ Church Anglican Cathedral in Ottawa.[44] An innovation which is certain to be included along with the standard civil and military involvement will be the integration of Indigenous observances such as smudging, drumming and throat singing. Given the enhanced connection between the Canadian Crown and Indigenous peoples, which has been fostered by the vice-regal family, and the special connection to the person of the Sovereign, this will be a natural and expected augmentation.

Similar accession ceremonies and memorial services are likely to take place in many provinces and territories, although the subnational jurisdictions have no official role in the legal mechanics of the demise of the Crown and the accession of a Sovereign. Citizens across Canada outside the National Capital Region will naturally have an expectation that their provinces and territories have some symbolic role in the transition. The various *Interpretation Acts*, which are in force federally and in each province, provide for such transformations of "Queen" to "King," so Queen's Councillors automatically become King's Councillors, the Court of Queen's Bench (in provinces where the superior court is known by this name) becomes the Court of King's Bench, commissions, proclamations and Bills come to be enacted in the King's name and not that of the Queen, and so on. In many provinces, as in 1952, lieutenant governors will preside over an accession proclamation ceremony, in the presence of their Premiers, Chief Justices and Clerks of the Executive Council. There will be official memorial services held under the aegis of the various provincial governments in most jurisdictions, and printed and electronic condolences books will be available for the public in addition to those provided by the Government of Canada and the Office of the Secretary to the Governor General.

When the period of mourning has concluded, the black ties and black armbands will be returned to storage and there will be a brief respite. This will be followed by an active period of planning for Canada's participation in the Coronation in London and official ceremonies to mark the Coronation of a new Sovereign in the national capital and the provinces. It is also reasonable to expect that the King will make a royal tour early in his reign. Of paramount importance will be the new Sovereign demonstrating his role as the King of Canada at the head of the Canadian Realm. While the Coronation in London is an important element of the Crown's shared history with other countries, the King's Canadian personality and character is of equal importance to his embodiment of the head of state-ship of fifteen other countries.

The Monarchy and Its Future

With the demise of the Crown comes the accession of a new Sovereign, and the corresponding Coronation ceremony in London and celebrations in each of the Realms. In time there will be the adoption of a new Royal Style and Title, a new Great Seal of Canada,[45] a new personal Canadian flag for the King, the effigy on coinage and banknotes will change, the text in the front of passports, on citizenship certificates, civil and military commissions, and the oath of allegiance will all be updated to reflect the transition to a new Sovereign. Following the obligatory period of mourning we can expect a royal tour by the new King, within a year there will be Coronation, and in short order Prince William, Duke of Cambridge, will be installed as the Prince of Wales. A great deal of importance will be placed on the continuity of the Crown, while also demonstrating the flexible and malleable nature of the overall institution – both in terms of the Royal Family and the vice-regal representatives across Canada.

Compared to the lengthy reign of Elizabeth II, in a relatively short period of time, say twenty years, there will be another demise of the Crown and the Duke of Cambridge will ascend to the throne, and eventually his son, Prince George will follow suit – barring abdication or other unforeseen events.[46] Thus, over the course of seven decades, Canada is likely to see three different Sovereigns. It is not dissimilar to the succession of monarchs following the death of Victoria in 1901 – so from historical experience, there is a familiarity to each lengthy reign being followed by a succession of much shorter ones. Of course, this all assumes that a republican option is not adopted in the United Kingdom or Canada.

As the third oldest continuous democracy in the world we must also acknowledge the inherent stability and predictability of this transition, even if we cannot divine its precise date, as is the case for the transfer of power in republics and some other monarchies. During the present Queen's reign, we have seen more societal change in Canada than during any previous period since Europeans first came to routinely reside on the part of the continent and interact with Indigenous peoples, nearly half a millennia ago. The Queen "is the latest link in a long golden chain that connects the Canadian Story,"[47] nevertheless, none of what we have reflected on in this book relies upon the person of Queen Elizabeth II. Certainly, Her Majesty has done an exemplary job of discharging her duties, while being practical and forward thinking, and the position of the Crown in Canada has been further enhanced by the adaptable and flexible nature of the role discharged by the governor general and lieutenant governors has helped to secure the Crown's position. The Crown today is a different Crown from when Princess Elizabeth ascended to the throne in 1952 – it is not the same institution and it has transformed for a host of reasons beyond symbol the style and substance of the person who has physically worn the Crown and as a living being, represented an international and multifaceted institution. The demise of the Crown is an inevitable facet of our system of government and the panoply of symbols which embody the Canadian state and broader civic identity.

While it will be a period of stability in a legal and constitutional sense, there will be a degree of change to the symbolic furniture of the nation. Nevertheless, the institution will continue and there will be a new "wearer" of the crown, if we can use that term. The person of the Sovereign – be it a Queen or King – is not the Crown; the Sovereign wears the Crown, heads and represents the institution, but the institution is much larger than a single person, even when that person has become profoundly associated with the Crown in the broadest sense, indeed that has been one of the principal reasons for this work, to demonstrate the ubiquitous and engrained nature of Canada's constitutional monarchy in Canada itself, hence the title of this book *Canada's Deep Crown.*

Postscript

This work has no formal "conclusion" as the Crown itself has no conclusion. The demise of the Crown brings with it the automatic succession of a new Sovereign, and the state continues to function. This is not a flippant observation; rather, it reflects the authors' premise throughout this work that the Crown's permanence needs to be comprehended more fully and that it be understood as foundational to the strength and resilience of Canada. The focus of this study has been on the continuing, indeed daily, activities of the Crown, carried out by its eleven Canadian representatives at any moment in time and the mechanics of how the Crown's authority is exercised and functions. We have sought to make clear the Crown's mutability and ubiquity. No longer is it a matter of Tudors and Stuarts issuing commands from on high (and off-shore) but rather of "a middle, and therefore unifying, voice" that speaks to and for all Canadians, nationally and in every part of the country, and which, it must be emphasized, is both effective and respected in the conduct of its duties.

The appointment of Mary May Simon as the 30th governor general and the first Indigenous person to represent the Queen at the federal level is the culmination of a long process whereby several Indigenous leaders have filled the vice-regal role in the provinces. The appointment is another illustration of the flexibility of the Crown as an institution, which provides for the representation and reflection of the diversity of the Canadian population in our oldest and highest offices and illustrates one of the themes of this book: governing practices that favour cultural and linguistic pluralism.

The influence of the Crown on Canada's political and territorial development is of over-riding importance in understanding the evolution of the country. Rather than being identified with inequality (class and rank), the Crown in Canada today promotes a culture of equality.

Notes

Preface

1 Those keen on tracing the historical roots of Canadian scholarship on the Crown are also likely to dig out R. MacGregor Dawson's *The Government of Canada*, along with subsequent updates undertaken by Norman Ward; Eugene Forsey's *The Royal Power of Dissolution in the British Commonwealth*; John Farthing's *Freedom Wears a Crown*; and Frank MacKinnon's *The Canadian Crown*.
2 John Fraser, *The Secret of the Crown: Canada's Affair with Royalty* (Toronto: House of Anansi Press, 2012).
3 D. Michael Jackson, ed., *The Canadian Kingdom* (Toronto: Dundurn, 2018).

Introduction

1 Christopher Lee, *Viceroys: The Creation of the British* (London: Constable, 2018), 171.
2 David E. Smith, *The Republican Option in Canada: Past and Present* (Toronto: University of Toronto Press, 1999); Colby Cosh, "Canadian Republicanism Is a Pathology, but It Won't Survive Past the Next Coronation," *National Post*, 29 December 2016, https://nationalpost .com/opinion/colby-cosh-canadian-republicanism-is-a-pathology-but-it -wont-survive-past-the-next-coronation.
3 CBC News, "Liberals Consider Break from Monarchy," 18 December 1998.
4 CBC News, "Liberals Consider Break from Monarchy."
5 Jean Chrétien, *My Years as Prime Minister* (Toronto: Vintage Canada, 2008), 249.

6 Robert Hazell and Bob Morris, "If the Queen Has No Reserve Powers Left, What Is the Modern Monarchy For?" *Review of Constitutional Studies: The Crown in the 21st Century* 22, no. 1 (2017): 18.

7 See, for instance, Terry Fenge and Jim Aldridge, eds., *Keeping Promises: The Royal Proclamation of 1763, Aboriginal Rights, and Treaties in Canada* (Montreal and Kingston: McGill-Queen's University Press, 2015).

8 David Arnot, "The Honour of the First Nations – The Honour of the Crown: The Unique Relationship of First Nations with the Crown," in *The Evolving Canadian Crown*, ed. Jennifer Smith and D. Michael Jackson, 155–73 (Montreal and Kingston: McGill-Queen's University Press, 2012).

9 *R v Secretary of State for Foreign and Commonwealth Affairs, ex parte Indian Association of Alberta and others*, [1982] 2 All ER 118 (CA).

10 Beurmond Benaville, "Acadians to Get Apology from Queen Elizabeth: Proclamation Acknowledges Deportation," *Bangor (Maine) Daily News*, 5 December 2003, https://www.acadian.org/history/acadians -get-apology-queen-elizabeth.

11 Yves Boisvert, "Hello, Victoria Day. Goodbye, Monarchy," *Globe and Mail*, 22 May 2017, A9; see too Martin Regg Cohn, "Maybe It's Time for Our Own Canadexit," *Toronto Star*, 25 June 2016, A6.

12 Leslie Young, "How Canada Could Break Up with the Monarchy," Globalnews.ca, 28 June 2017.

13 L.L. Blake, *The Prince and the Professor: A Dialogue on the Place of the Monarchy in the 21st Century* (London: Shepheard-Walwyn, 1995), 15.

14 Leslie Wayne, "The World Could Use More Kings and Queens, Monarchists Say," *New York Times*, 7 January 2018, 8.

15 Robert C. Vipond, *Liberty and Community: Canadian Federalism and the Failure of the Constitution* (Albany: State University of New York Press, 1991), 72.

16 In 2020, the top fifteen countries in descending order are: Finland, Denmark, Switzerland, Iceland, Norway, Netherlands, Sweden, New Zealand, Austria, Luxembourg, Canada, Australia, United Kingdom, Israel, and Costa Rica. John F. Helliwell, Richard Layard, Jeffrey Sachs, and Jan-Emmanuel De Neve, eds., *World Happiness Report 2020* (New York: Sustainable Development Solutions Network, 2020).

17 Helliwell et al., *World Happiness Report 2020*, 132–3.

18 Stephen Leacock, *My Discovery of England* (Toronto: McClelland and Stewart, 1961), 55.

19 Peter H. Russell and Lorne Sossin, eds., *Parliamentary Democracy in Crisis* (Toronto: University of Toronto Press, 2009); Robert Hazell and

Akash Paun, eds., *Making Minority Government Work: Hung Parliaments and the Challenges for Westminster and Whitehall* (London: Institute for Government, the Constitution Unit, 2009), 68.

20 Originally published as articles in *The Fortnightly Review* but later appearing in book form in the year of Confederation, 1867.

21 R. Macgregor Dawson, *The Government of Canada* (Toronto: University of Toronto Press, 1947), 169.

22 Vincent Massey, "Canada: Her Status and Stature," in *Speaking of Canada: Addresses by the Right Hon. Vincent Massey, Governor General of Canada, 1952–1959* (Toronto: Macmillan Canada, 1959), 25.

1 The Crown and Metaphor

1 James Wood, *The Broken Estate: Essays on Literature and Belief* (London: Jonathan Cape, 1999), 40; for an academic analysis of metaphor, see Elena Semino and Zsfia Demjén, eds., *The Routledge Handbook of Metaphor and Language* (New York: Routledge, 2017).

2 *Reference re Senate Reform*, [2014] 1 SCR 704, paras 26–7.

3 Andrew Coyne, "Supreme Court Ensures Widely Reviled Patronage House (the Senate) Will Stay Forever," *National Post*, 25 April 2014.

4 Ingrid D. Rowlands, "In the New Whitney," *New York Review of Books*, 26 June 2015, 14.

5 Stephen Leacock, *My Discovery of England* (New York: Dodd Mead, 1922), 59.

6 John Webster Grant, *The Canadian Experience of Church Union* (London: Butterworth, 1967).

7 Cynthia Ozick, *Fame and Folly* (New York: Vintage International, 1997), 87.

8 Mary Vipond, "Canadian National Consciousness and the Formation of the United Church of Canada," *Bulletin* 24 (1975), 10.

9 *Re Initiative and Referendum Act*, [1919] AC 935.

10 R. MacGregor Dawson, *The Government of Canada*, 5th ed. (Toronto: University of Toronto Press, 1970), 148.

11 John Charles Dent, *The Last Forty Years: Canada since the Union Act of 1841* (Toronto: George Virtue, 1881), 1:283.

12 J.R. Mallory, "The Continuing Evolution of Constitutionalism," in *Constitutionalism, Citizenship and Society in Canada*, ed. Alan Cairns and Cynthia Williams, 51–97 (Toronto: University of Toronto Press, in cooperation with the Royal Commission on the Economic Union and Development Prospects for Canada, 1985).

13 Bernard Bailyn, *To Begin the World Anew: The Genius and Ambiguities of the American Founders* (New York: Vintage Books, 2003).

14 Alan Cairns, ed., *The Politics of Gender, Ethnicity and Language in Canada*, Research Report, Royal Commission on the Economic Union and Development Prospects for Canada (Toronto: University of Toronto Press, 1986), 34:35.

15 Arthur G. Dorland, *Our Canada* (Toronto: Copp Clark, 1949), v.

16 Frank MacKinnon, *The Crown in Canada* (Calgary: Glenbow-Alberta Institute, McClelland and Stewart West, 1976), 30. Queen Elizabeth II has been particularly sensitive about being Queen of all of Canada, including French Canada and Quebec. See also Serge Joyal, "La Couronne au Québec, de credo rassurant à bouc émissaire commode," in *Canada and the Crown: Essays on Constitutional Monarchy*, ed. D. Michael Jackson and Philippe Lagassé, 33–62 (Montreal and Kingston: McGill-Queen's University Press, 2013).

17 Peter C. Oliver, *The Constitution of Independence: The Development of Constitutional Theory in Australia, Canada, and New Zealand* (Oxford: Oxford University Press, 2005), 132.

18 Sarah Katherine Gibson and Arthur Milnes, *Canada Transformed: The Speeches of Sir John A. Macdonald: A Bicentennial Celebration* (Toronto: McClelland and Stewart, 2014), 147.

19 Norman Penlington, *Canada and Imperialism, 1896–1899* (Toronto: University of Toronto Press, 1965).

20 Richard Gwyn, *John A.: The Man Who Made Us: The Life and Times of John A. Macdonald* (Toronto: Random House Canada, 2007), 1:389. The Crown meant that in British North America there were no "physical limits" to the emerging country. See, in contrast, Francisco Cantú, "Boundary Conditions: What Happens When the American Frontier Becomes a Wall?" *New Yorker*, 11 March 2019, 73–7.

21 David Malouf, "Made in England: Australia's British Inheritance," *Quarterly Essay* 12 (2003), 25–7.

22 Northrop Frye, *The Bush Garden: Essays in the Canadian Imagination* (Toronto: House of Anansi, 1971), x.

23 William Briggs, "Impressions of My Canadian Tour," 4 November 1919, *Empire Club Speeches* (Toronto: William Briggs, 1920), 387.

24 Harold A. Innis, "Decentralization and Democracy," in *Political Economy in the Modern State*, ed. Robert E. Babe and Edward A. Comor (Toronto: University of Toronto Press, 2018), 247.

25 W.L. Morton, *The Canadian Identity*, 2nd ed. (Toronto: University of Toronto Press, 1972), 5.

26 Bernard Ostry and Janice Yalden, eds., *Visions of Canada: The Alan B. Plaunt Memorial Lectures, 1958–1992* (Montreal and Kingston: McGill-Queen's University Press, 2004), 83.

27 E.E. Rich, *History of the Hudson's Bay Company, 1670–1870* (Toronto: McClelland and Stewart, 1960); see also E.E. Rich, ed., *The Hudson's Bay Company Booke of Letters, Commissions, Instructions Outward, 1688–1696* (London: Hudson's Bay Record Society, 1957); and Stephen Royale, *Company, Crown and Colony: The Hudson's Bay Company and Territorial Endeavour in Western Canada* (New York: I.B. Tauris, 2011).

28 Pierre Berton, *The Last Spike, 1881–1885* (Toronto: McClelland and Stewart, 1971), 1.

29 Clair Wills, "Prodigal Fathers," *New York Review of Books*, 20 December 2018, 38. The book under review was Colm Toibin, *Mad, Bad, Dangerous to Know: The Fathers of Wilde, Yeats and Joyce* (New York: Scribner, 2018).

30 R.C.B. Risk, "The Many Minds of W.P.M. Kennedy," *University of Toronto Law Journal* 48 (1998): 358.

31 Morton, *Canadian Identity*, 44.

32 See David E. Smith, *The Constitution in a Hall of Mirrors: Canada at 150* (Toronto: University of Toronto Press, 2017).

33 Richard Kelly, "Fixed-Term Parliaments Act 2011," House of Commons Library Briefing Paper No. 06111, 27 April 2017, 14. I would like to thank Professor Peter Neary for bringing this document to my attention.

34 *Conacher v Canada (Prime Minister)*, 2010 FCA 131.

35 José E. Igartua, *The Other Quiet Revolution: National Identities in English Canada, 1945–71* (Vancouver: UBC Press, 2006), 1.

36 Edward McWhinney, *The Governor General and the Prime Ministers: The Making and Unmaking of Governments* (Vancouver: Ronsdale, 2005), 16.

37 Donald Markwell, *Constitutional Conventions and the Headship of State: Australian Experience* (Redland Bay, QLD: Connor Court Publishing, 2016), 16.

38 2014 ONCA 578 (Docket C57775).

39 Bora Laskin, *The British Tradition in Canadian Law* (London: Stevens and Sons, 1969), 118–19.

40 Ben Pimlott, *The Queen: Elizabeth II and the Monarchy* (London: HarperCollins, 1996), 671.

41 Stefan Labbé, "End of a Royal Era," Open Canada, 29 September 2017, https://www.opencanada.org/features/end-royal-era/; Barbara Messamore, "Crown Proves Its Use: Far From Bending the Rules, It Ensures They Are Respected," *Globe and Mail*, 11 July 2017, A11.

42 Daniel Leblanc, "Former Astronaut Julie Payette to Be Governor General," *Globe and Mail*, 13 July 2017.
43 Campbell Clark, "Vice-Regal Role: A National Symbol," *Globe and Mail*, 14 July 2017, A9.
44 Clark, "Vice-Regal Role."
45 Peter Neary, "The Morning after a General Election: The Vice-Regal Perspective," *Canadian Parliamentary Review*, 35, no. 3 (Autumn 2012): 24.

2 A Realm of Opposites

1 Walter Bagehot, *The English Constitution* (London: Oxford University Press, 1958), 4. First published in 1867.
2 In Australia, augmentations to the office of the Queen, governor general, and governors cannot be implemented without national referenda, while in New Zealand and the other realms amendment to the office of the Queen or governor general can be made through a parliamentary vote.
3 J.W.F. Allison, *The English Historical Constitution: Continuity, Change and European Effects* (Cambridge: Cambridge University Press, 2007), 56–7.
4 F.W. Maitland, *The Constitutional History of England: A Course of Lectures Delivered* (Cambridge: Cambridge University Press, 1946), 418. See also *Town Investments Ltd v Department of the Environment*, [1978] AC 359 (HL), 397, per Lord Simon of Glaisdale, where the Crown was described as "a piece of jeweled headgear under guard at the Tower of London."
5 At the beginning of the First World War in 1914, aside from France, Portugal, and Switzerland, every country in Europe had a hereditary monarch as its head of state. By 1950 the monarchies had been reduced to just seven of twenty-five: Belgium, Britain, Denmark, Greece, Netherlands, Norway, Sweden. See John Van Der Kiste, *Crowns in a Changing World: The British and European Monarchies 1901–36* (London: Grange Books, 1993).
6 Vernon Bogdanor, *The Monarchy and the Constitution* (Oxford: Clarendon, 1995), 19.
7 Bogdanor, *The Monarchy and the Constitution*, 34, 37.
8 William Wade, "The Crown, Ministers and Officials: Legal Status and Liability," in *The Nature of the Crown: A Legal and Political Analysis*, ed. Maurice Sunkin and Sebastian Payne (Oxford: Oxford University Press, 1999), 31–2.
9 Peter Hogg, *Constitutional Law of Canada*, 5th ed. looseleaf (Scarborough, ON: Thompson Carswell, 2007–), vol. 1, ch. 10.

10 Anne Twomey, *The Chameleon Crown: The Queen and Her Australian Governors* (Sydney: Federation, 2006).

11 *McAteer v Canada (AG)*, 2014 ONCA 578 at para 62. See also *Roach v Canada (Minister of State for Multiculturalism and Citizenship)*, [1994] 2 FC 406 (CA), where the oath was described as a "solemn intention to adhere to the symbolic keystone of the Canadian Constitution as it has been and is, thus pledging an acceptance of the whole of our Constitution and national life."

12 *Giolla Chainnigh v Canada (AG)*, 2008 FC 69 at para 49.

13 Warren J. Newman, "Some Observations on the Queen, the Crown, the Constitution and the Courts," *Review of Constitutional Studies* 22, no. 1 (2017): 57–8. The quoted passage was an oblique reply to the insistence by Philippe Lagassé and James W.J. Bowden that the constitutionality of Canada's *Succession to the Throne Act, 2013* turns principally on the Crown's ostensible status as a corporation sole, a feature of the Crown that did not figure in either the reasons of the Superior Court or the Quebec Court of Appeal in upholding the validity of the legislation. See Philippe Lagassé and James W.J. Bowden, "Royal Succession and the Canadian Crown as a Corporation Sole: A Critique of Canada's *Succession to the Throne Act, 2013*," *Constitutional Forum* 23, no. 1 (2014): 17–26; *Motard c Procureur général du Canada*, 2019 QCCA 1826.

14 2017 SCC 40.

15 *Clyde River (Hamlet) v Petroleum Geo-Services Inc*, 2017 SCC 40, webcast of hearing at 2:20:58.

16 *Clyde River (Hamlet) v Petroleum Geo-Services Inc.*

17 *Clyde River (Hamlet) v. Petroleum Geo-Services Inc* at para 28.

18 *Clyde River (Hamlet) v Petroleum Geo-Services Inc* at para 29.

19 *Mikisew Cree First Nation v Canada (Governor General in Council)*, 2018 SCC 40.

20 Frederic William Maitland, *The Collected Papers of Frederic William Maitland*, ed. H.A.L. Fisher (Cambridge: Cambridge University Press, 1911), 3:158–9. Maitland ventured that "*et cetera*" probably meant "and (if future events shall so decide but not further or otherwise) of the Church of England and also of Ireland upon earth the Supreme Head." Maitland, *Collected Papers*, 1675.

21 J.W.F. Allison, *The English Historical Constitution: Continuity, Change and European Effects* (Cambridge: Cambridge University Press, 2007), 58.

22 It also removed the requirement for those after the first six persons in the line of succession to seek the sovereign's approval to marry in order to remain in the line of succession.

23 Legal challenges to both the Commonwealth heads of government agreement and Canada's *Succession to the Throne Act, 2013* have been unsuccessful. See *Teskey v Canada (AG)*, 2014 ONCA 612; *Motard c Procureur général du Canada*, 2019 QCCA 1826, application for leave to appeal to the Supreme Court dismissed with costs to the attorney general.

24 Robert MacGregor Dawson, "The Cabinet: Position and Personnel," *Canadian Journal of Economics and Political Science* 12, no. 3 (1946): 261–81. The exportation of the British system of government to Canada was also neither planned nor deliberate. Sir John Robert Seeley remarked that the British seemed to "have conquered and peopled half the world in a fit of absence of mind." John Robert Seeley, *The Expansion of England: Two Courses of Lectures* (Cambridge: Cambridge University Press, 2010), 8 (first published in 1883), quoted in Robert MacGregor Dawson, *The Government of Canada*, 1st ed. (Toronto: University of Toronto Press, 1947), 196.

25 Megan Specia, "Britain's Queen Is a Figurehead, but She Just Got Dragged into Brexit Politics," *New York Times*, 29 August 2019, https://www.nytimes.com/2019/08/29/world/europe/uk-queen-parliament-boris-johnson.html.

26 Gregory Tardi, *The Legal Framework of Government: A Canadian Guide* (Aurora, ON: Canada Law Book, 1992), 83.

27 Michelle Bellefontaine, "Alberta NDP Leader Rachel Notley Thrown Out of House in Bill 22 Stand-off," CBC News, 19 November 2019, https://www.cbc.ca/news/canada/edmonton/alberta-ndp-leader-rachel-notley-thrown-out-of-house-in-bill-22-stand-off-1.5365223.

28 Bagehot, *English Constitution*, 67.

29 Michael Valpy, "The 'Crisis': A Narrative," in *Parliamentary Democracy in Crisis*, ed. Peter H. Russell and Lorne Sossin (Toronto: University of Toronto Press, 2009), 16.

30 Adrienne Clarkson, *Heart Matters* (Toronto: Penguin, 2007), 208.

31 Vernon Bogdanor, *The Coalition and the Constitution* (Oxford: Hart Publishing, 2011), 23.

32 Norman Ward, review of *The Office of Lieutenant-Governor: A Study in Canadian Government and Politics*, by John T. Saywell, *Canadian Historical Review* 39, no. 3 (September 1958): 246–7.

33 *Re: Resolution to amend the Constitution*, [1981] 1 SCR 753, 882.

34 Andrew Heard, "The Governor General's Suspension of Parliament: Duty Done or a Perilous Precedent," in *Parliamentary Democracy in Crisis*, ed. Peter H. Russell and Lorne Sossin (Toronto: University of Toronto Press, 2009), 52–3.

35 Bogdanor, *The Monarchy and the Constitution*, 66.

36 Rideau Hall Foundation, www.rhf-frh.ca.

37 Serge Joyal, "The Changing Role of the Governor General, or How the Personality of the Office-Holder Is Changing the Perception of the Monarchy," in *Royal Progress: Canada's Monarchy in the Age of Disruption*, ed. D. Michael Jackson, 78–107 (Toronto: Dundurn, 2020).

38 Steven Point, "The Crown and First Nations in British Columbia: A Personal View," in *The Canadian Kingdom: 150 Years of Constitutional Monarchy*, ed. D. Michael Jackson (Toronto: Dundurn, 2018), 79.

39 Clarkson, *Heart Matters*, 187. More recently, officials at Rideau Hall, in the Offices of the Lieutenant Governors, and at the Department of Canadian Heritage and the Privy Council Office have taken steps to provide newly appointed vice-regals with more comprehensive information on their role in contemporary times. They have also established regular formal and informal channels of communication among the lieutenant governors and the governor general where issues can be discussed and best practices can be shared.

40 PC 1935–3374.

41 "Guidance for Deputy Ministers," https://www.canada.ca/en/privy -council/services/publications/guidance-deputy-ministers.html.

42 "Report of the Conference on the Operation of Dominion Legislation and Merchant Shipping Legislation, 1929," in *The Development of Dominion Status 1900–1936*, ed. Robert MacGregor Dawson (Oxford: University Press, 1937), 373.

43 Brian Slattery, "Aboriginal Rights and the Honour of the Crown," *Supreme Court Law Review: Osgoode's Annual Constitutional Cases Conference* 29 (2005): 435.

44 Robert MacGregor Dawson, ed., *The Development of Dominion Status 1900–1936* (Oxford: Oxford University Press, 1937), 331.

45 *Re: Resolution to amend the Constitution*, [1981] 1 SCR 753, 834; Gordon Robertson, *Memoirs of a Very Civil Servant: Mackenzie King to Pierre Trudeau* (Toronto: University of Toronto Press, 2000), 79.

46 *Haida Nation v British Columbia (Minister of Forests)*, [2004] 3 SCR 511 at para 25.

47 *Truth and Reconciliation Commission of Canada: Calls to Action*, 2015, http:// trc.ca/assets/pdf/Calls_to_Action_English2.pdf.

48 See generally Oliver, *Constitution of Independence*.

49 Andrew Heard, "The Crown in Canada: Is There a Canadian Monarchy?" in *The Canadian Kingdom: 150 Years of Constitutional Monarchy*, ed. D. Michael Jackson (Toronto: Dundurn, 2018), 114 (emphasis in original).

50 Norman Ward, *Dawson's The Government of Canada*, 6th ed. (Toronto: University of Toronto Press, 1987), 174.

51 Robert MacGregor Dawson, ed., *Constitutional Issues in Canada* (Oxford: Oxford University Press, 1933), 91–8.

52 Arthur Berriedale Keith, *Responsible Government in the Dominions*, 2nd ed. (Oxford: Clarendon, 1928), xiii.

53 *The Liquidators of the Maritime Bank of Canada v The Receiver-General of New Brunswick*, [1892] AC 437, 443.

54 Christopher Dummitt. *"Je me souviens* Too: Eugene Forsey and the Inclusiveness of 1950s' British Canadianism," *Canadian Historical Review* 100, no. 3 (2019): 384.

55 J.W. Pickersgill, *My Years with Louis St Laurent* (Toronto: University of Toronto Press, 1975), 161.

56 The appointment of lieutenant governors who were not residents of Canada (i.e., had not immigrated to the county permanently) ceased in 1870 following the appointment of Sir William C.F. Robinson, lieutenant governor of Prince Edward Island, who served in that role until 1873. Remarkably Robinson, who had previously served as governor of the Falkland Islands, would go on to serve variously as governor of the Leeward Islands, Western Australia on three separate occasions, then governor of Singapore and finally as governor of South Australia.

57 See, e.g., J.R. Mallory, "Seals and Symbols: From Substance to Form in Commonwealth Equality," *Canadian Journal of Economics and Political Science* 22, no. 3 (August 1956): 281–91.

58 Peter Stursberg, *Roland Michener: The Last Viceroy* (Toronto: McGraw-Hill Ryerson, 1989), 164; "Governors General Representing Canada at Home and Abroad," https://www.gg.ca/en/governors-general -representing-canada-home-and-abroad.

59 J.R. Mallory, *The Structure of Canadian Government* (Toronto: Gage Publishing, 1984), 37.

60 "Table of Titles to Be Used in Canada," https://www.canada.ca/en /canadian-heritage/services/protocol-guidelines-special-event/table -titles-canada.html.

61 Christopher McCreery, "Myth and Misunderstanding: The Origins and Meaning of the Letters Patent Constituting the Office of the Governor General," in *The Evolving Canadian Crown*, ed. Jennifer Smith and D. Michael Jackson (Montreal and Kingston: McGill-Queen's University Press, 2012), 52.

62 Philippe Lagassé, "The First and Last 'Queen of Canada," Policy Options, 9 September 2015, https://policyoptions.irpp.org/magazines/

september-2015/the-first-and-last-queen-of-canada/; *Ottawa Citizen*, "Canada's Independence Is at Stake," 6 July 2016.

63 "Proceedings of the Standing Senate Committee on Legal and Constitutional Affairs Issue 32 – Evidence for March 21, 2013," https:// sencanada.ca/en/Content/Sen/Committee/411/LCJC/32ev-50040-e . See also Peter W. Hogg, "Succession to the Throne," *National Journal of Constitutional Law* 33 (2014): 83–94; Mark D. Walters, "Succession to the Throne and the Architecture of the Constitution of Canada," in *The Crown and Parliament*, ed. Philippe Lagassé and Michel Bédard, 263–92 (Montreal: Éditions Yvon Blais, 2015).

64 See Heard, "Crown in Canada," 127.

65 Heard, "Crown in Canada," 127. See also John Fraser, D. Michael Jackson, Serge Joyal, and Michael Valpy, "The Supreme Court Reaffirms the Canadian Crown's Importance to Our Country's Sense of Order," *Globe and Mail*, 26 June 2020.

66 *Re The Initiative and Referendum Act*, [1919] AC 935 (JCPC). See also Stephen A. Scott, "Constituent Authority and the Canadian Provinces," 1966 *McGill Law Journal* 12, no. 4 (1966): 528, 542.

67 *Reference re Senate Reform*, 2014 SCC 32.

68 Christopher McCreery, "Subtle Yet Significant Innovations: The Vice-Regal Appointments Committee and the Secretary's New Role," in *The Crown and Parliament*, ed. Michael Bédard and Philippe Lagassé, 241–62 (Toronto: Thompson Reuters, 2015).

69 PC 2016-0011; SCC PC 2016-0693.

70 Government of Canada, "Canada's New Government Proposes Fixed Election Dates," news release, 30 May 2006, https://www.canada.ca /en/news/archive/2006/05/canada-new-government-proposes-fixed -election-dates.html.

71 *Canada Elections Act*, SC. 2000, c 9, s 56.1.

72 Warren J. Newman, "Of Dissolution, Prorogation, and Constitutional Law, Principle and Convention: Maintaining Fundamental Distinctions during a Parliamentary Crisis," *National Journal of Constitutional Law* 27 (2010): 217–29.

73 *Conacher v Canada (Prime Minister)*, 2010 FCA 131.

3 The Dispersal of Power

1 Craig Forcese, "The Executive, the Royal Prerogative, and the Constitution," in *The Oxford Handbook of the Canadian Constitution*, ed. Peter Oliver, Patrick Macklem, and Nathalie Des Rosier (Oxford: Oxford University Press, 2017), 151.

2 Peter H. Russell and Lorne Sossin, eds., *Parliamentary Democracy in Crisis* (Toronto: University of Toronto Press, 2009); Justin McElroy and Richard Zussman, "Showdown at Government House: The Meeting That Ended 16 Years of B.C. Liberal Rule," CBC News, 30 June 2017, https://www.cbc.ca/news/canada/british-columbia /government-house-stakeout-clark-horgan-guichon-1.4185404.

3 Robert MacGregor Dawson, described the prerogative as "very substantial" in Dawson, *The Government of Canada* (Toronto: University of Toronto Press, 1947), 170. A treatise on the Constitution of the United Kingdom notes, "In practical terms, the powers encompassed by the term 'prerogative' are of great importance for the effective working of government." See Peter Leyland, *The Constitution of the United Kingdom*, 2nd ed. (Oxford: Hart Publishing, 2012), 90.

4 See, e.g., *Abdelrazik v Canada (Minister of Foreign Affairs)*, 2009 FC 580; *Khadr v Canada (AG)*, 2006 FC 727; *Kamel v Canada (AG)*, 2009 FCA 21.

5 *Canadian Doctors for Refugee Care v Canada (AG)*, 2014 FC 651.

6 *Black v Canada (Prime Minister)*, 54 OR (3d) 215 (CA); *Black v Canada (Advisory Council for the Order)*, 2013 FCA 267; *Drabinsky v Canada (Advisory Council of the Order)*, 2015 FCA 5; *Chauvin v Canada*, 2009 FC 1202; *Canada v Chiasson*, 2003 FCA 155.

7 *Smith v Canada (AG)*, 2009 FC 228.

8 *Hupacasath First Nation v Canada (Foreign Affairs and International Trade Canada)*, 2015 FCA 4.

9 *Canada (Prime Minister) v Khadr*, 2010 SCC 3.

10 *Turp v Chrétien*, 2003 FC 301.

11 *Vancouver Island Peace Society v Canada*, [1994] 1 FC 102.

12 *Copello v Canada (Minister of Foreign Affairs)*, [2002] 3 FC 24.

13 *Kujan v Attorney General*, 2014 ONSC 966.

14 *Conacher v Canada (Prime Minister)*, 2010 FCA 131.

15 *Guergis v Novak*, 2013 ONCA 449.

16 *Robillard v Canada (Attorney General)*, 2016 FC 495.

17 William Anson, *The Law and Custom of the Constitution* (Oxford: Clarendon, 1886), 20.

18 F.W. Maitland, *The Constitutional History of England: A Course of Lectures Delivered* (Cambridge: Cambridge University Press, 1946), 196.

19 *Constitution Act, 1867*, s 10.

20 But see Frank Hardie, *The Political Influence of Queen Victoria, 1861–1901* (London: Frank Cass, 1935).

21 *Re: Resolution to amend the Constitution*, [1981] 1 SCR 753, 805.

22 As Viscount Radcliffe remarked in his dissenting reasons, the case was an anomaly because it related to acts done in Burma outside of the reach

of any of the UK statutes that provided for compensation for domestic property taken or damaged in wartime.

23 *Burmah Oil Company v Lord Advocate,* [1965] AC 75 (HL), 99.

24 *Burmah Oil Company v Lord Advocate,* 113.

25 *Petition of Right, In Re,* [1915] 3 KB 649; 31 TLR 569 (CA); [1916] 1 KB LT 419; 32 TLR 699 (HL); *AG v De Keyser's Royal Hotel Ltd,* [1920] AC 508 (HL).

26 *Burmah Oil Company v Lord Advocate,* 99.

27 *Burmah Oil Company v Lord Advocate,* 101.

28 Arthur Berriedale Keith, *Responsible Government in the Dominions* (Oxford: Clarendon, 1912), 1:146. There are a few peculiar historical Canadian prerogatives, such as the presentation to the sovereign of two elks and two black beavers by the governor of the Hudson's Bay Company as contemplated by the company's royal charter: "YEILDING AND PAYING yearly to Us, Our Heirs and Successors, for the same, two Elks and two black Beavers, whensoever, and as often as We, Our Heirs and Successors, shall happen to enter into the said Countries, Territories and Regions hereby granted." Hudson's Bay Company, "Royal Charter of the Hudson's Bay Company," http://www.hbcheritage.ca/things/artifacts/the-charter-and-text.

29 For non-exhaustive lists of recognized prerogatives, see Joseph Chitty, *A Treatise of the Law of the Prerogatives of the Crown; and the Relative Duties and Rights of the Subject*; H.V. Evatt, *The Royal Prerogative* (North Rydem NSW: Law Book, 1987); Paul Lordon, *Crown Law* (Toronto: Butterworths, 1991); Peter W. Hogg, Patrick J. Monahan, and Wade K. Wright, *Liability of the Crown*, 4th ed. (Toronto: Carswell, 2011), 23.

30 A.V. Dicey, *Introduction to the Study of the Law of the Constitution*, 9th ed. With an introduction and appendix by E.C.S. Wade (London: Macmillan, 1948), 424.

31 Dicey, *Introduction*, 425.

32 *Blackstone's Commentaries on the Laws of England* (Oxford: Clarendon, 1765), book 1 at 232.

33 A majority of the House of Lords favoured Dicey's definition in the *Burmah Oil* case, although Lord Reid pointed out that it "does not take us very far." See *Burmah Oil Company v Lord Advocate*, 99.

34 H.W.R. Wade, *Constitutional Fundamentals* (London: Stevens & Sons, 1980), 48.

35 Wade, *Constitutional Fundamentals*, 48.

36 Wade, *Constitutional Fundamentals*, 49.

37 Martin Loughlin, "The State, the Crown and the Law," in *The Nature of the Crown: A Legal and Political Analysis*, ed. Maurice Sunkin and Sebastian Payne (Oxford: Oxford University Press, 1999), 68.

38 On this point, see also George Winterton, "The Prerogative in Novel Situations," *Law Quarterly Review* 99 (July 1983): 409: "Both the Foreign Secretary and a private citizen could write to the President of Brazil requesting that he return a fugitive to stand trial; one letter would be treated as a request for extradition, the other would probably be ignored."

39 William Wade, "The Crown, Ministers and Officials: Legal Status and Liability," in *The Nature of the Crown: A Legal and Political Analysis*, ed. Maurice Sunkin and Sebastian Payne (Oxford: Oxford University Press, 1999), 31.

40 Hogg, *Constitutional Law of Canada*, 1:1–19.

41 *Council of Civil Service Unions v Minister for the Civil Service*, [1985] AC 374 (HL); *Hupacasath First Nation v Canada (AG)*, 2015 FCA 4.

42 Stephen Sedley, *Lions under the Throne: Essays on the History of English Public Law* (Cambridge: Cambridge University Press, 2015), 135.

43 See, e.g., *R (New College London Ltd) v Secretary of State for the Home Department*, [2013] UKSC 51.

44 *Verreault (JE) & Fils Ltée v Attorney General (Quebec)*, [1977] 1 SCR 41 at 47, Pigeon J.: "I know of no principle on the basis of which the general rules of mandate, including those of apparent mandate, would not be applicable to her." See also *Pharmaceutical Manufacturers Assn of Canada v British Columbia (AG)*, 149 DLR (4th) 613 (BCCA).

45 Sedley, *Lions under the Throne*, 137.

46 Sedley, *Lions under the Throne*, 137.

47 Sedley, *Lions under the Throne*, 139.

48 Sedley, *Lions under the Throne*, 139, 142.

49 Even natural persons have seen their powers subjected to public law. Take, for example, the educational trust established by Rueben Wells Leonard, which excluded "all who are not Christians of the White Race, and who are not of British Nationality or of British Parentage, and all who owe allegiance to any Foreign Government, Prince, Pope or Potentate, or who recognize any such authority, temporal or spiritual." The Court of Appeal for Ontario held that a trust "premised on these notions of racism and religious superiority contravenes contemporary public policy" and that it was empowered to sever the objectionable restrictions from the terms of the trust. *Canada Trust Co v Ontario Human Rights Commission*, (1990) 74 OR (2d) 481 (CA).

50 Relying on a word having "two or more possible meanings without sufficient specification of which meaning is intended" is what the

American historian David Hackett Fisher calls the fallacy of ambiguity: *Historians' Fallacies: Toward a Logic of Historical Thought* (New York: Harper & Row, 1970), 265.

51 F.W. Maitland, *The Constitutional History of England: A Course of Lectures Delivered* (Cambridge: Cambridge University Press, 1946), 418.

52 Philippe Lagassé, "Parliamentary and Judicial Ambivalence toward Executive Prerogative Powers in Canada," *Canadian Public Administration* 55, no. 2 (June 2012): 157, 161.

53 Lagassé, "Parliamentary and Judicial Ambivalence," 161–2.

54 *Department of the Environment Act*, RSC 1985, c E-10.

55 *Public Service Employment Act*, s 127.1(1). See, e.g., P.C. 2017-0106 appointing John Hannaford to be foreign and defence policy advisor to the prime minister as a deputy secretary to the Cabinet at the Privy Council Office and PC 2020-0172 appointing Kirsten Hillman as senior advisor to the Privy Council Office.

56 *Interpretation Act*, RSC 1985, c I-21, s 23.

57 Alpheus Todd, *On Parliamentary Government in England*, 2nd ed. (London: Longmans, Green, 1887), 609: the Crown is entrusted with the "power of creating such offices for carrying on the public service, or maintaining the dignity of the state, as may be required." Since Todd's time, statutes have overtaken much of this aspect of the prerogative, but the Supreme Court of Canada has recognized residual aspects of prerogative power over the public service. See, e.g., *Thomson v Canada (Deputy Minister of Agriculture)*, [1992] 1 SCR 385.

58 Forcese, "The Executive, the Royal Prerogative, and the Constitution," 159.

59 Forcese, "The Executive, the Royal Prerogative, and the Constitution," 160.

60 *Re: Resolution to amend the Constitution*, [1981] 1 SCR 753 at 882.

61 *Re: Resolution to amend the Constitution*, [1981] 1 SCR 753 at 882.

62 Recall the considerable difficulties that befell Prime Minister Meighen when he alone was appointed to the ministry following the resignation of Mackenzie King in 1926. Meighen attempted to rely on "acting ministers," which resulted in the defeat of his government. See Robert MacGregor Dawson, ed., *Constitutional Issues in Canada* (Oxford: University Press, 1933), 78–88.

63 *Letters Patent Constituting the Office of the Governor General, 1947; Guergis v Novak*, 2013 ONCA 449.

64 J.A. Corry, *Democratic Government and Politics*, 2nd ed. (Toronto: University of Toronto Press, 1951), 90.

65 Corry, *Democratic Government and Politics*, 90.

66 Classification also assists in answering long-serving British Labour MP Tony Benn's five democratic questions: "If one meets a powerful person … one can ask five questions: what power do you have; where did you get it; in whose interests do you exercise it; to whom are you accountable; and, how can we get rid of you?" UK House of Commons *Hansard* (16 November 1998), column 685.

67 *BBC v Johns*, [1964] 1 All ER 923.

68 *Abdelrazik v Canada (Minister of Foreign Affairs)*, 2009 FC 580.

69 *Kamel v Canada (AG)*, 2009 FCA 21; *Allen v Canada (AG)*, 2015 FC 213 at para 41; *Canadian Doctors for Refugee Care v Canada (AG)*, 2014 FC 651.

70 See, e.g., *Smith v Canada (AG)*, 2009 FC 228 where the Federal Court held that a Canadian on death row in the United States had a legitimate expectation that he would be given notice and afforded an opportunity to make submissions before the Government of Canada stopped advocating for clemency on his behalf.

71 *Reference re Remuneration of Judges of the Provincial Court (PEI)*, [1998] 2 SCR 4423 at para 10.

72 Colin Turpin and Adam Tomkins, *British Government and the Constitution*, 7th ed. (Cambridge: Cambridge University Press, 2011), 455, citing Terence Daintith, "Legal Analysis of Economic Policy," *Journal of Law and Society* 9 (1982): 191.

73 Turpin and Tomkins, *British Government and the Constitution*, 191.

74 As the English Court of Appeal held in *R v Criminal Injuries Compensation Board, ex p. Lain*, [1967] 2 QB 864 (CA), "Save within [a] narrow field" a proclamation issued pursuant to the royal prerogative "cannot deprive any subject of any rights to which he is entitled at common law or by statute, or grant to him any immunities to which he is not so entitled." The first of two Brexit cases in the UK Supreme Court turned on the prerogative to signal the government's intention to withdraw from the European Union not being exercisable due to the impact on UK domestic law, and in particular on the rights of those in the United Kingdom. See *Miller & Anor, R (on the application of) v Secretary of State for Exiting the European Union*, [2017] UKSC 5.

75 H.W.R. Wade and C.F. Forsyth, *Administrative Law*, 11th ed. (Oxford: Oxford University Press, 2014), 179.

76 Note, however, that this prerogative does not operate to deny compensation for the destroyed property: *Burmah Oil Company v Lord Advocate*, [1965] AC 75 (HL).

77 See, e.g., *Entick v Carrington* (1765) 19 St Tr 1030, 95 ER 807 (KB), where it was held that there is no general prerogative power of search and seizure.

78 See orders in council P.C. 2004-0850; P.C. 2003-2092; P.C. 2002-1322; P.C. 2002-0900; P.C. 2002-0033; and P.C. 1997-0983.

79 *Burmah Oil Company v Lord Advocate*, [1965] AC 75 (HL), 101.

80 *Ross River Dena Council Band v Canada*, [2002] 2 SCR 816 at para 54.

81 *Ross River Dena Council Band v Canada* at para 54.

82 There are few examples of these types of provisions, although one is found in s. 65 of the federal *Contraventions Act*, which provides that the "prerogative right of the Crown to refuse to issue a passport to a person, or to revoke the passport of a person, by reason only that the person is charged with or convicted of a contravention or of an offence committed outside Canada that, if committed in Canada, would constitute a contravention is abolished." *Contraventions Act*, SC 1992, c 47.

83 *Canada Elections Act*, s 56.1; *Conacher v Canada (Prime Minister)*, 2010 FCA 131.

84 *Criminal Code*, s 748, 749.

85 *Letters Patent, 1947*, clause 12. See order in council P.C. 2012-0212 for an example of a conditional pardon granted pursuant to statutory authority. Laura Payton, "Harper Pardons Farmers Arrested under Old Wheat Board Law," CBC News, 1 August 2012, https://www .cbc.ca/news/politics/harper-pardons-farmers-arrested-under -old-wheat-board-law-1.1146436.

86 *Official Languages Act*, RSC 1985, c 31.

87 Another example of this type of provision can be found in s. 29 of the federal *Statistics Act*, which requires the minister of public safety to inform the chief statistician about the exercise of the royal prerogative of mercy. It does not purport to restrain the prerogative of mercy, but it imposes statutory conditions on its exercise. *Statistics Act*, RSC 1985, c S-19.

88 *Criminal Records Act*, s 9.

89 *Ross River Dena Council Band v Canada*, [2002] 2 SCR 816.

90 *Galati v Canada (Governor General)*, 2015 FC 91 at para 56. The constitutional status of the power to grant royal assent has not prevented Parliament from enacting the *Royal Assent Act* to modernize the method through which royal assent may be signified. This is an example of the type of statute that Warren Newman has labelled organic or quasi-constitutional in the sense that it updates the procedure by which royal assent may be signified without altering the essential characteristics or the fundamentally constitutionally protected role of the governor general.

See W.J. Newman, "Defining the 'Constitution of Canada' Since 1982: The Scope of the Legislative Powers of Constitutional Amendment under Sections 44 and 45 of the *Constitution Act, 1982*" (2003) 22 SCLR (2d) 423.

91 The tipping point in the United Kingdom was Lord Diplock's speech in *Council of Civil Service Unions v Minister for the Civil Service*, [1984] 3 All ER 935 (HL), while the Canadian approach can be found in *Operation Dismantle Inc v Canada*, [1985] 1 SCR 441; *Black v Canada (Prime Minister)*, 54 OR (3d) 215 (CA); and, *Hupacasath First Nation v Canada (Foreign Affairs and International Trade Canada)*, 2015 FCA 4.

92 *Friends of the Earth v Canada (Governor in Council)*, 2008 FC 1183, aff'd 2009 FCA 297.

93 *Khadr v Canada (AG)*, 2006 FC 727.

94 *Chiasson v Canada*, 2003 FCA 155.

95 *Black v Canada (Advisory Council for the Order)*, 2013 FCA 267; *Drabinsky v Canada (Advisory Council of the Order)*, 2015 FCA 5.

96 *Miller, R (on the application of) v The Prime Minister* [2019] UKSC 41.

97 *Miller, R (on the application of) v The Prime Minister* [2019] UKSC 41 at para. 1.

98 *Miller, R (on the application of) v The Prime Minister* [2019] UKSC 41 at para. 34.

99 A legal challenge to the 2008 Canadian prorogation, albeit by a less sophisticated litigant, was dismissed on a preliminary motion without lengthy argument about the nature of the prerogative or whether it was justiciable. It was a complete answer to plaintiff's private law action for $33 million in damages to demonstrate to the court that the governor general was in fact legally authorized to prorogue Parliament, and that none of the statutes or other legal instruments cited in argument appreciably limited this power in the circumstances. See *Daniel Kujan v The Attorney General of Canada*, 2014 ONSC 966.

100 Evatt was particularly concerned with the cables to the dominions of Arthur Berriedale Keith. See H.V. Evatt, *The King and His Dominion Governors*, 2nd ed. (London: Frank Cass, 1967), 3.

4 Beyond All that Glitters

1 Maurice Sunkin and Sebastian Payne, "The Nature of the Crown: An Overview," in *The Nature of the Crown: A Legal and Political Analysis*, ed. Sunkin and Payne (Oxford: Oxford University Press, 1999), 3. The quotation arises in the context of a discussion about one of the book's chapters: Martin Loughlin, "The State, the Crown, and the Law," 33–76.

2 Walter Bagehot, *The English Constitution* (Garden City, NY: Dolphin Books, 1961). It is this edition of Bagehot that will be cited in this chapter.

3 K.C. Wheare, "'Walter Bagehot,' Lectures on a Master Mind," *Proceedings of the British Academy* 60 (1974). (Oxford: Oxford University Press, 1975), 195.

4 Ferdinand Mount, *The British Constitution Now: Recovery or Decline?* (London: Mandarin, 1992), 94.

5 See, for instance, Stefan Collini, Donald Winch, and John Burrow, *That Noble Science of Politics: A Study in Nineteenth-Century Intellectual History* (Cambridge: Cambridge University Press, 1983), 161–81.

6 Vernon Bogdanor, *The New British Constitution* (Oxford: Hart Publishing, 2009), 276.

7 Joseph Pope, *Correspondence of John A. Macdonald: Selections from the Correspondence of the Rt. Hon. Sir John A. Macdonald, G.C.B.* (Toronto: Oxford University Press, 19[21]), 172–4; and Campbell to Macdonald, 7 March 1888, John A. Macdonald Papers, Library and Archives Canada (hereafter LAC), 83495–8.

8 M.J.C. Vile, *Constitutionalism and the Separation of Powers* (Oxford: Clarendon, 1967), 224–7.

9 *The Governance of England* (London: T. Fisher Unwin, 1904), cited in Bogdanor, *New British Constitution*, 12.

10 Henry Fairlie, *The Life of Politics* (London: Methuen, 1968), 194.

11 Louis St. Laurent to Alan Macnaughton, 28 October 1949, St. Laurent Papers, LAC, file N-10-5(a), National Status. For the incident in question, see Canada, House of Commons, *Debates*, 12–13 November 1945, 2020 and 2075–8.

12 Memoranda: "Record of Interview. Prime Minister of Canada," 12 October 1939, and "The Crown and Canada," 12 April 1939, Records of the Governor General's Office, LAC, files 1850A and 1850B. The author of the memoranda was Sir Arthur Shuldham Redfern, who between 1936 and 1946 served as secretary to the governor general, and previously as governor of Kassala Province in the Anglo-Egyptian Sudan.

13 Tony Benn, *Letters to My Grandchildren: Thoughts on the Future* (London: Arrow Books, 2010), 56.

14 R.F.V. Heuston, *Essays in Constitutional Law*, 2nd ed. (London: Stevens and Sons, 1964), 170.

15 Vernon Bogdanor has suggested that "it may be inherent in the notion of constitutional monarchy that these powers should remain undefined

in scope." See "The United Kingdom," in *Sovereigns and Surrogates: Constitutional Heads of State in the Commonwealth*, ed. David Butler and D.A. Low (London: Macmillan, 1991), 19.

16 Patricia Cline Cohen, *A Calculating People: The Spread of Numeracy in Early America* (Chicago: University of Chicago Press, 1982).

17 For compilations of federal and provincial royal commissions, see George Fletcher Henderson, *Federal Royal Commissions in Canada: A Checklist* (Toronto: University of Toronto Press, 1967); and Lise Maillet, compiler, *Provincial Royal Commissions and Commissions of Inquiry, 1867–1982: A Selective Bibliography* (Ottawa: National Library of Canada, 1986).

18 R. MacGregor Dawson, *The Principle of Official Independence* (London: P.S. King and Son, 1922), 179–80. The phrase comes from Graham Wallas, *The Great Society: A Psychological Analysis* (London: Macmillan, 1932), 238.

19 Thomas J. Lockwood, "A History of Royal Commissions," *Osgoode Hall Law Journal* 5 (1967), 174.

20 W.H. McConnell, *Commentary on the British North America Act* (Toronto: Macmillan, 1977), 191.

21 Royal Commission on Dominion-Provincial Relations, *Report of Proceedings*, 3846.

22 Kathy Kelso, Alamar Education, *Electronic Legal Information: Exploring Access Issues* (Toronto: Canadian Legal Information Centre, 1991), 23–33.

23 *Federal Government Reporting Study: A Joint Study by the Office of Auditor General of Canada and the United States Government Administration Office* (Ottawa: Auditor General's Office, 1986), 6.

24 David E. Smith, *Clarifying the Doctrine of Ministerial Responsibility as It Applies to the Government of Canada and the Parliament of Canada* (Restoring Accountability, Research Studies, Vol. 1: Parliament, Ministers and Deputy Ministers), Commission of Inquiry into the Sponsorship Program and Advertising Activities (Ottawa: Public Works and Government Services, 2006), 133.

25 Bagehot, *English Constitution*, 64.

26 Monarchist League, "The Case for the Crown," https://www.monarchist .ca/index.php/our-monarchy/canada-s-monarchy/the-case-for-the -crown.

27 An examination of existing practice in cabinet manuals or similar documents is found in James W.J. Bowden and Nicholas A. MacDonald, "Writing the Unwritten: The Officialization of Constitutional Convention in Canada, the United Kingdom, New Zealand and Australia," *Journal of Parliamentary and Political Law* 6 (2012): 365–400. See also Andrew Blick, *The Codes of the Constitution* (Oxford: Hart Publishing, 2016).

28 P.H. Russell, "Learning to Live with Minority Parliaments," in *Parliamentary Democracy in Crisis,* ed. P.H. Russell and L. Sossin (Toronto: University of Toronto Press, 2009), 136.

29 D.J. Heasman, "Queen's Prerogative," *Times,* 24 October 1985.

30 Elgin to Grey, 13 July 1847 and Elgin to Grey, 14 January 1850, in *The Elgin-Grey Papers, 1846–1852,* ed., Arthur G. Doughty, 2 vols. (Ottawa: King's Printer, 1937), 1:58 and 2:577.

31 Vincent Massey, "Canada: Her Status and Stature," in *Speaking of Canada: Addresses by the Right Hon. Vincent Massey, Governor General of Canada, 1952–1959* (Toronto: Macmillan Canada, 1959), 23.

32 Heasman, "Queen's Prerogative."

5 The Vice-Regal Family

1 David Johnston, governor general 2010–17, speaking at a luncheon for the lieutenant governors and territorial commissioners at Rideau Hall the day following his installation, 2 October 2010.

2 David E. Smith, *The Invisible Crown: The First Principle of Canadian Government* (Toronto: University of Toronto Press, 1995), 13.

3 Fraser, *Secret of the Crown,* 10.

4 Charles Dickens, *American Notes for General Circulation* (London: Chapman and Hall, 1913), 21.

5 While certain major elements of the ceremony were borrowed from Westminster, there were other very significant differences. No mace, no black rod, small group of legislative councillors, irresponsible government, similar procedure, no heralds or wool sack.

6 Cecilia Morgan, *Building Better Britains? Settler Societies in the British World, 1783–1920* (Toronto: University of Toronto Press, 2017), 171.

7 Richard Gwyn, *Nation Maker, Sir John A. Macdonald: His Life, Our Times* (Toronto: Vintage Canada, 2012), 2:323.

8 R. MacGregor Dawson, *Constitutional Issues in Canada, 1900–1931* (London: Oxford University Press, 1933), 60.

9 Dawson, *Constitutional Issues in Canada, 1900–1931,* 58.

10 Goldwin Smith, *Canada and the Canadian Question* (London: Macmillan, 1891), 157.

11 J. Murray Beck, *The Government of Nova Scotia* (Toronto: University of Toronto Press, 1957), 184.

12 Edward McWinney, "Democracy in the 21st Century: The Future of the Crown in Canada," *Canadian Parliamentary Review* (Autumn 2005):

2–3. McWinney's piece fails to make any reference of the role of the Crown in the provincial sphere. Bill C-60, also known as an *Act to Amend the Canadian Constitution, 1978*, sought to deem the governor general as the "first Canadian" and to have lieutenant governors appointed after the federal government consulted with the provincial executive council. This prospect had Eugene Forsey asking if such changes would relegate lieutenant governors to be the "second Canadians."

13 A long-time observer of the vice-regal offices, John Fraser, in his 2012 book *The Secret of the Crown*, developed "two models or styles for the role of national regent" (70). The *Crown Legatee*, who behaves as though "the person of the Sovereign is far less important than the person representing the Crown" (70), and the *Right Royal*, who "reveres the Sovereign, regardless of who sits on the throne, and carries out his or her duties in the name of the King or Queen but never forgets – or lets the people forget – where the 'font of honour' rests" (70). Massey and Vanier were stellar examples of the Right Royal typology of governor general, while Clarkson and Jean represent the Crown Legatee sort of governor general. While this dichotomy works well for the sovereign's federal representative, it is not easily applied to the lieutenant governors, who almost invariably fall into the Right Royal classification, given their more limited resources and the persistent marginalization of the offices. Also see D. Michael Jackson, *The Crown and Canadian Federalism* (Toronto: Dundurn, 2013), 204–8.

14 One of the most formal efforts to elevate the role of the governor general to a presidential sort of plane was proposed in Bill C-60, *An Act to Amend the Constitution of Canada*. Among the provisions included in the broad-ranging amendments proposed was designating the governor general as the "First Canadian."

15 Fraser, *Secret of the Crown*, xvi.

16 John T. Saywell, *The Office of the Lieutenant Governor* (Toronto: University of Toronto Press, 1957), 265.

17 Saywell, *Office of the Lieutenant Governor*, 265.

18 Jackson, *The Crown and Canadian Federalism*, 132.

19 Colin Cosgrove, British high commissioner to Ottawa, in a dispatch to the Foreign and Commonwealth Office; see Philip Murphy, *Monarchy & the End of Empire* (Oxford: Oxford University Press, 2013), 99.

20 Beck, *Government of Nova Scotia*, 183.

21 Smith, *Invisible Crown*, 4.

22 *Globe and Mail*, "Canada's Distant, Abstract and Remarkably Successful Monarchy," 18 May 2019.

23 At Confederation in 1867, three of the four founding provinces had lieutenant governors appointed who were born outside Canada and were not permanent residents – Quebec being the only province with a Canadian-born vice-regal. The appointment of lieutenant governors who were not residents of Canada (i.e., had not immigrated to the county permanently) ceased in 1870 following the appointment of William C.F. Robinson, lieutenant governor of Prince Edward Island, who served in that role until 1873. Remarkably Robinson, who had previously served as governor of the Falkland Islands, would go on to serve variously as governor of the Leeward Islands, Western Australia, on three separate occasions, then governor of Singapore, and finally as governor of South Australia.

24 R. MacGregor Dawson, *The Government of Canada*, 4th ed., rev. Norman Ward (Toronto: University of Toronto Press 1964), 178.

25 Barbara Messamore, *Canada's Governors General, 1847–1878: Biography and Constitutional Evolution* (Toronto: University of Toronto Press, 2006), 19.

26 Loughlin, "The State, the Crown and the Law," 44.

27 William Smith and Arthur G. Doughty, *The Evolution of Government in Canada: Confederation Memorial Volume* (Ottawa: King's Printer, 1928), 8.

28 F.R. Scott, "The End of Dominion Status," *American Journal of International Law* 38, no. 1 (1944): 41. It would later be used with some frequency by Louis St-Laurent's lieutenant J.W. Pickersgill. J.W. Pickersgill, *My Years with Louis St-Laurent: A Political Memoir* (Toronto: University of Toronto Press, 1975), 159.

29 Philip Murphy, *Monarchy & the End of Empire: The House of Windsor, the British Government and the Postwar Commonwealth* (Oxford: Oxford University Press, 2013), 7.

30 Dummitt. "*Je me souviens* Too," 376.

31 Quoted in David Cannadine, *Ornamentalism: How the British Saw Their Empire* (Oxford: Oxford University Press, 2000), 32.

32 The last being Rear-Admiral Richard Trowbridge, appointed as governor of Western Australia in 1980. Also see Twomey, *Chameleon Crown*, 44–54.

33 Alison Quentin-Baxter and Janet McLean, *This Realm of New Zealand: The Sovereign, the Governor General and the Crown* (Auckland: Auckland University Press, 2017), 118.

34 Cris Shore and David V. Williams, eds., *The Shapeshifting Crown: Locating the State in Postcolonial New Zealand, Australia, Canada and the UK* (Cambridge: Cambridge University Press, 2019), 76.

35 MacKinnon, *Crown in Canada*, 69.

36 In addition to the various vice-regals who have held jurisdiction over British North America, Canada, and the current ten provinces and their antecedents, this aggregate includes the lieutenant governors of territories that would eventually be absorbed into other provinces: Cape Breton Island, Vancouver Island and British Columbia, and the Northwest Territories. Since Confederation there have been 280 governors general and lieutenant governors and, since Elizabeth II ascended the throne, 140 have served.

37 Brian C. Cuthbertson, *The Loyalist Governor: Biography of Sir John Wentworth* (Halifax: Petheric, 1983), 107.

38 Noble Frankland, *Witness of a Century: The Life and Times of Prince Arthur Duke of Connaught, 1850–1942* (London: Shepeard-Walwyn, 1993), 352.

39 Theo Aronson, *Princess Alice, Countess of Athlone* (London: Cassel, 1981), 140, 255. Lester B. Pearson went so far as to describe her as "easy and welcoming."

40 *Canadian Monarchist News* 23 (Spring 2005).

41 Philip Murphy, *Monarchy & the End of Empire* (Oxford: Oxford University Press, 2013), 151–2. Cannadine, *Ornamentalism*, 168.

42 The suggestion appeared in an article by Brigitte Pellerin: "How to Save the Monarchy: Make Prince Harry Canada's next GG," *Ottawa Citizen*, 12 December 2019. Further reflection on having Prince Harry appointed governor general and the torpid performance of Payette was examined by Dale Smith: "Can Canada Put Harry and Meghan to Work?" *Maclean's*, 14 January 2020.

43 Regular citizens who, after leaving office, retain the style Right Honourable or Honourable, depending on whether they have served as governor general or lieutenant governor. In most cases, vice-regals also leave office with more honours than when they start, as federally and in every province (save Quebec) the vice-regal serves as chancellor of the respective order in the jurisdiction.

44 The Duke of Windsor, the short-reigning Edward VIII (1936–7); Diana, Princess of Wales; Sara, Duchess of York; and most recently in late 2020, Prince Andrew, Duke of York – all provide examples of how members of the Royal Family have been marginalized.

45 The funding agreement ultimately decided upon was a onetime grant of $2 million, plus a dollar-per-dollar matching of additional funds raised to support the establishment of the institute. It took nearly six months for Cabinet to agree upon how to financially support the new organization. The funding scheme was specifically developed without the input of Governor General Georges Vanier, at the direction of Prime Minister

Pearson, as a "symbol of the recognition of the Governor General," RG 2, Privy Council Office Series, A-5-a, vol. 6271, 22 December 1965. See also RG 2, Privy Council Office Series A-5-a, vol. 6271, 12 December 1965, and vol. 6321, 17 May 1966.

46 The list of foundations to date include: the Michener Institute of Education; the Jeanne Sauvé Foundation (for youth leadership); the Hnatysnyn Foundation (focused on the arts); the Institute for Canadian Citizenship (established by Adrienne Clarkson and her husband John Ralston Saul) and the Fondation Michaële Jean, which focuses on youth, arts, and culture. While no government-supported foundation was established in the name of Jules Léger, a series of fellowships and universities chairs were endowed with funds from the Government of Canada.

47 In 1979 Cabinet approved the provision of funding for former governors general, RG 2, Privy Council Office Series, A-5-a, vol. 26845, 18 January 1979.

48 Department of Canadian Heritage, *The Lieutenant Governor's Briefing Book*, 2012.

49 Through a variety of political, diplomatic, and academic postings, Massey came to the post as highly trained as anyone to live in Rideau Hall before or after. Having experienced not only the governmental and constitutional role, the diplomatic aspect of serving in high office, but also the minutia of protocol and ceremonial, he was uniquely suited to become the first Canadian to hold the office. Claude Bissell, *The Imperial Canadian: Vincent Massey in Office* (Toronto: University of Toronto Press, 1986), 10. Those who have overtly lusted after vice-regal office have almost invariably failed, as notably demonstrated by George Ignatieff, who was very nearly appointed as the governor general to succeed Jules Léger in 1979.

50 Bogdanor, *The Monarchy and the Constitution*, 48–50.

51 During the present reign, four governors general have served for seven years: Massey, Vanier, Michener, and Johnston, while eight lieutenant governors have served for seven to ten years: John Bowles, 1950–9, Alberta; Thomas Prowse, 1950–8, Prince Edward Island; John MacEwan, 1966–74, Alberta; Robert Hanbidge, 1963–70, Saskatchewan; Hédard Robichaud, 1971–81, New Brunswick; Lise Thibault, 1997–2007, Quebec; Pierre Duschene, 2007–15, Quebec; Elizaebth Dowdswell, 2014–, Ontario.

52 Christopher McCreery, "Confidant and Chief of Staff: The Governor's Secretary," in *The Evolving Canadian Crown*, ed. Jennifer Smith and D. Michael Jackson, 197–218 (Montreal and Kingston: McGill-Queen's University Press, 2013).

53 The appointment of exempt staff – those brought in from outside the federal public service or Canadian Armed Forces – only became common following the appointment of Adrienne Clarkson in 1999. While governors general often brought with them a correspondence secretary or a trusted advisor, they merely augmented the existing staffing establishment and were not placed in senior roles (the notable exception in the modern era being Vincent Massey's appointment of his son Lionel Massey as private secretary, 1952–9). This approach that became common in the 2000s occasionally injected a well-needed external "beyond Ottawa/outside of government" view, but it also had the potential of creating a parallel management structure and group of advisors, separate from the permanent staff. This became an acute problem in the final year of Michaëlle Jean's tenure as governor general, when the secretary to the governor general and some senior staff were made veritable exiles from the strategic direction of the governor general's program.

54 Joyal, "Changing Role of the Governor General," 94.

55 The main exceptions have been Sir Shuldham Redfern, who served from 1935 to 1946 under Lords Tweedsmuir and Athlone; Esmond Butler, who served from 1959 to 1985 under Massey, Vanier, Michener, Léger, Schreyer, and the first year of Sauvé; and Judith LaRocque, who served from 1990 to 1999 under Hnatyshyn and LeBlanc. The main outlier to the entire set of post-Confederation secretaries to the governor general was Assunta di Lorenzo, who served as secretary to governor general Julie Payette from 2 February 2018 to 22 January 2021, resigning from office on the same day as her governor general. It is also worth noting that di Lorenzo was the only person to hold the position of secretary to the governor general who had no previous experience in the public service or military.

56 This does not include the Queen's first private secretary, Sir Allan Lascelles, or the present private secretary to the Queen, Sir Edward Young, who was appointed in 2017. The Queen's private secretaries have served from between four and nineteen years in the position.

57 For example, the Queen's first private secretary, Sir Allan Lascelles, started as assistant private secretary to the Prince of Wales from 1920 to 1929, then served as secretary to the governor general of Canada from 1931 to 1935, as assistant private secretary to King George VI from

1935 to 1943, and then as private secretary to the King from 1943 until 1952, finishing his career as private secretary to the Queen for a year. Lascelles's successor, Sir Michael Adeane, began his royal service in 1930 as an aide-de-camp to the governor general of Canada, and then, following his war service, in 1945 became assistant private secretary to the King, and then as the Queen's private secretary from 1953 to 1972. His successor, Sir Martin Charteris, was private secretary to Princess Elizabeth, then assistant private secretary to the Queen from 1972 to 1977. All but one of the Queen's other private secretaries had previous careers of between five and twenty years in the private secretary's office.

58 The most notable exception to this pattern in the federal sphere was Esmond Butler, who served first as press secretary to Vincent Massey from 1955 to 1957, then as assistant press secretary to the Queen from 1957 to 1959, and then as secretary to the governor general from 1959 to 1985. While several aides-de-camp in the provinces have gone on to serve as private secretary, this has not been the norm since the 1960s. As the size of the provincial lieutenant governor's establishments have grown and become more professionalized, there have been a few occasions when long-serving senior staff have been promoted into the role of private secretary: notably Anthony Hylton, who was appointed private secretary to the lieutenant governor of Ontario in 2014 following seven years' service in the office of the lieutenant governor; and Jerymy Brownridge, who was appointed private secretary to the lieutenant governor of British Columbia in 2015 after six years as director of operations for Government House Victoria.

59 Colin Coates, ed., *Majesty in Canada: Essays on the Role of Royalty* (Toronto: Dundurn, 2006), 15.

60 Andrew Heard, *Canadian Constitutional Conventions: The Marriage of Law & Politics* (Don Mills, ON: Oxford University Press, 2014), 36.

61 Peter Boyce explains this as "the derivative nature of the vice regal office" in *The Queen's Other Realms: The Crown and Its legacy in Australia, Canada and New Zealand* (Sydney: Federation, 2008), 38.

62 Peter Zimonjic, Ryan Patrick Jones, and Ashley Burke, "Report into Julie Payette's Conduct at Rideau Hall Finds Toxic Environment, Public Humiliations," CBC News, 27 January 2021, https://www.cbc.ca/news/politics/julie-payette-workplace-report-1.5890757.

63 See Andrew J.B. Johnston, "Popery and Progress: Anti-Catholicism in Mid-Nineteenth-Century Nova Scotia," *Dalhousie Review* 4, no. 1 (1984): 159.

64 Johnston, "Popery and Progress," 159.

65 Richard Myers, "The Crown in Democracy Revisited," *Dalhousie Review* 74, no. 1 (1994): 16. Frank MacKinnon, author of *The Crown in Canada*, took exception to this trend and responded to Myers, "I don't believe it. That is not the function of a head of state, and his or her personal qualifications to fill the office should be paramount without the conflicting demands of group patronage." "A Response," *Dalhousie Review* 74, no. 6 (1994): 21.

66 Kathleen Wynn, premier of Ontario, became the first openly gay head of government in Canadian history in 2013.

67 Lieutenant Governor of Ontario Elizabeth Dowdswell (2014); Lieutenant Governor of New Brunswick Joycelin Roy Vinneau; Lieutenant Governor of Manitoba Janice Filmon (2015); Lieutenant Governor of Alberta Lois Mitchell (2015); Governor General Mary May Simon (2021); Lieutenant Governor of British Columbia Janet Austin (2018); Lieutenant Governor of Prince Edward Island Antoinette Perry (2017); Lieutenant Governor of Newfoundland & Labrador Judy Foote (2018).

68 Boyce, *Queen's Other Realms*, 97.

69 This is the period for which Statistics Canada provides the most detailed data.

70 The following tables outline the statistics related to the age of vice-regal appointees at the time they assumed office.

Table 5.2. Vice-Regal Age at Time of Appointment during Specific Periods

	Confederation to 1966		1967 to 2019		Confederation to 2019	
	Average	Median	Average	Median	Average	Median
Governors general	53.7	53	58.9	61	55.5	56
Lieutenant governors	62.1	62	57.8	62	62.7	63
Governors general and lieutenant governors	61.4	62	57.8	64	62	63

Table 5.3. Vice-Regal Age at Time of Appointment during Specific Periods, by Jurisdiction

	Confederation to 1966		1967 to 2019		Confederation to 2019	
	Average	Median	Average	Median	Average	Median
Ontario	61.3	60	63.4	63	62	60
Quebec	64.5	62	63.5	65	62.1	64
Nova Scotia	68.9	64	63.1	61	64.6	64
New Brunswick	65.1	65	62.8	64	64.3	65
Manitoba	60.0	57	57.9	59	59.2	61
British Columbia	59.3	59	65.3	65	61.3	61
Prince Edward Island	59.4	57	64.6	64	61.2	62
Saskatchewan	62.5	59	63.4	61	63	63
Alberta	66.9	72	71.3	72	69.3	72
Newfoundland	53.3	50	63.6	66	61.4	62

71 Yves Decady and Lawson Greenberg, "Ninety Years of Change in Life Expectancy, 1921–2011," Statistics Canada, 2014, https://www150 .statcan.gc.ca/n1/pub/82-624-x/2014001/article/14009-eng.htm.

72 Statistics Canada, *Profile of the Canadian Population by Age and Sex: Canada Ages, 2001*, 28, http://publications.gc.ca/Collection/Statcan/96F0030X /96F0030XIE2001002.pdf.

73 Since Confederation six Government Houses have been shuttered, two of which – Chorley Park in Ontario and Spencer Wood in Quebec – were razed.

74 Alan Lascelles, *Government House Ottawa* (Ottawa: King's Printer, 1934), 12.

75 Ontario Premier Mitchell Hepburn described such events as limited to the "smart set" of society and made up in part his reason for closing Government House Toronto and marginalizing the role of the lieutenant governor in Ontario in the late 1930s. Neil McKenty, *Mitch Hepburn* (Toronto: McClelland and Stewart, 1967), 139.

76 For a broader discussion, see Ian Radforth, *Royal Spectacle: The 1860 Visit of the Prince of Wales to Canada and the United States* (Toronto: University of Toronto Press, 2004); Tom MacDonnell, *Daylight upon Magic: The Royal Tour of Canada, 1939* (Toronto: Macmillan, 1989); and Phillip Buckner,

"The Last Great Royal Tour: Queen Elizabeth II's 1959 Royal Tour to Canada," in *Canada and the End of Empire*, ed. Buckner, 66–93 (Vancouver: University of British Columbia Press, 2005).

77 Cannadine, *Ornamentalism*, 16.

78 In 1967, the governor general and lieutenant governors served as patrons of 240 organizations, charities, and causes. By 2019 this number had grown to 748. While there is overlap between organizations that have both a federal and provincial presence (e.g., the Red Cross, St. John Ambulance, and the Duke of Edinburgh's International Award), the array of organizations has become greatly diversified since the Centennial year.

79 The banishing of the four olds was a concept developed during the cultural revolution in Communist China during the 1960s.

80 Canadian Broadcasting Corporation, *The Schreyers' New Life at Rideau Hall*, television documentary, 3 August 1973.

81 John Fraser, "The Governor General's Man," *Saturday Night Magazine*, April 1990, 7.

82 Mark Francis, *Governors and Settlers: Images of Authority in the British Colonies, 1820–1860* (London: Macmillan, 1992), 196.

83 Francis, *Governors and Settlers*, 196.

84 Sydenham died from injuries received after falling off his horse while riding in front of the legislature in Kingston, Upper Canada. Adam Shortt, *The Makers of Canada: Lord Sydenham* (Toronto: Morang, 1908), 340; George Poulett Scroupe, *Memoir of the Life of the Right Honourable Charles, Lord Sydenham; With a Narrative of His Administration in Canada* (London: John Murray, 1844), 247.

85 Norman Chester, *The English Administrative System, 1780–1870* (Oxford: Clarendon, 1981), 97.

86 Beginning in 1887 the Colonial Office commenced holding periodic conferences of the colonial governors from throughout the British Empire. Stephanie Williams, *Running the Show: Governors of the British Empire* (London: Viking, 2011), 23.

87 LAC, MG 31 E80, vol. 4, Esmond Butler Papers, Conference of the Governor General and Lieutenant Governors, 197 and 1975.

88 Christopher McCreery, *The Canadian Honours System* (Toronto: Dundurn, 2015), 344–64.

89 Arthur Berriedale Keith, *The Sovereignty of the British Dominions* (London: McMillan, 1929), 267.

90 Christopher McCreery, *The Order of Canada: Genesis of an Honours System* (Toronto: University of Toronto Press, 2018), 23.

91 McCreery, *Order of Canada*, 130.

92 Christopher P. McCreery, "The Provincial Crown: The Lieutenant Governor's Expanding Role," in *The Evolving Canadian Crown*, ed. Jennifer Smith and D. Michael Jackson (Montreal and Kingston: McGill-Queen's University Press, 2013), 147.

93 *McAteer v Canada (AG)*, 2014 ONCA 578.

94 James K. Bartleman, "Native Youth," address to the legislature, Debates of the Legislative Assembly of Ontario, 7 December 2006.

95 David Johnston, *Trust: Twenty Ways to Build a Better Country* (Toronto: Penguin, 2018), 189.

96 Steve Paikin, "It's One of the Most Important Jobs in Ontario – but Few People Understand It," TVO, 6 February 2019, https://www.tvo.org /article/its-one-of-the-most-important-jobs-in-ontario-but-few-people -understand-it.

97 Francis, *Governors and Settlers*, 35.

6 Yet Symbols Still Matter

1 The Canadian citizenship ceremony requires that a portrait of the Queen be on display, new citizens take the citizenship oath, which is an oath of allegiance to the Queen of Canada, and the citizenship certificates display a large representation of the Royal Arms of Canada at the top.

2 H.V. Nelles, *The Art of Nation-Building: Pageantry and the Spectacle at Quebec's Tercentenary* (Toronto: University of Toronto Press, 1999), 229.

3 Roger Milton, *The English Ceremonial Book: A History of Robes Insignia and Ceremonies still in Use in England* (New York: Drake Publishers, 1972), 9.

4 Michael E. Geisler, ed., *National Symbols, Fractured Identities: Contesting the National Narrative* (Hanover: University of New England Press, 2005), x.

5 John R. Matheson, *Canada's Flag: A Search for a Country* (Boston: G.K. Hall, 1980), 122; House of Commons, *Debates* 14 December, 1964 (Ottawa: Queen's Printer, 1964), 11139; J.L. Granatstein *1957–1967: The Years of Uncertainty and Innovation* (Toronto: McClelland and Stewart, 1986), 201–8.

6 McCreery, *Order of Canada*, 45.

7 José E. Igartua, *The Other Quiet Revolution: National Identities in English Canada, 1945–72* (Vancouver: University of British Columbia Press, 2006), 90.

8 *National Post*, "Queen Elizabeth Deserves a Place of Honour on Our Walls," 24 May 2019; *Huffington Post*, "The Government Won't Send You Free Pictures of the Queen Anymore," 24 May 2019; CTV News, "Federal

Government Stops Sending Photos of Queen to Canadians," 23 May 2019.

9 Judy S. DeLoache, "Early Understanding and Use of Symbols: The Model Model," *Current Directions in Psychological Science* 4, no. 4 (August 1995): 110.

10 Francis, *Governors and Settlers*, 35.

11 Clifford Geertz, *Negara: The Theatre State in Nineteenth-Century Bali* (Princeton: Princeton University Press, 1980), 13.

12 Norman Bonney, *Monarchy, Religion and the State: Civil Religion in the United Kingdom, Canada, Australia and the Commonwealth* (Manchester: Manchester University Press, 2013), 12.

13 Eric Hobsbawm and Terence Raner, *The Invention of Tradition* (Cambridge: Cambridge University Press, 1983); David Cannadine and Simon Price, *Rituals of Royalty: Power and Ceremonial in Traditional Societies* (Cambridge: Cambridge University Press, 1992); Cannadine, *Ornamentalism*.

14 Buckner, "Last Great Royal Tour"; Radforth, *Royal Spectacle*; Nelles, *Art of Nation-Building*.

15 Cecilia Morgan, *Commemorating Canada: History, Heritage and Memory, 1850s–1990s* (Toronto: University of Toronto Press, 2016).

16 MacKinnon, *Crown in Canada*, 136.

17 As observed by the British high commissioner to Canada of the period, Colin Cosgrove, in a dispatch to the Foreign and Commonwealth Office; see Philip Murphy, *Monarchy & the End of Empire* (Oxford: Oxford University Press, 2013), 99.

18 John Maynard Keynes, "Art and the State," *Listener*, 26 August 1936.

19 Jacques Monet, *The Canadian Crown* (Toronto: Clarke, Irwin, 1978), 13.

20 The exception to this statement is, however, the province of Quebec, which will be examined further along in this chapter.

21 Thomas Chandler Haliburton, *Sam Slick's Wise Saws and Modern Instances; Or, What He Said, Did or Invented* (London: Hurst and Blackett, 1859), 244.

22 It is worthwhile noting that the inclusion of Indigenous elements of ceremony and participants is a tradition that dates back to the time of Prince Edward, Duke of Kent (Queen Victoria's father) and his service in Canada as commander-in-chief at the beginning of the nineteenth century.

23 Cannadine and Price, *Rituals of Royalty*, 138.

24 Messamore, *Canada's Governors General, 1847–1878*, 19.

25 For instance, the Papal Decree, negotiated between Archbishop Laval and Governor General Lord Grey, which endorsed the Tercentenary of Quebec celebrations of 1908. Nelles, *Art of Nation-Building*, 116.

26 Frederick H. Armstrong, *Handbook of Upper Canadian Chronology* (Toronto: Dundurn, 1985), 14.

27 James Curran and Stuart Ward, *The Unknown Nation: Australia after Empire* (Melbourne: Melbourne University Press, 2010), 20.

28 Murphy, *Monarchy & the End of Empire*, 7.

29 Following the accession of the Queen in 1952 and in discussions surrounding the royal style and title that would be taken by the new sovereign, Canadian officials were "known to object to the expression 'British Dominions beyond the Seas.'" Philip Murphy, "Breaking the Bad News: Plans for the Announcement to the Empire of the Death of Elizabeth II and the Proclamation of Her Successor, 1952–67," *Journal of Imperial and Commonwealth History* 34, no. 1 (2006): 143.

30 Murphy, "Breaking the Bad News," 143.

31 Keith, *Sovereignty of the British Dominions*, 267.

32 In his study "The Strange Demise of British Canada" C.P. Champion notes the alacrity with which the maple leaf flag was accepted in English Canada, and that it "remains one of the modern world's most successful and popular invented traditions." Christian P. Champion, *The Strange Demise of British Canada: The Liberals and Canadian Nationalism, 1964–1968* (Montreal and Kingston: McGill-Queen's University Press, 2010), 223. See also Richard Nimijean and L. Pauline Rankin, "Marketing the Maple Leaf: The Curious Case of National Flag of Canada Day," in *Celebrating Canada*, ed. Matthew Hayday and Raymond Blake (Toronto: University of Toronto Press, 2016), 1:414.

33 Conrad Swan, *Canadian Symbols of Sovereignty* (Toronto: University of Toronto Press, 1976), 79.

34 A number of other flags rank ahead of the national flag of Canada; these are all "distinguishing flags" to denote the presence of the Queen, the governor general, or a lieutenant governor.

35 Aside from a period from 1932 to 1935 and 1942 to 1946.

36 Canada's establishment of its own office for the design and approval of official symbols, the Canadian Heraldic Authority, is another example of the Crown's ability to adapt in relation to new symbols and ceremonies. The establishment of the Canadian Heraldic Authority came in 1988 and essentially patriated the last element of the Crown's prerogative, in this case the granting of arms, flags, and badges. This was done through a simple ceremony at Rideau Hall whereby Prince Edward, on behalf of the Queen, conveyed to the governor general letters patent signed by the Queen establishing the Canadian Heraldic Authority – meaning Canadians no longer had to petition the College of Arms in London

or the Court of the Lord Lyon in Edinburgh to be granted a coat of arms. It also brought a more structured and regulated approach to the development, design, and adoption of flags, badges, and other symbols for both Canadian institutions and individuals.

37 LAC, RG 2, series A-5-a, vol. 2653, 18 December 1953, Cabinet Conclusions: "The Cabinet agreed that the Secretary of State make the necessary arrangements to have made, in Canada, a new Great Seal, bearing the figure of Queen Elizabeth II and suitable inscriptions in English and in French rather than in Latin as had previously been the case." Also RG 2, series A-5-a, vol. 2659, Cabinet Conclusions, 3 November 1955; and Order-in-Council 1955-1661, 3 November 1955.

38 Swan, *Canadian Symbols of Sovereignty*, 74–5.

39 Cannadine and Price, *Rituals of Royalty*, 1.

40 Ian Moncreiffe and Don Pottinger, *Simple Custom: Cheerfully Illustrated* (London: Thomas Nelson & Sons, 1954), 4.

41 Herbert J. Spiro, *Government by Constitution* (New York: Random House, 1959), 377.

42 Obviously if there is a coup or entire change of regime, as was the case during the American, French, and Russian Revolutions, there is a desire to remake all the symbols and ceremonies of the state. It is telling that these attempts at remaking the symbols and ceremonies almost invariably come to follow the previous pattern – albeit with different designations given to the ceremonies.

43 Edward Shils and Michael Young, "The Meaning of the Coronation," *Sociological Review* 1, no. 2 (1953): 63–81.

44 The Coronation of Queen Elizabeth II in 1953 saw Canada (and the other realms) added to the Coronation Oath. The heads of government for the Queen's realms were included in the actual ceremony and were not simply guests, as had been the case in 1937, 1911, and 1902, and the banner of arms of each of the realms was included in the procession into Westminster Abbey. This was a significant departure from previous coronations.

45 Cannadine, *Ornamentalism*, 38.

46 Francis, *Governors and Settlers*, 35.

47 Norman Bonney, *Monarchy, Religion and the State: Civil Religion in the United Kingdom, Canada, Australia and the Commonwealth* (Manchester: Manchester University Press, 2013), 17.

48 Bonney, *Monarchy, Religion and the State*.

49 *Toronto Star*, "Olympics Will Miss Queen's Touch," 8 November 2009.

50 It is worthwhile noting that aside from the military and diplomatic roles, the ceremonial aspects and activities of the two levels of government are remarkably similar.

51 See Brendan Sexton, *Ireland and the Crown, 1922–1936: The Governor Generalship of the Irish Free State* (Ann Arbor: University of Michigan Press, 1989).

52 T. Dunbar Moodie, *The Rise of Afrikanerdom: Power, Apartheid and the Afrikaner Civil Religion* (Berkeley: University of California Press, 1975), 22.

53 The lieutenant governor of Quebec has also lacked an official residence since 1997.

54 Robert Holland, Susan Williams, and Terry Barringer, *The Iconography of Independence: Freedoms at Midnight* (New York: Routledge, 2010), 19.

55 Murphy, *Monarchy & the End of Empire,* 20.

56 During the period from 1947 to 1976 when thirty-two – more than a majority – Commonwealth countries gained their independence, the Queen and members of the Royal Family visited Canada officially forty-seven times.

57 Robert Holland, Susan Williams, and Terry Barringer, eds., *Iconography of Independence "Freedoms at Midnight"* (London: Routledge, 2013), quoting Prime Minister Jawaharlal Nehru, 15 August 1947.

58 Holland, Williams, and Barringer, *Iconography of Independence,* 4.

59 Holland, Williams, and Barringer, *Iconography of Independence,* 4.

60 As part of the 2002 diamond jubilee, the Queen started her Canadian tour in Nunavut to honour the establishment of the new territory.

61 This had previously been done in 1967 for the Centennial Celebrations.

62 Boyce, *Queen's Other Realms,* 114.

63 Shore and Williams, *Shapeshifting Crown,* 119.

64 Samuel Clarke, *Distributing Status: The Evolution of State Honours in Western Europe* (Montreal and Kingston: McGill-Queen's University Press, 2017), 14.

65 McCreery, *Order of Canada,* 243–7. See also Peter Galloway, *The Order of the British Empire* (Woodstock: Writersworld, 2017), 62–5.

66 McCreery, *Order of Canada,* 221.

67 Although they may come in the form of a medal that can be worn, awards are not honours – they confer no postnominals and are not given in the name of the Queen, nor are they created by the Queen or established on formal advice. Generally speaking, awards can be created or abolished without formal advice from a head of government or the sovereign, and they tend to recognize specific acts or contributions that do not meet the bar of an official honour of the Crown.

68 The conferral of recognition, "Presenting awards in your province that recognize special achievement and contributions of citizens," was deemed important by 81 per cent of respondents in a 2019 Ipsos poll, up 13 per cent since 2012. Ipsos, *Understanding Canadians*, 2012 and 2019.

69 Johnston, *Trust*, 96.

70 Freeman Clowery, *Medals of Governors General* (Toronto: Charlton, 1981), 13–15.

7 A Moment in Transition

1 Proclamation announcing Demise of Late Sovereign and Accession of New Sovereign, 6 February 1952, reproduced in *The Manual of Official Procedure of the Government of Canada* (Ottawa: Queen's Printer, 1968), 2:829.

2 Along with Canada, Australia, New Zealand, Pakistan, Sri Lanka (then Ceylon), and the United Kingdom are the only realms that have experienced the demise of the Crown as independent countries, although Pakistan and Sri Lanka now possess republican forms of government. When King George VI died on 6 February 1952 the other members of the Commonwealth that are today realms had not yet achieved independence and had no formal role in the accession of Queen Elizabeth II: Antigua and Barbuda, Bahamas, Barbados, Belize, Grenada, Jamaica, Papua New Guinea, Saint Lucia, St. Vincent and the Grenadines, St. Kitts and Nevis, Solomon Islands, Tuvalu.

3 Murphy, "Breaking the Bad News."

4 McCreery interview with the Gordon Robertson, 6 December 2001; McCreery interview with Jacques Monet, 24 October 2016. Also see "Sovereign," *Manual of Official Procedure of the Government of Canada*, 561–99.

5 Anne Twomey, "Regency in the Realms," *Public Law Review* 27, no. 3 (2016): 198.

6 This concept has most notably been proposed by Edward McWhinney, *The Governor General and Prime Ministers* (Vancouver: Ronsdale, 2005), and also Citizens for a Canadian Republic, http://www.canadian-republic.ca/faq.html.

7 The plaintiffs in the challenge to the *Succession to the Throne Act, 2013* were clear that their motive was not related to the monarchy, but rather to force the federal government to negotiate other constitutional amendments with the provinces, in particular with the province of Quebec. Stéphanie Marin, "La Loi sur la succession du trône sera

contestée en Cour lundi," *La Presse*, 31 May 2015, https://www.lapresse.
ca/actualites/politique/politique-canadienne/201505/31/01-4874043
-la-loi-sur-la-succession-du-trone-sera-contestee-en-cour-lundi.php: "Car
si le gouvernement refuse d'ouvrir la Constitution pour les demandes
du Québec et des Autochtones, il n'aura peut-être pas le choix cette
fois face au respect de la monarchie et de ses obligations envers le
Commonwealth."

8 Philippe Lagassé, "The Monarchy's Rights, Privileges and Symbols in
Canada Can Be Changed," *Policy Options*, 21 January 2020.

9 Smith, *Republican Option in Canada*, xiii.

10 Hazell and Morris, "If the Queen Has No Reserve Powers Left," 18.

11 Hazell and Morris, "If the Queen Has No Reserve Powers Left," 5.

12 Bogdanor, *The Monarchy and the Constitution*, ch. 2; *O'Donahue v Canada*,
[2003] OJ No 2764 (SC), aff'd [2005] OJ No 965 (CA); *Motard v Canada
(AG)*, 2016 QCCS 588 aff'd 2019 QCCA 1826, leave to appeal to the
Supreme Court denied with costs to the Attorney General of Canada.

13 Warren J. Newman, "The Succession to the Throne in Canada" in *Royal
Progress: Canada's Monarchy in the Age of Disruption*, ed. D. Michael
Jackson, 127–52 (Toronto: Dundurn, 2020).

14 Norman Ward, *Dawson's The Government of Canada*, 6th ed. (Toronto:
University of Toronto Press, 1987), 173.

15 This provision was repealed in 1893, when housekeeping amendments
were made to the British statute book to remove, among other things,
provisions that had become unnecessary. In 1889, the UK Parliament
enacted the *Interpretation Act 1889* (the long title of which was "An
Act for consolidating enactments relating to the Construction of Acts
of Parliament and for further shortening the Language used in Acts
of Parliament)," which provided a general rule of construction for the
sovereign rendering s. 2 of the *Constitution Act, 1867* redundant and
superfluous: "30. In this Act and in every other Act, whether passed
before or after the commencement of this Act, references to the Sovereign
reigning at the time of the passing of the Act or to the Crown shall,
unless the contrary intention appears, be construed as references to
the Sovereign for the time being, and this Act shall be binding on the
Crown."

16 *Interpretation Act*, RSC, 1985, c I-21, s 35.

17 *Parliament of Canada Act*, RSC, 1985, c P-1, s 2.

18 *Interpretation Act*, 1985, c I-21, s 46.

19 Robertson would later serve as clerk of the Privy Council and secretary
to the Cabinet from 1963 to 1975.

20 *Manual of Official Procedure of the Government of Canada*, vol. 1.

21 The chief justice had been proclaimed as administrator of the Government of Canada and was acting in the stead of the governor general, as Lord Alexander had returned to England to take up the post of secretary of state for defence, and the governor general designate, Vincent Massey, had not yet been sworn into office.

22 McCreery interview with Gordon Robertson.

23 Pope's extraordinary presence in the development of the machinery of government, relationship with the Crown, vice-regals, and even state ceremonial reached back to his youth when as a ten-year-old boy: his father – William Henry Pope, a Father of Confederation from PEI – took him onboard the *Queen Victoria* during the Charlottetown Conference in 1864.

24 Joseph Pope, *Public Servant: The Memoires of Sir Joseph Pope*, ed. Maurice A. Pope (Toronto: Oxford University Press, 1960).

25 Robertson joked to one of the authors, "Young fellow, you had better finish this PhD and get to the Privy Council Office before Elizabeth II dies; then the chain of memory reaching back to Victoria will be unbroken!" Robertson briefed his successor, Michael Pitfield, on the file as well. Pitfield had acquired some knowledge of the file during his posting as attaché to Governor General Georges Vanier from 1962 to 1964.

26 Bogdanor, *The Monarchy and the Constitution*, 46.

27 Rodney Brazier, "Royal Incapacity and the Constitutional Continuity: The Regent and Counsellors of State," *Cambridge Law Journal* 64, no. 2 (2005): 362. Bogdanor notes several restrictions on the powers of counsellors of state, including that they cannot "have any functions with regard to the other realms of which the sovereign is head of state." Bogdanor, *The Monarchy and the Constitution*, 49.

28 Brazier, "Royal Incapacity and the Constitutional Continuity," 371. Also see *Regency Act, 1937*, s 2(1).

29 *Regency Act*, s 2.

30 Being held captive or reduced to puppet status by an invading power. *Regency Act*, s 2.

31 Royal sources have refuted speculation surrounding the Queen's "retirement": Jackie Dunham, "Prince Charles' Office Issues Statement about Queen's Retirement," CTV News, 7 December 2019, https://www.ctvnews.ca/world/prince-charles-office-issues-statement-about-queen-s-retirement-1.4719891: "'There are no plans for any change in arrangements at the age of 95 – or any other age,' the Clarence House spokesperson told CTVNews.ca in an email on Saturday."

32 W.P.M. Kennedy, "The Regency Acts, 1937–1953," *University of Toronto Law Journal* 10, no. 2 (1954): 248; Bogdanor, *The Monarchy and the Constitution*, 49–50; *Manual of Official Procedure of the Government of Canada*, 565.

33 Commonwealth Relations Office Telegram, cited in McCreery, "Myth and Misunderstanding," 45.

34 McCreery, "Myth and Misunderstanding," 39. Twomey notes that the use of the Letters Patent "also constituted a cunning way of avoiding the question of the head of legislative power to support the enactment of regency legislation by the Canadian Parliament." Twomey, "Regency in the Realms," 206.

35 *Manual of Official Procedure*, 1:566.

36 Anne Twomey, *The Veiled Sceptre: Reserve Powers of Heads of State in Westminster Systems* (Cambridge: Cambridge University Press, 2018), 836–8.

37 McCreery, "Myth and Misunderstanding," 52.

38 The lieutenant governor of Quebec, Luc Letellier, was dismissed in 1879 and the lieutenant governor of British Columbia, Thomas Robert McInnes, was dismissed in 1900, both for disregarding the principles of responsible government.

39 Twomey, *Veiled Sceptre*, ch. 11.

40 *Canada Gazette*, Part II, vol. 86 extra (6 February 1952).

41 Pickersgill, *My Years with Louis St Laurent*, 162.

42 Vincent Massey, *What's Past Is Prologue: The Memoirs of Vincent Massey* (Toronto: Macmillan, 1963), 247–8.

43 There is no indication that a similar printed program was created for the 1910 or 1935 services.

44 It is also worth noting that by the time Centre Block is due to reopen, the Queen will be 103. The Queen Mother's 2002 Canadian memorial service, which was held by the federal government, was held at Christ Church Anglican Cathedral in Ottawa, as was the Canadian memorial service for the Duke of Edinburgh in 2021.

45 Also new Great Seals will have to be commissioned in a number of provinces where their Great Seals include Queen Elizabeth II in their inscription: Newfoundland and Labrador, Saskatchewan, and British Columbia. The Great Seals used in Ontario, Quebec, Nova Scotia, New Brunswick, Prince Edward Island, Manitoba, and Alberta will not require any alteration.

46 Something that even the most trained constitutional mind cannot predict.

47 Fraser, *Secret of the Crown*, 204.

Select Bibliography

Interviews

Jacques Monet
Gordon Robertson
Michael Pitfield

Primary Documents

Library and Archives Canada, MG 31 E80, vol. 4, Esmond Butler Papers,
Conference of the Governor General and Lieutenant Governors.

Books and Articles

Allison, J.W.F. *The English Historical Constitution: Continuity, Change and
European Effects*. Cambridge: Cambridge University Press, 2007.
Anson, William. *The Law and Custom of the Constitution*. Oxford: Clarendon,
1886.
Armstrong, Frederick H. *Handbook of Upper Canadian Chronology*. Toronto:
Dundurn, 1985.
Arnot, David. "The Honour of the First Nations – The Honour of the
Crown: The Unique Relationship of First Nations with the Crown." In
The Evolving Canadian Crown, edited by Jennifer Smith and D. Michael
Jackson, 155–76. Montreal and Kingston: McGill-Queen's University
Press, 2012.
Aronson, Theo. *Princess Alice, Countess of Athlone*. London: Cassel, 1981.
Bagehot, Walter. *The English Constitution*. London: Oxford University Press,
1958.

Bailyn, Bernard. *To Begin the World Anew: The Genius and Ambiguities of the American Founders*. New York: Vintage Books, 2003.

Beck, J. Murray. *The Government of Nova Scotia*. Toronto: University of Toronto Press, 1957.

Benn, Tony. *Letters to My Grandchildren: Thoughts on the Future*. London: Arrow Books, 2010.

Berton, Pierre. *The Last Spike, 1881–1885*. Toronto: McClelland and Stewart, 1971.

Bissell, Claude. *The Imperial Canadian: Vincent Massey in Office*. Toronto: University of Toronto Press, 1986.

Blackstone, William. *Blackstone's Commentaries on the Laws of England*. Oxford: Clarendon, 1765.

Blake, L.L. *The Prince and the Professor: A Dialogue on the Place of the Monarchy in the 21st Century*. London: Shepheard-Walwyn, 1995.

Blick, Andrew. *The Codes of the Constitution*. Oxford: Hart Publishing, 2016.

Bogdanor, Vernon. *The Coalition and the Constitution*. Oxford: Hart Publishing, 2011.

– *The Monarchy and the Constitution*. Oxford: Oxford University Press, 1998.

– *The New British Constitution*. Oxford: Hart Publishing, 2009.

Bonney, Norman. *Monarchy, Religion and the State: Civil Religion in the United Kingdom, Canada, Australia and the Commonwealth*. Manchester: Manchester University Press, 2013.

Bowden, James, and Nicholas A. MacDonald. "Writing the Unwritten: The Officialization of Constitutional Convention in Canada, the United Kingdom, New Zealand and Australia." *Journal of Parliamentary and Political Law* 6 (2012): 365–400.

Boyce, Peter. *The Queen's Other Realms: The Crown and Its Legacy in Australia, Canada and New Zealand*. Sydney: Federation, 2008.

Brazier, Rodney. "Royal Incapacity and the Constitutional Continuity: The Regent and Counsellors of State." *Cambridge Law Journal* 64, no. 2 (2005): 352–87.

Briggs, William. "Impressions of My Canadian Tour," 4 November 1919, *Empire Club Speeches*. Toronto: William Briggs, 1920.

Buckner, Phillip. "The Last Great Royal Tour: Queen Elizabeth II's 1959 Royal Tour to Canada." In *Canada and the End of Empire*, edited by Buckner, 66–93. Vancouver: University of British Columbia Press, 2005.

Butler, David, and D.A. Low, eds. *Sovereigns and Surrogates: Constitutional Heads of State in the Commonwealth*. London: Macmillan, 1991.

Cairns, Alan, and Cynthia Williams, research coordinators. *The Politics of Gender, Ethnicity and Language in Canada*, vol. 34, Research Report, Royal

Commission on the Economic Union and Development Prospects for
Canada. Toronto: University of Toronto Press, 1986.

Cannadine, David. "Churchill and the British Monarchy." *Transactions of the
Royal Historical Society* 11 (2001): 249–72

– *Ornamentalism: How the British Saw Their Empire*. Oxford: Oxford
University Press, 2001.

Cannadine, David, and Simon Price. *Rituals of Royalty: Power and Ceremonial
in Traditional Societies*. Cambridge: Cambridge University Press, 1992.

Champion, Christian P. *The Strange Demise of British Canada: The Liberals and
Canadian Nationalism, 1964–1968*. Montreal and Kingston: McGill-Queen's
University Press, 2010.

Chester, Norman. *The English Administrative System, 1780–1870*. Oxford:
Clarendon, 1981.

Chitty, Joseph. *A Treatise of the Law of the Prerogatives of the Crown; and the
Relative Duties and Rights of the Subject*. London: Butterworth, 1820.

Chrétien, Jean. *My Years as Prime Minister*. Toronto: Knopf, 2007.

Clarke, Samuel. *Distributing Status: The Evolution of State Honours in Western
Europe*. Montreal and Kingston: McGill-Queen's University Press, 2017.

Clarkson, Adrienne. *Heart Matters*. Toronto: Penguin, 2007.

Clowery, Freeman. *Medals of Governors General*. Toronto: Charlton, 1981.

Coates, Colin, ed. *Majesty in Canada: Essays on the Role of Royalty*. Toronto:
Dundurn, 2006.

Cohen, Patricia Cline. *A Calculating People: The Spread of Numeracy in Early
America*. Chicago: University of Chicago Press, 1982.

Collini, Stefan, Donald Winch, and John Burrow. *That Noble Science of
Politics: A Study in Nineteenth-Century Intellectual History*. Cambridge:
Cambridge University Press, 1983.

Corry, James. *Democratic Government and Politics*. 2nd ed. Toronto: University
of Toronto Press, 1951.

Curran, James, and Stuart Ward. *The Unknown Nation: Australia after Empire*.
Melbourne: Melbourne University Press, 2010.

Cuthbertson, Brian C. *The Loyalist Governor: Biography of Sir John Wentworth*.
Halifax: Petheric, 1983.

Dawson, Robert MacGregor. "The Cabinet: Position and Personnel."
Canadian Journal of Economics and Political Science 12, no. 3 (1946): 261–81.

– *Constitutional Issues in Canada, 1900–1931*. London: Oxford University
Press, 1933.

–, ed.*The Development of Dominion Status 1900–1936*. Oxford: Oxford
University Press, 1937.

– *The Government of Canada*. Toronto: University of Toronto Press, 1947.

– *The Government of Canada.* 4th ed., rev. Norman Ward. Toronto: University of Toronto Press, 1964.

– *The Government of Canada.* 5th ed., rev. Norman Ward. Toronto: University of Toronto Press, 1970.

– *The Principle of Official Independence.* London: P.S. King and Son, 1922.

DeLoache, Judy S. "Early Understanding and Use of Symbols: The Model Model." *Current Directions in Psychological Science* 4, no. 4 (August 1995): 109–11.

Dent, John Charles. *The Last Forty Years: Canada since the Union Act of 1841.* Toronto: George Virtue, 1881.

Dicey, A.V. *Introduction to the Study of the Law of the Constitution.* 9th ed. London: Macmillan, 1948.

Dickens, Charles. *American Notes for General Circulation.* London: Chapman and Hall, 1913.

Dorland, Arthur G. *Our Canada.* Toronto: Copp Clark, 1949.

Doughty, Arthur, ed. *The Elgin-Grey Papers, 1846–1852.* Ottawa: King's Printer, 1937.

Dummitt, Christopher. "*Je me souviens* Too: Eugene Forsey and the Inclusiveness of 1950s' British Canadianism." *Canadian Historical Review* 100, no. 3 (2019): 376–96.

Evatt, Herbert Vere. *The Royal Prerogative.* Sydney: Law Book, 1987.

Fairlie, Henry. *The Life of Politics.* London: Methuen, 1968.

Fenge, Terry, and Jim Aldridge, eds. *Keeping Promises: The Royal Proclamation of 1763, Aboriginal Rights, and Treaties in Canada.* Montreal and Kingston: McGill-Queen's University Press, 2015.

Finer, Herman. *The Theory and Practice of Modern Government.* 2nd ed. London: Methuen, 1946.

Fischer, David Hackett. *Historians' Fallacies: Toward a Logic of Historical Thought.* New York: Harper & Row, 1970.

Forcese, Craig. "The Executive, the Royal Prerogative, and the Constitution." In *The Oxford Handbook of the Canadian Constitution,* edited by Peter Oliver, Patrick Macklem, and Nathalie Des Rosier, 151–69. Oxford: Oxford University Press, 2017.

Francis, Mark. *Governors and Settlers: Images of Authority in the British Colonies, 1820–1860.* London: Macmillan, 1992.

Frankland, Noble. *Witness of a Century: The Life and Times of Prince Arthur Duke of Connaught, 1850–1942.* London: Shepeard-Walwyn, 1993.

Frye, Northrop. *The Bush Garden: Essays in the Canadian Imagination.* Toronto: House of Anansi, 1971.

Geertz, Clifford. *Negara: The Theatre State in Nineteenth-Century Bali.*
Princeton: Princeton University Press, 1980.

Geisler, Michael E. *National Symbols, Fractured Identities: Contesting the
National Narrative.* Hanover: University of New England Press, 2005.

Gibson, Sarah Katherine, and Arthur Milnes. *Canada Transformed: The
Speeches of Sir John A. Macdonald: A Bicentennial Celebration.* Toronto:
McClelland and Stewart, 2014.

Granatstein, Jack L. *1957–1967: The Years of Uncertainty and Innovation.*
Toronto: McClelland and Stewart, 1986.

Grant, John Webster. *The Canadian Experience of Church Union.* London:
Lutterworth, 1967.

Gwyn, Richard. *John A.: The Man Who Made Us: The Life and Times of John A.
Macdonald.* Toronto: Random House Canada, 2007.

– *Nation Maker, Sir John A. Macdonald: His Life, Our Times.* Toronto: Vintage
Canada, 2012.

Haliburton, Thomas Chandler. *Sam Slick's Wise Saws and Modern Instances;
Or, What He Said, Did or Invented.* London: Hurst and Blackett, 1859.

Hardie, Frank. *The Political Influence of Queen Victoria, 1861–1901.* London:
Frank Cass, 1935.

Hayday, Matthew, and Raymond B. Blake. *Celebrating Canada.* Toronto:
University of Toronto Press, 2016.

Hazell, Robert, and Bob Morris. "If the Queen Has No Reserve Powers Left,
What Is the Modern Monarchy For?" *Review of Constitutional Studies: The
Crown in the 21st Century* 22, no. 1 (2017): 5–32.

Hazell, Robert, and Akash Paun, eds. *Making Minority Government Work:
Hung Parliaments and the Challenges for Westminster and Whitehall.* London:
Institute for Government, the Constitution Unit, 2009.

Heard, Andrew. *Canadian Constitutional Conventions: The Marriage of Law &
Politics.* Don Mills, ON: Oxford University Press, 2014.

– "The Crown in Canada: Is There a Canadian Monarchy?" In *The Canadian
Kingdom: 150 Years of Constitutional Monarchy,* edited by D. Michael
Jackson, 113–32. Toronto: Dundurn, 2018.

Helliwell, John F., Richard Layard, Jeffrey Sachs, and Jan-Emmanuel
De Neve, eds. *World Happiness Report 2020.* New York: Sustainable
Development Solutions Network, 2020.

Henderson, George Fletcher. *Federal Royal Commissions in Canada: A
Checklist.* Toronto: University of Toronto Press, 1967.

Henderson, George Fletcher, and Lise Maillet. *Provincial Royal Commissions
and Commissions of Inquiry, 1867–1982: A Selective Bibliography.* Ottawa:
National Library of Canada, 1986.

Heuston, R.F.V. *Essays in Constitutional Law.* 2nd ed. London: Stevens and
 Sons, 1964.
Hobsbawm, Eric, and Terence Ranger. *The Invention of Tradition.* Cambridge:
 Cambridge University Press, 1983.
Hogg, Peter W. *Constitutional Law of Canada.* 5th ed. Scarborough, ON:
 Thompson Carswell, 2007.
– "Succession to the Throne." *National Journal of Constitutional Law*
 33 (2014): 83.
Hogg, Peter W., and Patrick J. Monahan. *The Liability of the Crown.* 3rd ed.
 Toronto: Carswell, 2000.
Holland, Robert, Susan Williams, and Terry Barringer, eds. *Iconography of*
 Independence "Freedoms at Midnight." London: Routledge, 2011.
Houston, William. *Documents Illustrative of the Canadian Constitution.*
 Toronto: Carswell, 1891.
Igartua, José E. *The Other Quiet Revolution: National Identities in English*
 Canada, 1945–72. Vancouver: University of British Columbia Press, 2006.
Innis, Harold A. "Decentralization and Democracy." In *Political Economy in*
 the Modern State, edited by Robert E. Babe and Edward A. Comor, 103–44.
 Toronto: University of Toronto Press, 2018.
Jackson, D. Michael. *The Crown and Canadian Federalism.* Toronto: Dundurn,
 2013.
Johnston, Andrew J.B. "Popery and Progress: Anti-Catholicism in Mid-
 Nineteenth-Century Nova Scotia." *Dalhousie Review* 4, no. 1 (1984): 146–54.
Johnston, David. *Trust: Twenty Ways to Build a Better Country.* Toronto:
 Penguin, 2018.
Joyal, Serge. "The Changing Role of the Governor General, or How the
 Personality of the Office-Holder Is Changing the Perception of the
 Monarchy." In *Royal Progress: Canada's Monarchy in the Age of Disruption,*
 edited by D. Michael Jackson, 108–26. Toronto: Dundurn, 2020.
– "La Couronne au Québec, de credo rassurant á bouc émissaire commode."
 In *Canada and the Crown: Essays on Constitutional Monarchy,* edited by D.
 Michael Jackson and Philippe Lagassé, 33–62. Montreal and Kingston:
 McGill-Queen's University Press, 2013.
Keith, Arthur Berriedale. *Responsible Government in the Dominions.* 1st ed.
 Oxford: Clarendon Press, 1912.
– *Responsible Government in the Dominions.* 2nd ed. Oxford: Clarendon, 1928.
– *The Sovereignty of the British Dominions.* London: McMillan, 1929.
Kelso, Kathy. *Electronic Legal Information: Exploring Access Issues.* Toronto:
 Canadian Legal Information Centre, 1991.

Kennedy, W.P.M. "The Regency Acts, 1937–1953." *University of Toronto Law Journal* 10, no. 2 (1954): 248–54.

Lagassé, Philippe. "Parliamentary and Judicial Ambivalence toward Executive Prerogative Powers in Canada." *Canadian Public Administration* 55, no. 2 (June 2012): 157–80.

Lagassé, Philippe, and James W.J. Bowden. "Royal Succession and the Canadian Crown as a Corporation Sole: A Critique of Canada's *Succession to the Throne Act, 2013*." *Constitutional Forum* 23, no. 1 (2014): 17-26.

Lascelles, Alan. *Government House Ottawa*. Ottawa; King's Printer, 1934.

Laskin, Bora. *The British Tradition in Canadian Law*. London: Stevens and Sons, 1969.

Leacock, Stephen. *My Discovery of England*. Toronto: McClelland and Stewart, 1961.

Lee, Christopher. *Viceroys: The Creation of the British*. London: Constable, 2018.

Leyland, Peter. *The Constitution of the United Kingdom*. 2nd ed. Oxford: Hart Publishing, 2012.

Lockwood, Thomas J. "A History of Royal Commissions." *Osgoode Hall Law Journal* 5 (1967): 172–207.

Lordon, Paul. *Crown Law*. Toronto: Butterworths, 1991.

Loughlin, Martin. "The State, the Crown and the Law." In *The Nature of the Crown: A Legal and Political Analysis*, edited by Maurice Sunkin & Sebastian Payne, 33–76. Oxford: Oxford University Press, 1999.

Low, Sidney. *The Governance of England*. London: T. Fisher Unwin, 1904.

MacDonnell, Tom. *Daylight upon Magic: The Royal Tour of Canada, 1939*. Toronto: Macmillan, 1989.

MacKinnon, Frank. *The Crown in Canada*. Calgary: McClelland and Stewart West, 1976.

Maitland, Frederick William. *The Collected Papers of Frederic William Maitland*. Edited by H.A.L. Fisher. Cambridge: Cambridge University Press, 1911.

– *The Constitutional History of England: A Course of Lectures Delivered*. Cambridge: Cambridge University Press, 1946.

Mallory, J.R. "The Continuing Evolution of Constitutionalism." In *Constitutionalism, Citizenship and Society in Canada*, edited by Alan Cairns and Cynthia Williams, 51–97. Toronto: University of Toronto Press, in cooperation with the Royal Commission on the Economic Union and Development Prospects for Canada, 1985.

– "Seals and Symbols: From Substance to Form in Commonwealth Equality." *Canadian Journal of Economics and Political Science* 22, no. 3 (August 1956): 281–91.

– *The Structure of Canadian Government*. Toronto: Gage Publishing, 1984.

Malouf, David. "Made in England: Australia's British Inheritance." *Quarterly Essay* 12 (2003): 1–66.

Massey, Vincent. "Canada: Her Status and Stature." In *Speaking of Canada: Addresses by the Right Hon. Vincent Massey, Governor General of Canada, 1952–1959*, 21–5. Toronto: Macmillan, 1959.

– *What's Past Is Prologue*. Toronto: MacMillan, 1963.

Matheson, John R. *Canada's Flag: A Search for a Country*. Boston: G.K. Hall, 1980.

McConnell, W.H. *Commentary on the British North America Act*. Toronto: Macmillan, 1977.

McCreery, Christopher. *The Canadian Honours System*, 2nd ed. Toronto: Dundurn, 2015.

– "The Lieutenant Governor's Expanding Role." In *Canada and the Crown*, edited by D. Michael Jackson and Philippe Lagassé, 141–60. Montreal and Kingston: McGill-Queen's University Press, 2013.

– "Myth and Misunderstanding: The Origins and Meaning of the Letters Patent Constituting the Office of the Governor General." In *The Evolving Canadian Crown*, edited by Jennifer Smith and D. Michael Jackson, 31–56. Montreal and Kingston: McGill-Queen's University Press, 2012.

– *The Order of Canada: Genesis of an Honours System*. Toronto: University of Toronto Press, 2018.

– "Subtle yet Significant Innovations: The Vice-Regal Appointments Committee and the Secretary's New Role." In *The Crown and Parliament*, edited by Michael Bédard and Philippe Lagassé, 241–62. Toronto: Thompson Reuters, 2015.

McKenty, Neil. *Mitch Hepburn*. Toronto: McClelland and Stewart, 1967.

McWinney, Edward. "Democracy in the 21st Century: The Future of the Crown in Canada." *Canadian Parliamentary Review* 28, no. 3 (Autumn 2005): 2–3.

– *The Governor General and Prime Ministers*. Vancouver: Ronsdale, 2005.

Messamore, Barbara. *Canada's Governors General, 1847–1878: Biography and Constitutional Evolution*. Toronto: University of Toronto Press, 2006.

Milton, Roger. *The English Ceremonial Book: A History of Robes Insignia and Ceremonies Still in Use in England*. New York: Drake Publishers, 1972.

Monet, Jacques. *The Canadian Crown*. Toronto: Clarke, Irwin, 1978.

Moodie, T. Dunbar. *The Rise of Afrikanerdom: Power, Apartheid and the Afrikaner Civil Religion*. Berkeley: University of California Press, 1975.

Morgan, Cecilia. *Building Better Britains? Settler Societies in the British World, 1783–1920*. Toronto: University of Toronto Press, 2017.

– *Commemorating Canada: History, Heritage and Memory, 1850s–1990s*. Toronto: University of Toronto Press, 2016.

Morton, W.L. *The Canadian Identity*. 2nd ed. Toronto: University of Toronto Press, 1972.

Mount, Ferdinand. *The British Constitution Now: Recovery or Decline?* London: Mandarin, 1992.

Murphy, Phillip. "Breaking the Bad News: Plans for the Announcement to the Empire of the Death of Elizabeth II and the Proclamation of Her Successor, 1952–67." *Journal of Imperial and Commonwealth History* 34, no. 1 (2006): 245–65.

– *Monarchy & the End of Empire: The House of Windsor, the British Government and the Postwar Commonwealth*. Oxford: Oxford University Press, 2013.

Neary, Peter. "The Morning after a General Election: The Vice-Regal Perspective." *Canadian Parliamentary Review* 35, no. 3 (Autumn 2012): 23–9.

Nelles, H.V. *The Art of Nation-Building: Pageantry and the Spectacle at Quebec's Tercentenary*. Toronto: University of Toronto Press, 1999.

Newman, Warren J. "Of Dissolution, Prorogation, and Constitutional Law, Principle and Convention: Maintaining Fundamental Distinctions during a Parliamentary Crisis." *National Journal of Constitutional Law* 27 (2010): 217–29.

– "Some Observations on the Queen, the Crown, the Constitution and the Courts." *Review of Constitutional Studies* 22 (2017): 1.

– "The Succession to the Throne in Canada." In *Royal Progress: Canada's Monarchy in the Age of Disruption*, edited by D. Michael Jackson, 127–52. Toronto: Dundurn, 2020.

Oliver, Peter. C. *The Constitution of Independence: The Development of Constitutional Theory in Australia, Canada, and New Zealand*. Oxford: Oxford University Press, 2005.

Ostry, Bernard, and Janice Yalden, eds. *Visions of Canada: The Alan B. Plaunt Memorial Lectures, 1958–1992*. Montreal and Kingston: McGill-Queen's University Press, 2004.

Ozick, Cynthia. *Fame and Folly*. New York: Vintage International, 1997.

Payne, Sebastian. "The Royal Prerogative." In *The Nature of the Crown: A Legal and Political Analysis*, edited by Maurice Sunkin & Sebastian Payne, 77–110. Oxford: Oxford University Press, 1999.

Penlington, Norman. *Canada and Imperialism, 1896–1899*. Toronto: University of Toronto Press, 1965.

Pickergsill, J.W. *My Years with Louis St-Laurent: A Political Memoir*. Toronto: University of Toronto Press, 1975.

Pimlott, Ben. *The Queen: Elizabeth II and the Monarchy*. London: HarperCollins, 1996.

Point, Steven. "The Crown and First Nations in British Columbia: A Personal View." In *The Canadian Kingdom: 150 Years of Constitutional Monarchy*, edited by D. Michael Jackson, 77–88. Toronto: Dundurn, 2018.

Pope, Joseph. *Correspondence of John A. Macdonald: Selections from the Correspondence of the Rt. Hon. Sir John A. Macdonald, G.C.B.* Toronto: Oxford University Press, 1921.

– *Public Servant: The Memoires of Sir Joseph Pope*. Edited by Maurice A. Pope. Toronto: Oxford University Press, 1960.

Poulett Scroupe, George. *Memoir of the Life of the Right Honourable Charles, Lord Sydenham; With a Narrative of His Administration in Canada*. London: John Murray, 1844.

Quentin-Baxter, Alison, and Janet McLean. *This Realm of New Zealand: The Sovereign, the Governor General and the Crown*. Auckland: Auckland University Press, 2017.

Radforth, Ian. *Royal Spectacle: The 1860 Visit of the Prince of Wales to Canada and the United States*. Toronto: University of Toronto Press, 2004.

Rich, E.E., ed. *History of the Hudson's Bay Company, 1670–1870*. Toronto: McClelland and Stewart, 1960.

– *The Hudson's Bay Company Booke of Letters, Commissions, Instructions Outward, 1688–1696*. London: Hudson's Bay Record Society, 1957.

Risk, R.C.B. "The Many Minds of W.P.M. Kennedy." *University of Toronto Law Journal* 48 (1998): 353–86.

Royale, Stephen. *Company, Crown and Colony: The Hudson's Bay Company and Territorial Endeavour in Western Canada*. New York: I.B. Tauris, 2011.

Russell, Peter H., and Lorne Sossin, eds. *Parliamentary Democracy in Crisis*. Toronto: University of Toronto Press, 2009.

Saywell, John T. *The Office of the Lieutenant Governor*. Toronto: University of Toronto Press, 1957.

Scott, Francis Reginald. "The End of Dominion Status." *American Journal of International Law* 38, no. 1 (1944): 34–49.

Scott, Stephen A. "Constituent Authority and the Canadian Provinces." *McGill Law Journal* 12, no. 4 (1966): 529–72.

Sedley, Stephen. *Lions under the Throne: Essays on the History of English Public Law*. Cambridge: Cambridge University Press, 2015.

Semino, Elena, and Zsfia Demjén, eds. *The Routledge Handbook of Metaphor and Language*. New York: Routledge, 2017.

Sexton, Brendan. *Ireland and the Crown, 1922–1936: The Governor Generalship of the Irish Free State*. Ann Arbor: University of Michigan Press, 1989.

Shils, Edward, and Michael Young. "The Meaning of the Coronation." *Sociological Review* 1, no. 2 (1953): 63–81.

Shore, Cris, and David V. Williams, eds. *The Shapeshifting Crown: Locating the State in Postcolonial New Zealand, Australia, Canada and the UK*. Cambridge: Cambridge University Press, 2019.

Shortt, Adam. *The Makers of Canada: Lord Sydenham*. Toronto: Morang, 1908.

Slattery, Brian Slattery. "Aboriginal Rights and the Honour of the Crown." Supreme Court Law Review: Osgoode's Annual Constitutional Cases Conference 29 (2005): 434–45.

Smith, David E. "Clarifying the Doctrine of Ministerial Responsibility as It Applies to the Government of Canada and the Parliament of Canada." In *Restoring Accountability, Research Studies*, vol. 1, *Parliament, Ministers and Deputy Ministers*, Commission of Inquiry into the Sponsorship Program and Advertising Activities, 101–43. Ottawa: Public Works and Government Services, 2006.

– *The Constitution in a Hall of Mirrors: Canada at 150*. Toronto: University of Toronto Press, 2017.

– *The Invisible Crown: The First Principle of Canadian Government*. Toronto: University of Toronto Press, 1995.

– *The Republican Option in Canada, Past and Present*. Toronto: University of Toronto Press, 1999.

Smith, Goldwin. *Canada and the Canadian Question*. London: Macmillan, 1891.

Smith, Jennifer, and D. Michael Jackson, eds. *The Evolving Canadian Crown*. Montreal and Kingston: McGill-Queen's University Press, 2013.

Smith, William, and Arthur G. Doughty. *The Evolution of Government in Canada: Confederation Memorial Volume*. Ottawa: King's Printer, 1928.

Spiro, Herbert J. *Government by Constitution*. New York: Random House, 1959.

Strusberg, Peter. *Roland Michener: The Last Viceroy*. Toronto: McGraw-Hill Ryerson, 1989.

Sunkin, Maurice, and Sebastian Payne, eds. *The Nature of the Crown: A Legal and Political Analysis*. Oxford: Oxford University Press, 1999.

– "The Nature of the Crown: An Overview." In *The Nature of the Crown: A Legal and Political Analysis*, edited by Sunkin and Payne, 1–21. Oxford: Oxford University Press, 1999.

Swan, Conrad. *Canadian Symbols of Sovereignty*. Toronto: University of Toronto Press, 1976.

Tardi, Gregory. *The Legal Framework of Government: A Canadian Guide*. Aurora, ON: Canada Law Book, 1992.

Todd, Alpheus. *On Parliamentary Government in England*. 2nd ed. London: Longmans, Green, 1887.

Turpin, Colin, and Adam Tomkins. *British Government and the Constitution*. Cambridge: Cambridge University Press, 2007.

Twomey, Anne. *The Chameleon Crown: The Queen and Her Australian Governors*. Sydney: Federation, 2006.

– "Regency in the Realms." *Public Law Review* 27, no. 3 (2016): 198–217.

– *The Veiled Sceptre: Reserve Powers of Heads of State in Westminster Systems*. Cambridge: Cambridge University Press, 2018.

Vile, M.J.C. *Constitutionalism and the Separation of Powers*. Oxford: Clarendon, 1967.

Vipond, Mary. "Canadian National Consciousness and the Formation of the United Church of Canada." *Bulletin* 24 (1975): 5–27.

Vipond, Robert C. *Liberty and Community: Canadian Federalism and the Failure of the Constitution*. Albany: State University of New York Press, 1991.

Wade, H.W.R. *Constitutional Fundamentals*. London: Stevens & Sons, 1980.

Wade, H.W.R., and C.F. Forsyth. *Administrative Law*. 11th ed. Oxford: Oxford University Press, 2014.

Wade, William. "The Crown, Ministers and Officials: Legal Status and Liability." In *The Nature of the Crown: A Legal and Political Analysis*, edited by Maurice Sunkin and Sebastian Payne, 23–32. Oxford: Oxford University Press, 1999.

Ward, Norman. *Dawson's The Government of Canada*, 6th ed. Toronto: University of Toronto Press, 1987.

– Review of *The Office of Lieutenant-Governor: A Study in Canadian Government and Politics*, by John T. Saywell. *Canadian Historical Review* 39, no. 3 (September 1958): 246–7.

Walters, Mark D. "Succession to the Throne and the Architecture of the Constitution of Canada." In *The Crown and Parliament*, edited by Philippe Lagassé and Michel Bédard, 263–92. Montreal: Éditions Yvon Blais, 2015.

Wheare, K.C. "'Walter Bagehot': Lectures on a Master Mind." *Proceedings of the British Academy* 60 (1974): 173–97. London: Oxford University Press, 1975.

Williams, Stephanie. *Running the Show: Governors of the British Empire*. London: Viking, 2011.

Willis, Claire. "Prodigal Fathers." *New York Review of Books*, 20 December 2018, 38–40.

Wood, James. *The Broken Estate: Essays on Literature and Belief.* London: Jonathan Cape, 1999.

Government Documents

Bill C-60. *An Act to Amend the Constitution of Canada.*

Department of Canadian Heritage. *The Lieutenant Governor's Briefing Book,* 2012.

Federal Government Reporting Study: A Joint Study by the Office of Auditor General of Canada and the United States Government Administration Office. Ottawa: Auditor General's Office, 1986.

"Guidance for Deputy Ministers." https://www.canada.ca/en/privy -council/services/publications/guidance-deputy-ministers.html.

Kelly, Richard. "Fixed-term Parliaments Act 2011." House of Commons Library Briefing Paper No. 06111, 27 April 2017, 14.

Manual of Official Procedure of the Government of Canada. Ottawa: Queen's Printer, 1968.

Markwell, Donald. *Constitutional Conventions and the Headship of State: Australian Experience.* Redland Bay, QLD: Connor Court Publishing, 2016.

Proceedings of the Standing Senate Committee on Legal and Constitutional Affairs. Issue 32 – Evidence for March 21, 2013. https://sencanada.ca/en /Content/Sen/Committee/411/LCJC/32ev-50040-e.

Royal Commission on Dominion-Provincial Relations. *Report of Proceedings.*

"Table of Titles to Be Used in Canada." https://www.canada.ca/en /canadian-heritage/services/protocol-guidelines-special-event/table -titles-canada.html.

Truth and Reconciliation Commission of Canada: Calls to Action. 2015. http://trc .ca/assets/pdf/Calls_to_Action_English2.pdf.

Media Articles

Banville, Beurmond. "Acadians to Get Apology from Queen Elizabeth: Proclamation Acknowledges Deportation." *Bangor (Maine) Daily News,* 5 December 2003. https://www.acadian.org/history/acadians -get-apology-queen-elizabeth.

Bellefontaine, Michelle. "Alberta NDP Leader Rachel Notley Thrown Out of House in Bill 22 Stand-off." CBC News, 19 November 2019. https://

www.cbc.ca/news/canada/edmonton/alberta-ndp-leader-rachel-notley-thrown-out-of-house-in-bill-22-stand-off-1.5365223.

Boisvert, Yves. "Hello, Victoria Day. Goodbye, Monarchy." *Globe and Mail*, 22 May 2017, A9.

Canadian Broadcasting Corporation. *The Schreyers' New Life at Rideau Hall*, 3 August 1973.

Canadian Monarchist News 23 (Spring 2005).

Cantú, Francisco. "Boundary Conditions: What Happens When the American Frontier Becomes a Wall?" *New Yorker*, 11 March 2019, 73–7.

Cohn, Martin Regg. "Maybe It's Time for Our Own Canadexit." *Toronto Star*, 25 June 2016, A6.

Cosh, Colby. "Canadian Republicanism Is a Pathology, but It Won't Survive Past the Next Coronation." *National Post*, 29 December 2016.

Coyne, Andrew. "Supreme Court Ensures Widely Reviled Patronage House (the Senate) Will Stay Forever." *National Post*, 25 April 2014.

CTV News. "Federal Government Stops Sending Photos of Queen to Canadians," 23 May 2019.

Fraser, John D. "The Governor General's Man." *Saturday Night Magazine*, April 1990.

Fraser, John D, D. Michael Jackson, Serge Joyal, and Michael Valpy. "The Supreme Court Reaffirms the Canadian Crown's Importance to Our Country's Sense of Order." *Globe and Mail*, 26 June 2020.

Globe and Mail. "Harry and Meghan and Why Members of the Royal Family Can't Live in Canada," 13 January 2020.

– "Vice-regal Role: A National Symbol," 14 July 2017, A9.

Government of Canada. "Canada's New Government Proposes Fixed Election Dates." News release, 30 May 2006. https://www.canada.ca/en/news/archive/2006/05/canada-new-government-proposes-fixed-election-dates.html.

Heasman, D.J. "Queen's Prerogative." *Times*, 24 October 1985.

Huffington Post. "The Government Won't Send You Free Pictures of the Queen Anymore." 24 May 2019.

Keynes, John Maynard. "Art and the State." *Listener*, 26 August 1936.

Labbé, Stefan. "End of a Royal Era." Open Canada, 29 September 2017. https://www.opencanada.org/features/end-royal-era/29 September 2017.

Lagassé, Philippe. "The First and Last 'Queen of Canada"? Policy Options politiques, 9 September 2015. https://policyoptions.irpp.org/magazines/september-2015/the-first-and-last-queen-of-canada/.

LeBlanc, Daniel. "Former Astronaut Julie Payette to Be Governor General." *Globe and Mail*, 13 July 2017.

McElroy, Justin, and Richard Zussman. "Showdown at Government House: The Meeting That Ended 16 Years of B.C. Liberal Rule." CBC News, 30 June 2017. https://www.cbc.ca/news/canada/british-columbia /government-house-stakeout-clark-horgan-guichon-1.4185404.

Messamore, Barbara. "Crown Proves Its Use: Far from Bending the Rules, It Ensures They Are Respected." *Globe and Mail*, 11 July 2017, A11.

Monarchist League. "The Case for the Crown." https://www.monarchist .ca/index.php/our-monarchy/canada-s-monarchy/the-case-for-the -crown.

National Post. "Queen Elizabeth Deserves a Place of Honour on Our Walls," 24 May 2019.

Ottawa Citizen. "Canada's Independence Is at Stake," 6 July 2016.

Payton, Laura. "Harper Pardons Farmers Arrested under Old Wheat Board Law." CBC News, 1 August 2012. https://www.cbc.ca/news/politics /harper-pardons-farmers-arrested-under-old-wheat-board-law-1.1146436.

Pellerin, Brigitte. "How to Save the Monarchy: Make Prince Harry Canada's Next GG." *Ottawa Citizen*, 12 December 2019.

Rowlands, Ingrid D. "In the New Whitney." *New York Review of Books*, 26 June 2015, 14.

Smith, Dale. "Can Canada Put Harry and Meghan to Work?" *Maclean's Magazine*, 14 January 2020.

Toronto Star. "Olympics Will Miss Queen's Touch," 8 November 2009.

Wayne, Leslie. "The World Could Use More Kings and Queens, Monarchists Say." *New York Times*, 7 January 2018.

Young, Leslie. "How Canada Could Break Up with the Monarchy." Globalnews.ca, 28 June 2017. https://globalnews.ca/news/3559289/how -canada-could-break-up-with-the-monarchy/.

Court Decisions

Abdelrazik v Canada (Minister of Foreign Affairs), 2009 FC 580

AG v De Keyser's Royal Hotel Ltd, [1920] AC 508 (HL)

BBC v Johns, [1964] 1 All ER 923

Black v Canada (Advisory Council for the Order), 2013 FCA 267

Black v Canada (Prime Minister), 54 OR (3d) 215 (CA)

Burmah Oil Company v Lord Advocate, [1965] AC 75 (HL)

Canada v Chiasson, 2003 FCA 155.

Canadian Doctors for Refugee Care v Canada (AG), 2014 FC 651.

Chauvin v Canada, 2009 FC 1202.

Chiasson v Canada, 2003 FCA 155.

Clyde River (Hamlet) v Petroleum Geo-Services Inc, 2017 SCC 40.
Conacher v Canada (Prime Minister), 2009 FC 920, aff'd 2010 FCA 131.
Copello v Canada (Minister of Foreign Affairs), [2002] 3 FC 24.
Council of Civil Service Unions v Minister for the Civil Service, [1985]
    AC 374 (HL).
Drabinsky v Canada (Advisory Council of the Order), 2015 FCA 5.
Friends of the Earth v Canada (Governor in Council), 2008 FC 1183, aff'd 2009
    FCA 297.
Galati v Canada (Governor General), 2015 FC 91.
Giolla Chainnigh v Canada (AG), 2008 FC 69.
Guergis v Novak, 2013 ONCA 449.
Haida Nation v British Columbia (Minister of Forests), [2004] 3 SCR 511.
Hupacasath First Nation v Canada (AG), 2015 FCA 4.
Kamel v Canada (AG), 2009 FCA 21.
Khadr v Canada (AG), 2006 FC 727.
Kujan v Attorney General, 2014 ONSC 966.
*The Liquidators of the Maritime Bank of Canada v The Receiver-General of New
    Brunswick*, [1892] AC 437.
McAteer v Canada (AG), 2014 ONCA 578.
Mikisew Cree First Nation v Canada (Governor General in Council), 2018 SCC 40.
Motard c Procureur général du Canada, 2019 QCCA 1826.
Operation Dismantle Inc v Canada, [1985] 1 SCR 441.
Petition of Right, In Re, [1915] 3 KB 649; 31 TLR 569 (CA); [1916 1 KB LT 419; 32
    TLR 699 (HL).
*R (on the application of Miller) (Appellant) v The Prime Minister (Respondent);
    Cherry and Others (Respondents) v Advocate General for Scotland (Appellant)*,
    [2019] UKSC 41.
Reference re Remuneration of Judges of the Provincial Court (PEI), [1998] 2 SCR
    4423.
Reference re Senate Reform, 2014 SCC 32.
Re: Resolution to amend the Constitution, [1981] 1 SCR 753.
Re The Initiative and Referendum Act, [1919] AC 935 (JCPC).
Roach v Canada (Minister of State for Multiculturalism and Citizenship), [1994]
    2 FC 406 (CA).
Robillard v Canada (Attorney General), 2016 FC 495.
Ross River Dena Council Band v Canada, [2002] 2 SCR 816.
R v Criminal Injuries Compensation Board, [1967] 2 QB 864 (CA).
*R v Secretary of State for Foreign Affairs ex parte Indian Association of Alberta et
    al*, [1982] 2 All ER 122.
Smith v Canada (AG), 2009 FC 228.
Teskey v Canada (AG), 2014 ONCA 612.

Thomson v Canada (Deputy Minister of Agriculture), [1992] 1 SCR 385.
Tunda v Canada, 2001 FCA 151.
Turp c Chrétien, [2003] JQ no 7019
Vancouver Island Peace Society v Canada, [1994] 1 FC 102.
Verreault (JE) & Fils Ltée v Attorney General (Quebec), [1977] 1 SCR 41.

Legislation

Canada Elections Act, SC 2000, c 9.
Canadian Passport Order, SI/81–86.
Contraventions Act, SC 1992, c 47.
Criminal Records Act, RSC 1985, c C-47.
Department of the Environment Act, RSC 1985, c E-10.
Interpretation Act, RSC 1985, c I-21.
Official Languages Act, RSC 1985, c 31.
Statistics Act, RSC 1985, c S-19.

Index